IMAGES
of America

LAURENS COUNTY

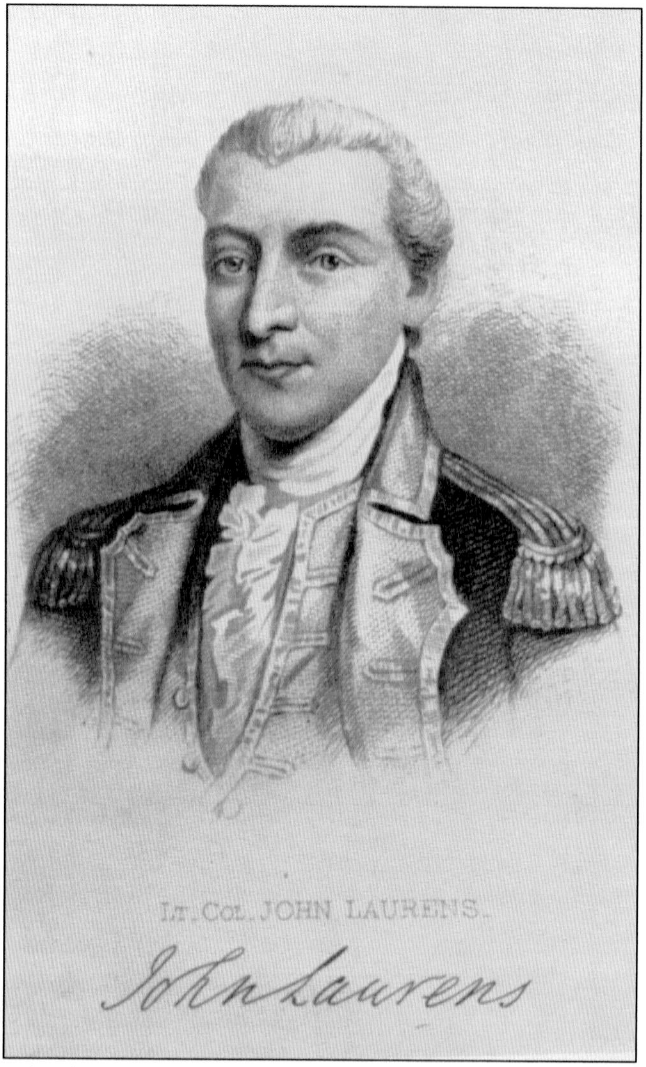

John Laurens. Col. John Laurens served as an aide to Gen. George Washington throughout most of the American Revolution. He was captured and taken prisoner by the British after the fall of Charleston, South Carolina. After he was exchanged, Laurens was given a diplomatic mission to work with Benjamin Franklin to seek more money, arms, and material from the French government. As a result of his efforts, the Continental Army was able to capture the British Army at Yorktown, Virginia, in 1781. Colonel Laurens continued to serve in the Continental Army. He was mortally wounded at Combachee, South Carolina, his native state, on August 27, 1782, by members of a British patrol. The State of Georgia honored Colonel Laurens by naming its newest county, Laurens County, after him on December 10, 1807.

IMAGES
of America

LAURENS COUNTY

Scott Thompson

ARCADIA
PUBLISHING

ISBN 978-0-7385-0638-8

Published by Arcadia Publishing
Charleston, South Carolina

Printed in the United States of America

Library of Congress Catalog Card Number: 00-106960

For all general information contact Arcadia Publishing at:
Telephone 843-853-2070
Fax 843-853-0044
E-Mail sales@arcadiapublishing.com
For customer service and orders:
Toll-Free 1-888-313-2665

Visit us on the Internet at www.arcadiapublishing.com

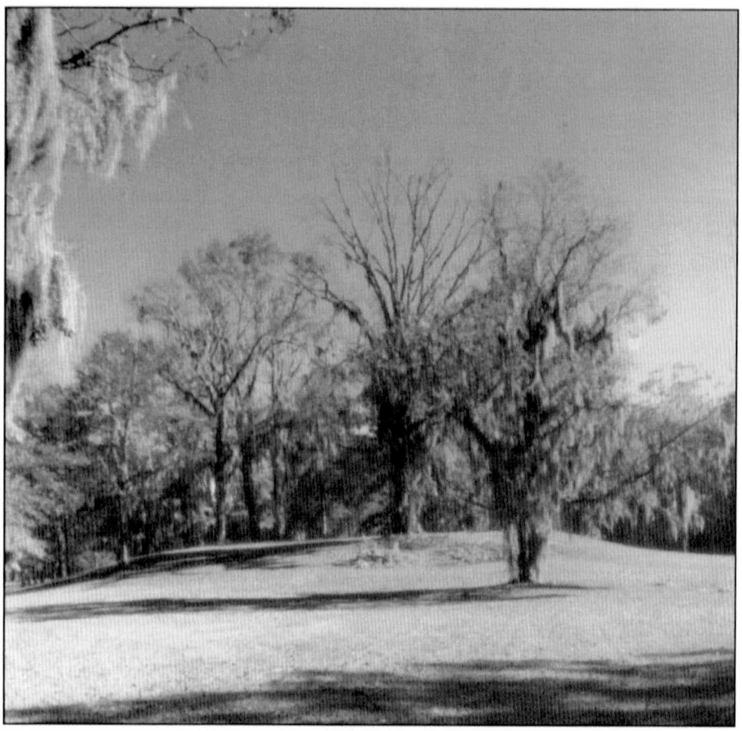

The Indian Mounds at Fish Trap Cut. The southern or ceremonial mound is one of two Mississippian Periods at Fish Trap Cut, which is located a couple miles south of Interstate 16 on the Oconee River. The mounds, which were constructed in the 13th century, are listed on the National Register of Historic Places and surround the oldest known Woodland Period village site in Georgia, which dates back to the first or second centuries, B.C. (Photo courtesy of Don Lamb.)

Contents

ACKNOWLEDGMENTS

I would like to thank all of the people of Laurens County over the last 193 years who have worked to make our county a better place in which to live. Laurens Countians have always been there ready to serve—to serve their community, to serve their country, and to serve their God. It would be impossible to print a photograph of every major event, business, church, or outstanding citizen in the history of our county. In this book, I have attempted to show a few glimpses of how we lived over the last two centuries. It is my sincere desire that this book will inspire others to preserve the history of our county and its citizens. History can be found anywhere you look. It is in your home and family. It is in your church and your school. It is in your neighborhood and your community. No one's history is more important than anyone else's. No matter how old you are, you should study it, preserve it, and never forget it.

INTRODUCTION

Laurens County, Georgia, which was created on December 10, 1807, was named for Col. John Laurens, an aide to Gen. George Washington during the American Revolution. He also worked with Benjamin Franklin in securing men and material from the French king to defeat the British Army. The original county seat was located at Sumpterville, about 5 miles west of Dublin near the banks of Turkey Creek. In 1811, after a large portion of the county's lands were cut off to form other counties, the State of Georgia ceded a portion of Washington and Montgomery counties to form the eastern portion of present-day Laurens County. The county seat was moved to a small community formerly known as Sandbar on the Oconee River. A new town was established on the site and was name Dublin by Jonathan Sawyer, Dublin's first postmaster, in honor of his recently deceased wife, who was a native of Dublin, Ireland.

Gen. David Blackshear of Laurens County led a large contingent of Georgia forces during the War of 1812 when Laurens County was threatened by Indian attacks. George Troup moved into the area after the war and served in public office for over 25 years as a congressman, senator, and governor. The plantation system, which flourished in Laurens County from the 1820s until the 1860s, stretched across the northern part of the county. During the decades before the Civil War, most Laurens Countians, of whom nearly half were slaves, lived on these plantations while the town of Dublin was virtually uninhabited.

Laurens Countians voted over two-to-one not to secede from the Union in an 1860 election. Despite that fact, over 800 Laurens County men served in the various units of the Confederate States. Laurens Countians fought in every major battle of the war. One Laurens County man earned a remarkable distinction for his service. Bill Yopp, a slave of Capt. Thomas Yopp, served as the regimental drummer of the 14th Georgia Infantry and is the only African-American Confederate soldier buried in the National Cemetery in Marietta, Georgia.

After the war, Laurens Countians managed to cope with the lack of food and money. During the Reconstruction period, county residents elected Rev. George Linder to the Georgia House of Representatives, making him the only African American to represent the county in the legislature. The county saw virtually no growth until the rail lines of the Wrightsville & Tennille; Macon, Dublin & Savannah; and Oconee & Western Railroads were run into Dublin in 1891.

As the railroads came, so did more people and money. The rich virgin pine forests of southwestern Laurens County were cleared, and cotton was planted. By the second decade of the 20th century, Laurens County was one of the top two cotton producers in the state, setting an all-time record of 30 million pounds in 1911. The 1900 census revealed that Laurens was the 12th largest county in Georgia. By 1910, Laurens County was the 7th largest county in Georgia.

The year 1918 brought a cataclysmic change in the economy of Laurens County. With many of its men serving in the Armed Forces during World War I, Laurens County was devastated by the coming of the boll weevil, which destroyed the cotton crop and sent the local economy into a severe depression for nearly 20 years. Tenant farmers, who had so vitally contributed to the economy of the county, began leaving in masses. One such family was the Walker Smith family who moved to Detroit. Walker Smith Jr. became a professional fighter and changed his name to Sugar Ray Robinson, a six-time world boxing champion. The coming of U.S. Highway 80 helped the economy grow as the railroads began to decline in the county. Laurens Countians turned to movies, sports, and politics as forms of entertainment during the Depression. Many prominent Laurens Countians left the county to serve in high political positions and as prominent journalists.

During World War II Laurens Countians served their country with unparalleled patriotism, gallantry, and courage. Capt. Bobbie E. Brown was awarded the Congressional Medal for his heroism at Aachen, Germany. Many other Laurens Countians were awarded Silver Stars and Service Crosses for extraordinary heroism. Nearly ten dozen men lost their lives during the war. During the war, German and Italian prisoners were kept in the county to work the farms. The United States Navy established a long-term recovery hospital in Dublin in 1945. The hospital is now a Veterans Administration Hospital and still remains an integral part of our county's economy.

A major shift in Laurens County's economy occurred in the post-war years when many veterans returned home and started their own businesses. The establishment of J.P. Stevens & Co. began a shift from a nearly total agricultural economy to a mixture of agriculture and industry. During the next five decades the shift only accelerated. Dublin is still experiencing a half-century period of slow but steady growth, due mainly to the cooperation between local governments, the chamber of commerce, and other community leaders.

The people of Laurens County are avid sports fans. Minor League baseball was played in Dublin between 1949 and 1962. Basketball teams from Cedar Grove, Dexter, and Dudley dominated their classes in the 1950s and 1960s. Dublin's football program was one of the best in the state during the decade of the 1960s. Laurens Countians have participated in nearly every major professional sport, including being top draft choices and playing in championship games.

As Laurens County enters the 21st century, we can look back on nearly two centuries of her history, and hers is a story of people. A people who are patriotic. A people who are industrious. A people who are kind. The story of her future is yet to be written. The deep-rooted history of the county will serve as a guide to lead her citizens throughout the centuries to come.

One

THE EARLY YEARS

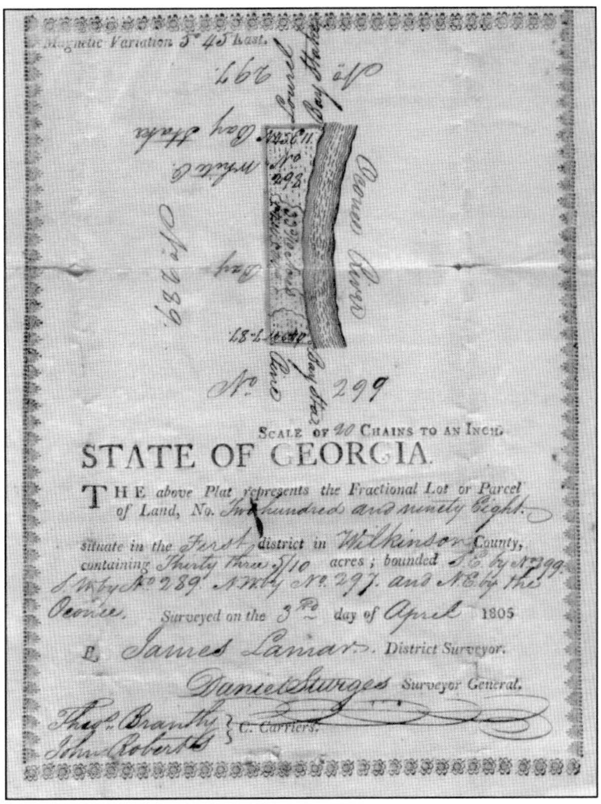

LAND GRANT. The State of Georgia acquired all of the land of present-day Georgia, which lies between the Oconee and Ocmulgee River, from the Indian Tribes under a treaty signed in 1802. This survey for Land Lot 298 of the First Land District (which was then Wilkinson County) was done in April of 1805, long before the lands of present-day Laurens County were settled. The land is located about a mile above Blackshear's Ferry and was granted to Elijah Blackshear, who, in conjunction with his brother General David Blackshear, established the first Blackshear's Ferry.

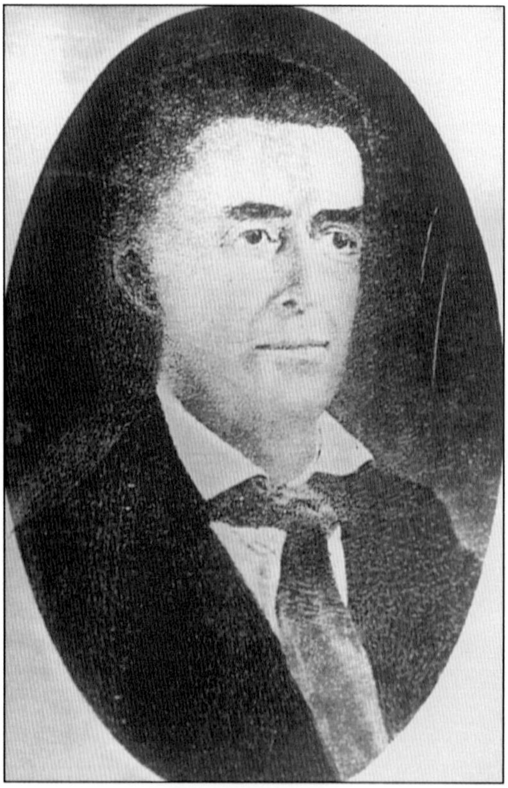

Gen. David Blackshear. David Blackshear moved from North Carolina to present-day Laurens County in 1790. He served in the Georgia Senate from Laurens County for many years. Blackshear served as a presidential elector committed to Andrew Jackson in 1828 and 1832. The general became prominent in Georgia military affairs as a brigadier general during the War of 1812, when he commanded the Georgia forces based at Fort Hawkins in Macon.

George M. Troup. George M. Troup was one of Georgia's most honored and important political leaders of the first half of the 19th century. He served in Congress and the United States Senate before, during, and after the War of 1812. Troup moved to Laurens County near the end of his first term in the Senate and served as governor of Georgia from 1823 to 1827. He nearly took Georgia into a war with the United States over the question of whether a state had the right to purchase Indian lands and forcibly remove their inhabitants. He returned to the Senate and became one of the founders of the State's Rights movement in the country. Governor Troup lived on his plantation, "Valdosta," a few miles south of East Dublin.

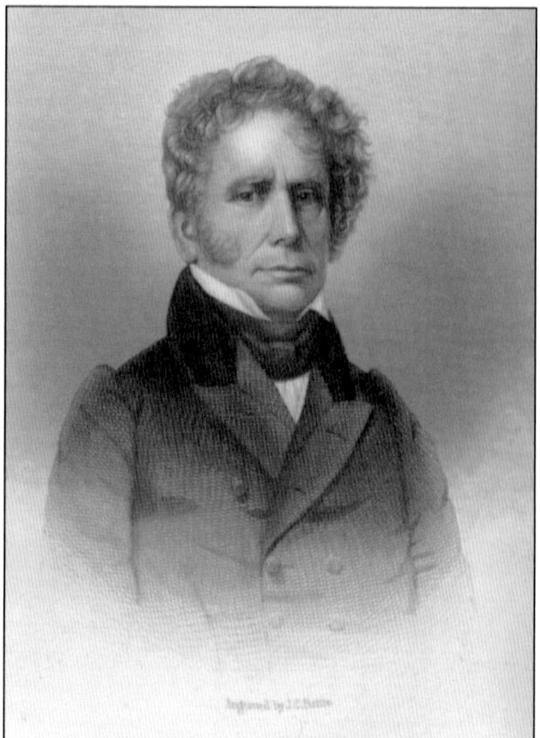

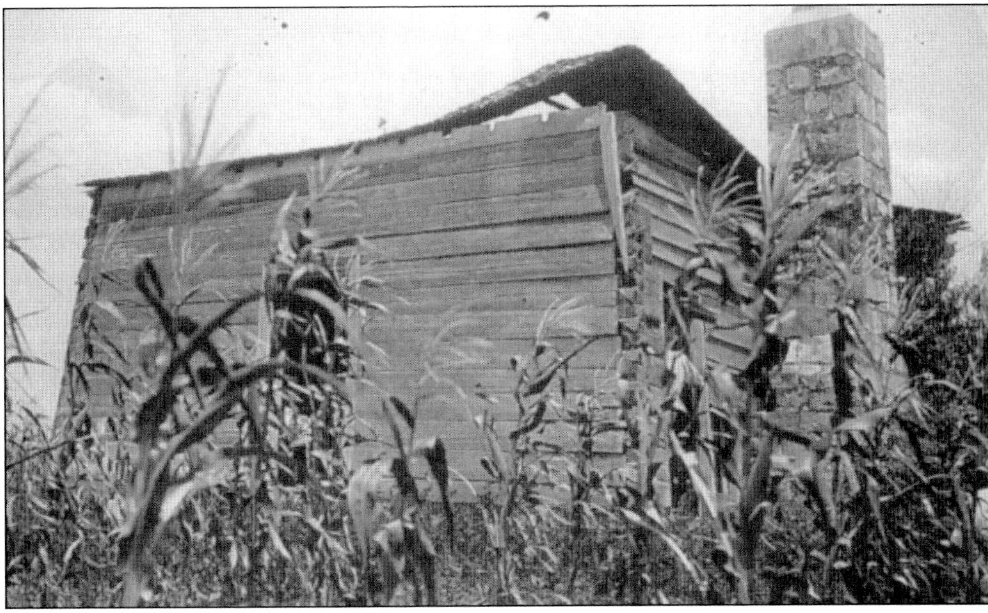

VALDOSTA. The simple log structure shown in this *c.* 1900 photograph shows the ruins of George Troup's home, Valdosta, which sat on a high hill with a commanding view of the Oconee River Valley. The home was the site of many important political meetings and was frequented by high-ranking politicians on their travels along the old Milledgeville-to-Darien Road.

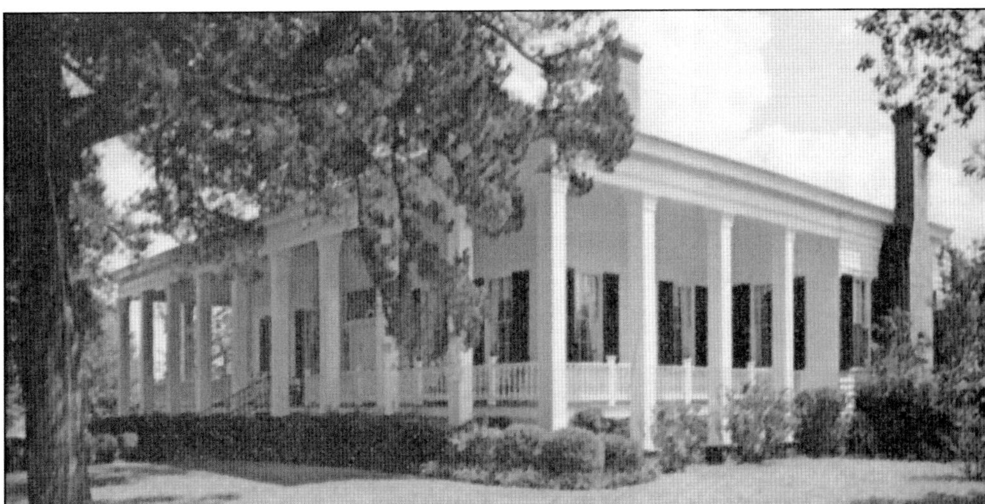

WHITEHALL. This Greek Revival home, located near the Bleckley County line on Georgia Highway 26, was built by Maj. Joseph McKee White in the mid-1800s. The house has been associated with the President's House in Athens and the Hermitage in Savannah as being rarely surpassed in the sheer grace of its architecture. Joseph White was commissioned a major in the Provisional Army of the Confederate States of America. He served his community by supervising the distribution of food in the area. The home and a large portion of the original plantation have been purchased and beautifully maintained by Bill Holmes, a direct descendant of Major White.

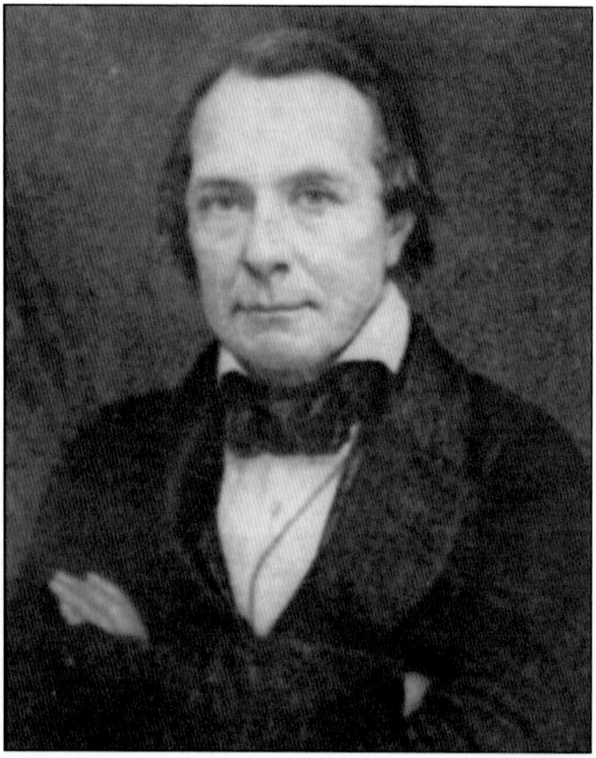

MIRABEAU LAMAR. Lamar, a native of Jefferson County, Georgia, served as the personal secretary of George Troup during his term as governor of Georgia. Lamar lived in the Troup household in Laurens County before he moved to Columbus to publish a newspaper favorable to the Troup political faction of the Democratic Party. Lamar moved to Texas during the great migration to that territory in the 1830s. He joined the Texas Army as a private and rose to the rank of commander-in-chief. Lamar was elected as the second president of the Republic of Texas and is still widely known for his contributions to the educational systems of Texas.

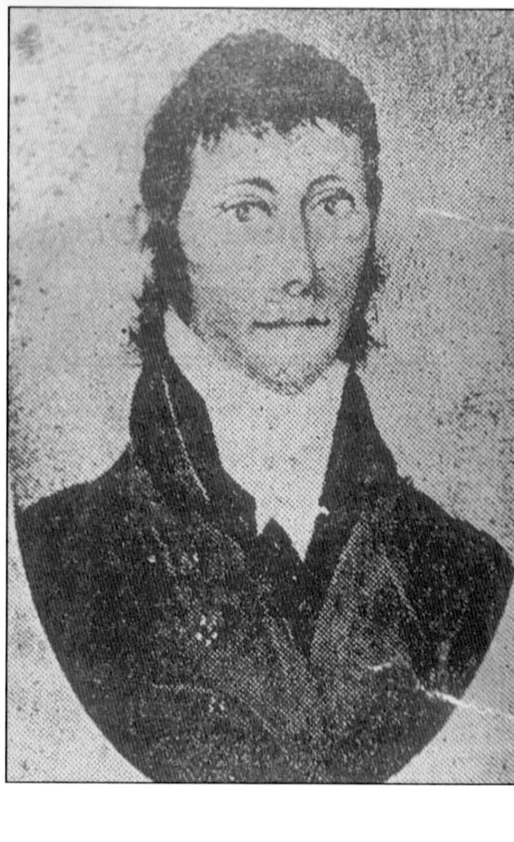

JONATHAN SAWYER. Sawyer, known as the founder of Dublin, moved to this area around 1804, when the land now known as East Dublin was known as Sandbar. A local merchant, he was appointed the first postmaster of Dublin in 1811, giving him the honor of naming the post office and consequently the new county seat. Sawyer chose Dublin in honor his recently deceased wife, Elizabeth McCormick Sawyer of Dublin, Ireland. Sawyer owned a large portion of northeastern Dublin and remained in the area until he moved to Darien, where he became a director of the Bank of Darien, which once claimed to be the largest bank south of Philadelphia.

THOMAS MCCALL. Thomas McCall, a soldier of the American Revolution, served as the surveyor general of Georgia from 1786 to 1795. He moved to Laurens County in the early 19th century and became known statewide for his skills as a winemaker. The graves of McCall and his wife are among the oldest known graves in the old Dublin city cemetery.

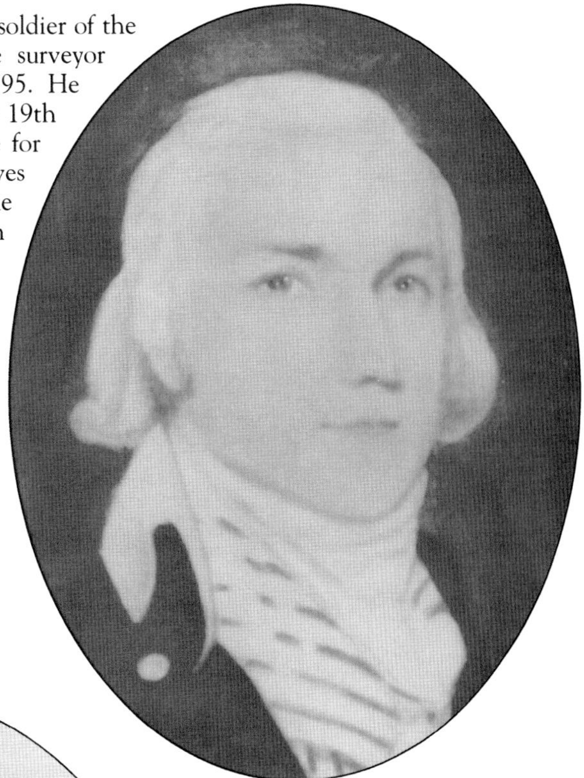

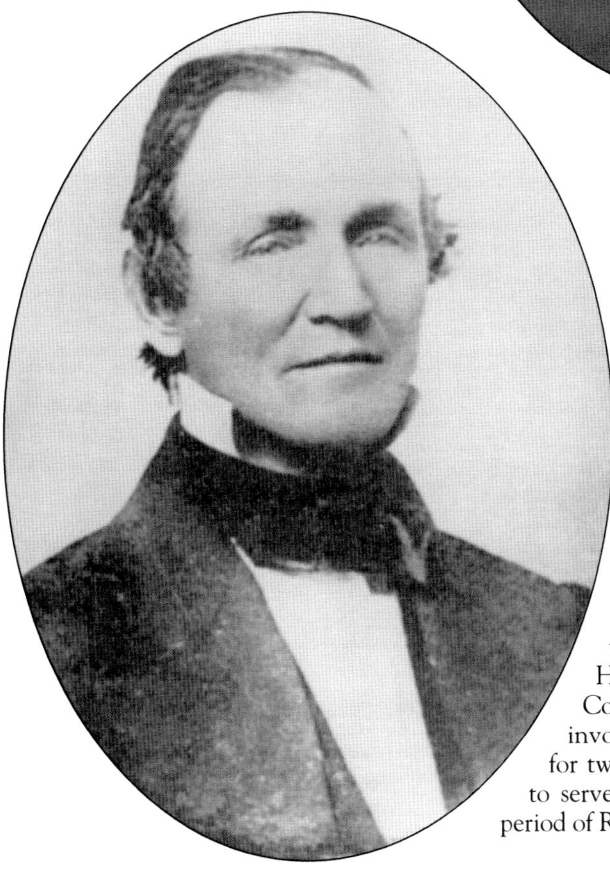

JAMES L. SEWARD. Seward, a native of Dublin, left Laurens County along with dozens of other families to settle in Thomas County, Georgia. He served in the United States Congress from 1853 to 1859 and was involved in Georgia state government for two decades. Seward declined an offer to serve as governor of Georgia during the period of Reconstruction after the Civil War.

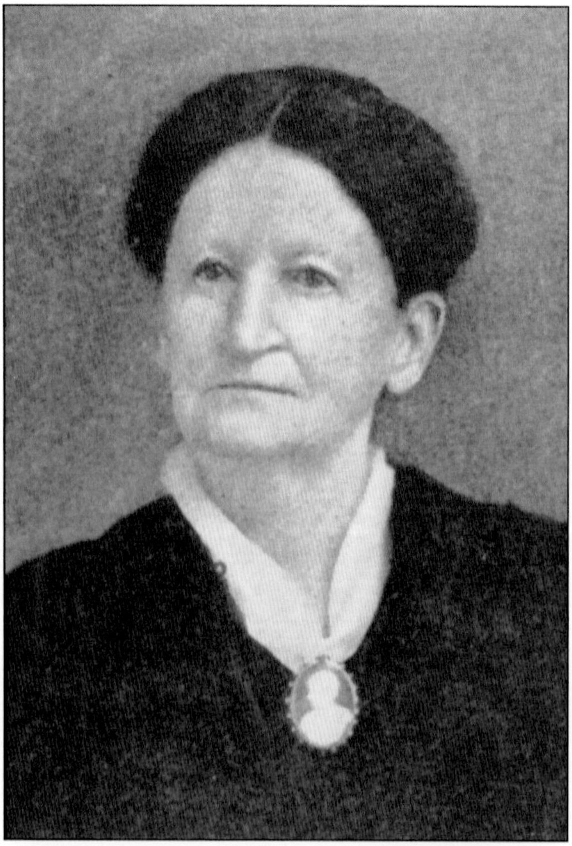

EUGENIA TUCKER COCHRAN FITZGERALD. Eugenia Tucker, daughter of Dr. Nathan Tucker, a wealthy plantation owner in the Buckeye District, founded the Adelphean Society at Wesleyan College in Macon in 1851. The society evolved into Alpha Delta Pi Sorority and was the first collegiate women's sorority in the United States.

CHAPPELL'S MILL. Originally known as Gilbert's Mill and then Stanley's Mill, Chappell's Mill operated for most of the 19th and 20th centuries. During the "March to the Sea" in the waning months of the Civil War, the mill was threatened by Union cavalry forces and was reportedly saved by Maj. James B. Duggan, who burned the Lightwood Knot Bridges to deceive the cavalry into thinking that he and an old slave woman were Gen. Joseph Wheeler's Confederate cavalry.

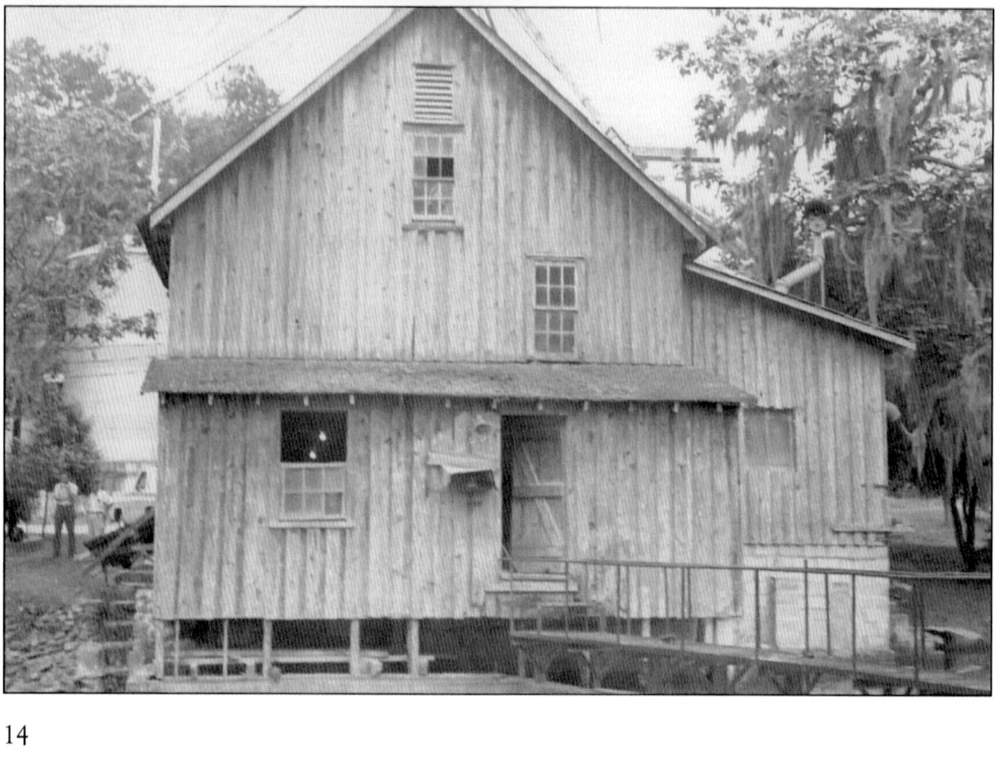

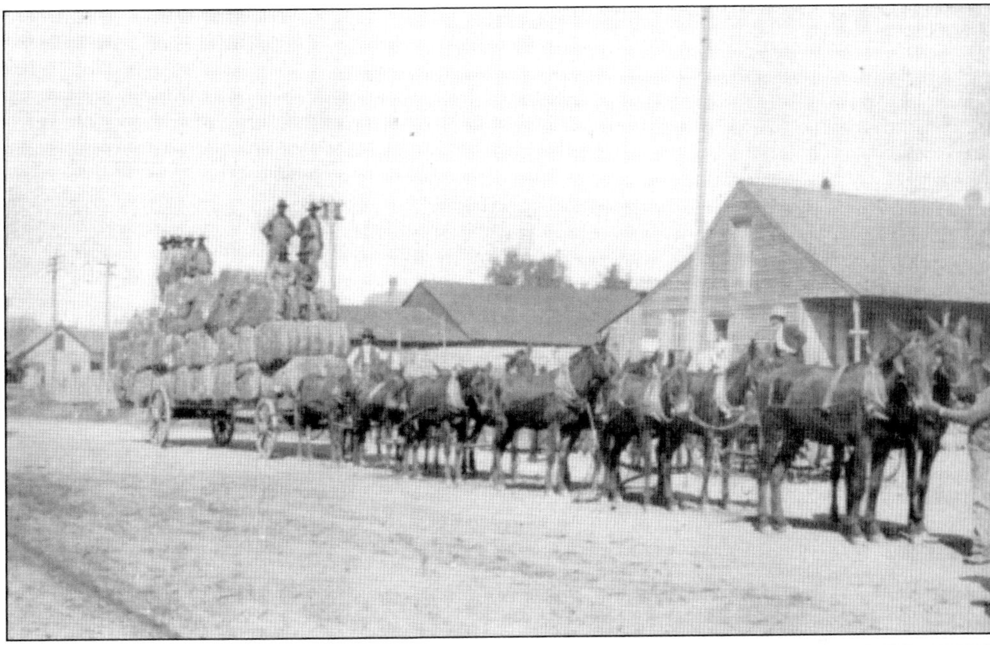

COTTON. Cotton was the lifeblood of Laurens County for more than a century. This photograph shows a large load of cotton being hauled through Dublin at the turn of the 20th century.

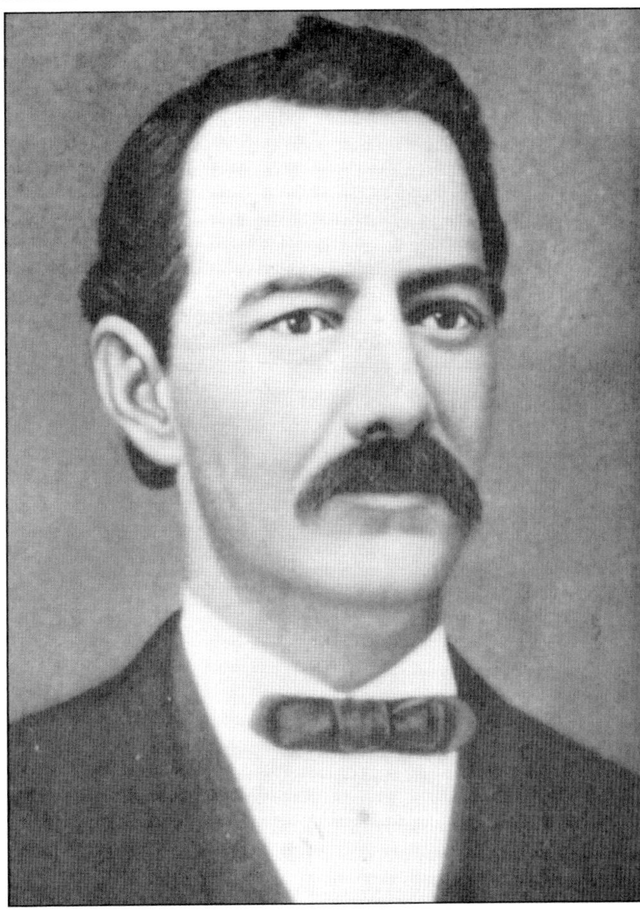

COL. WHITEFORD S. RAMSAY. Whiteford S. Ramsay, a Dublin school teacher, Baptist minister, and Laurens County's first school superintendent, served as lieutenant colonel of the 14th Georgia Infantry Regiment in 1861. Ramsay, who only served a brief period in the army before resigning his commission, was one of the youngest colonels in the Confederate Army.

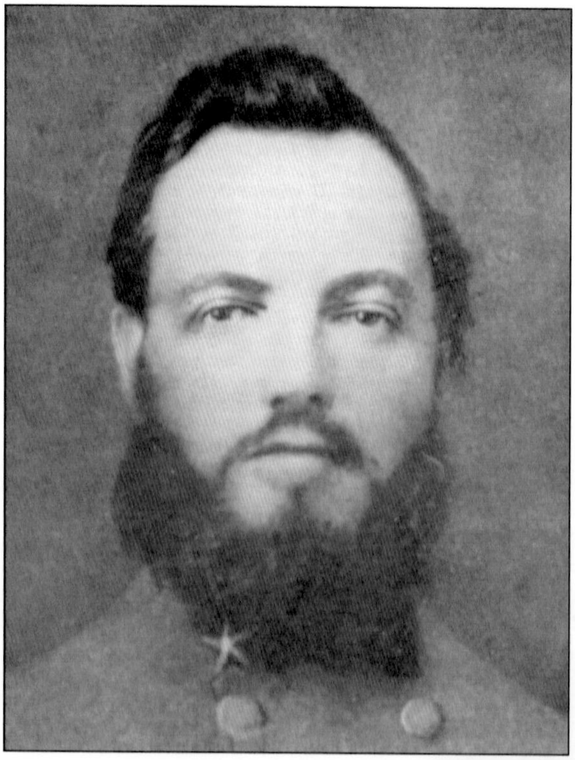

Col. Cinncinatus Saxon Guyton. C.S. Guyton, as he was commonly known, was the son of a wealthy eastern Laurens County plantation owner. Guyton served as second in command of the 57th Georgia Infantry during the siege of Vicksburg in 1863. In July of 1864, Colonel Guyton led the 57th Georgia on an all-night march and the ensuing attack on the Federal left flank, which began the Battle of Atlanta.

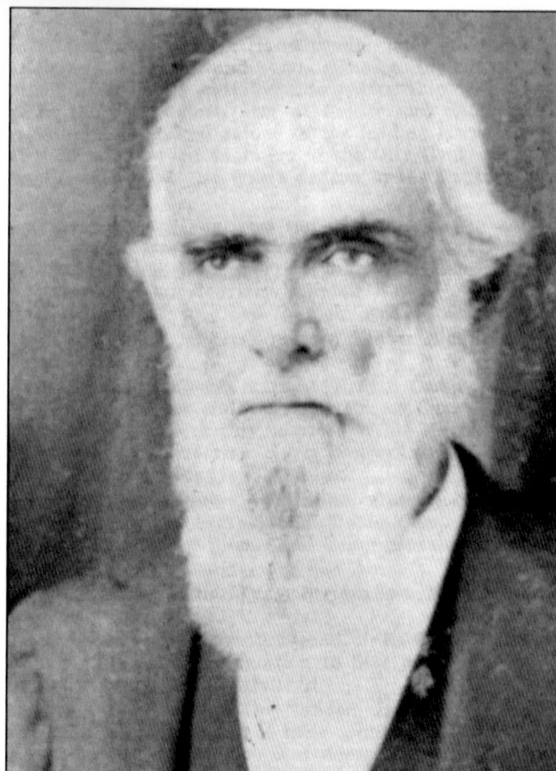

Capt. Thomas H. Rowe. Rowe served as lieutenant in the Blackshear Guards during the Battle of Manassas in July of 1861. He resigned his commission and was elected captain of the Georgia Militia company based in Laurens County, which saw action in the defense of Atlanta and the "March to the Sea."

PRIVATE BENJAMIN F. BALLARD. Private Ballard served in the Blackshear Guards, Co. F., 14th Georgia Infantry, for most of the war. He fought in all the major battles of the Army of Northern Virginia.

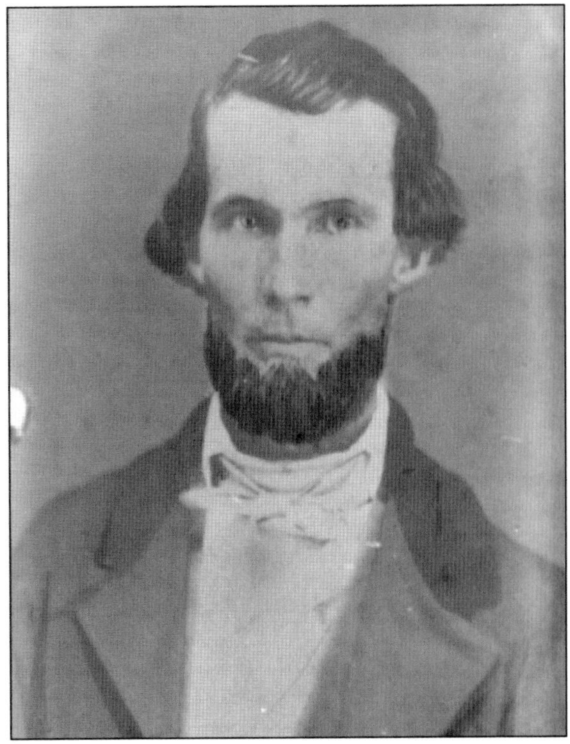

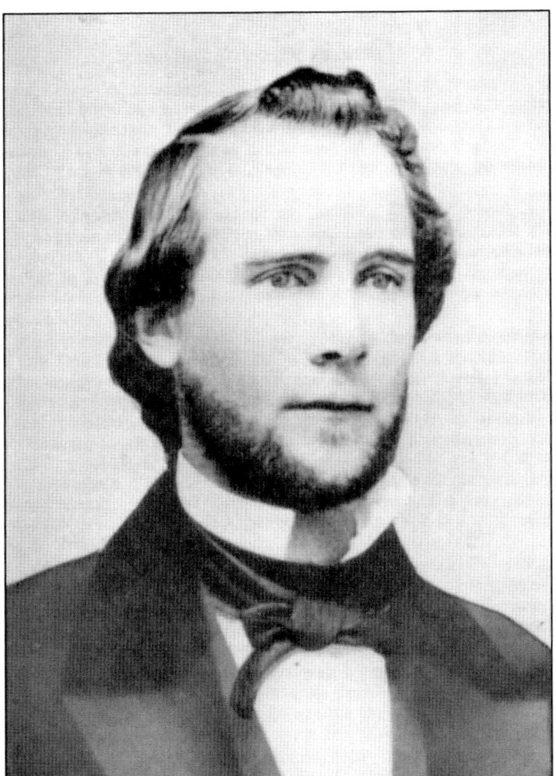

CAPTAIN ROLLIN A. STANLEY. Stanley, who served as judge of the Court of Ordinary of Laurens County from 1891 to 1893, served as captain of Company A, 2nd Georgia Militia. He was elected major of the 16th Military District, but the war ended before he was commissioned.

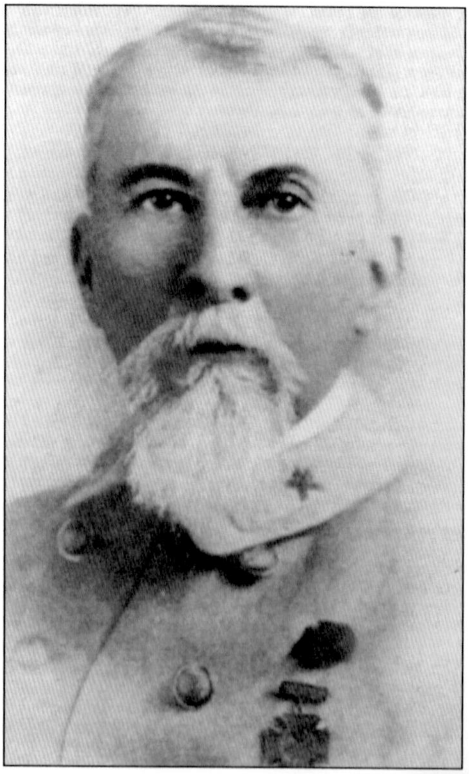

Capt. Hardy Smith. Smith, who served as clerk of Laurens County Superior Court and judge of the Court of Ordinary of Laurens County, served as a sergeant in the Blackshear Guards. In June 1862, at the Battle of Mechanicsville, Smith suffered a severe wound in his right arm that necessitated amputation. Following the war, Smith made his home in western Dublin on a small farm. His home is the subject of a restoration effort by concerned citizens who are seeking to convert his home into a memorial for all Laurens Countians who have served in the military forces of the United States and Confederate States of America.

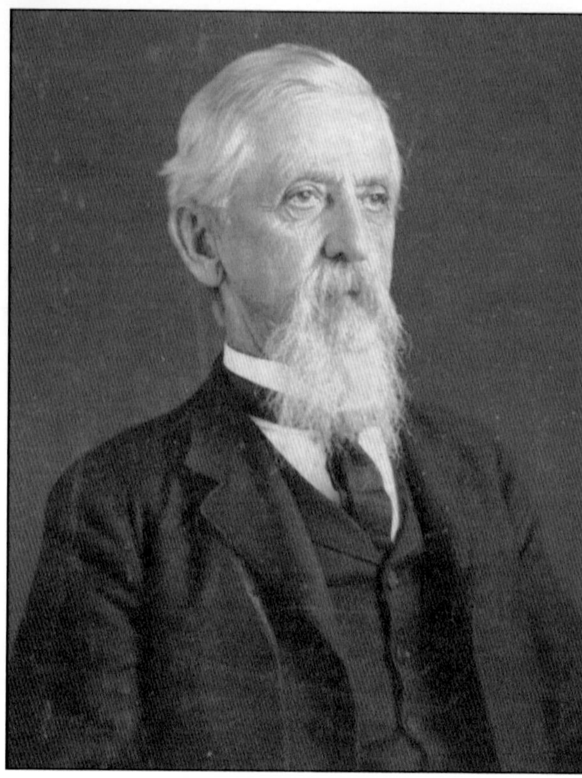

Thomas Hartley Hall. Dr. Hall served in the Confederate Army as a physician. After the war he practiced medicine in Laurens County for over 50 years. He was chosen as the first Laurens County health officer when the first Laurens County Board of Health was created.

Two

Laurens County Communities

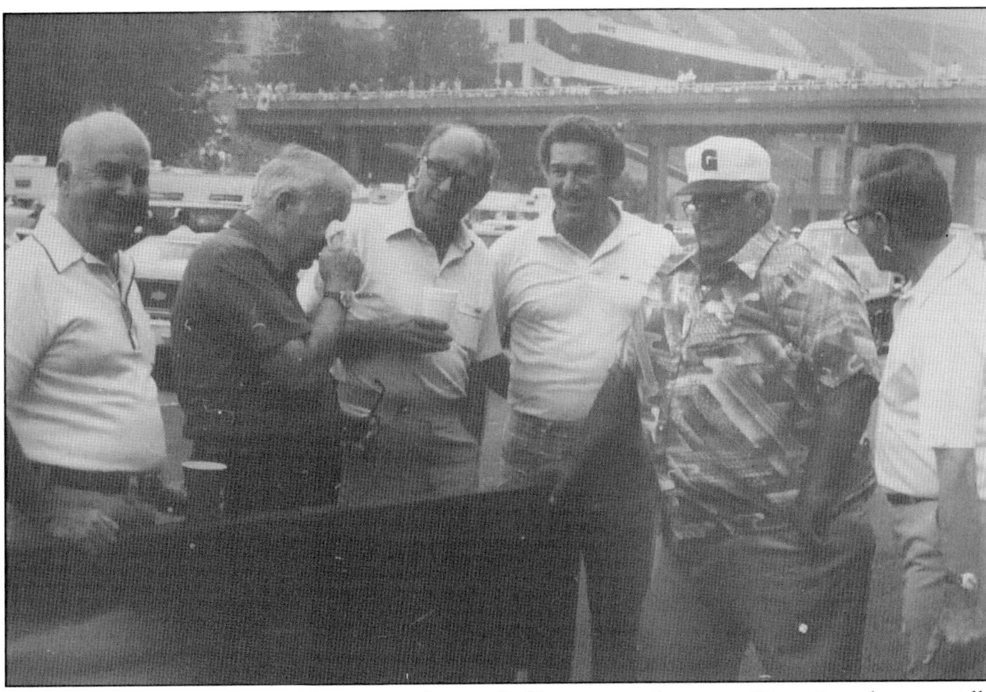

Georgia Bulldog Fans. For more than a half century, Laurens Countians have avidly followed the games of the Georgia Bulldogs. Shown in this 1970s photograph are, from left to right, Thomas Curry, Dale Thompson, Frank Seatonk, Ray Prosperi, the parking lot guard, and Don Lamb. Prosperi is a former Bulldog who played quarterback for the team in the early 1950s.

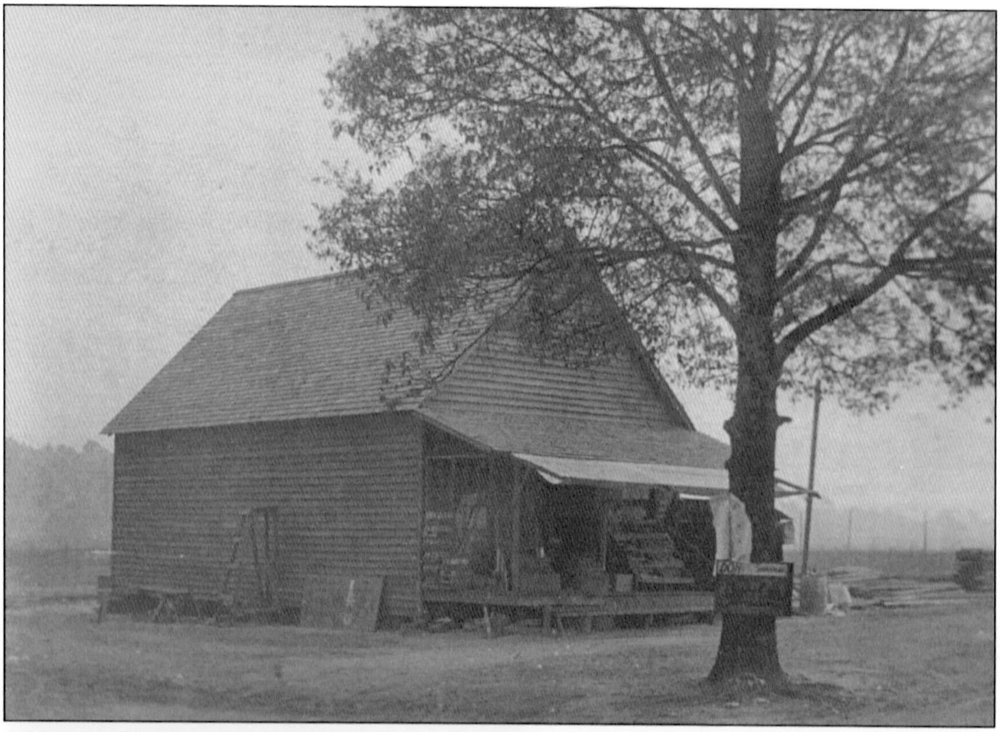

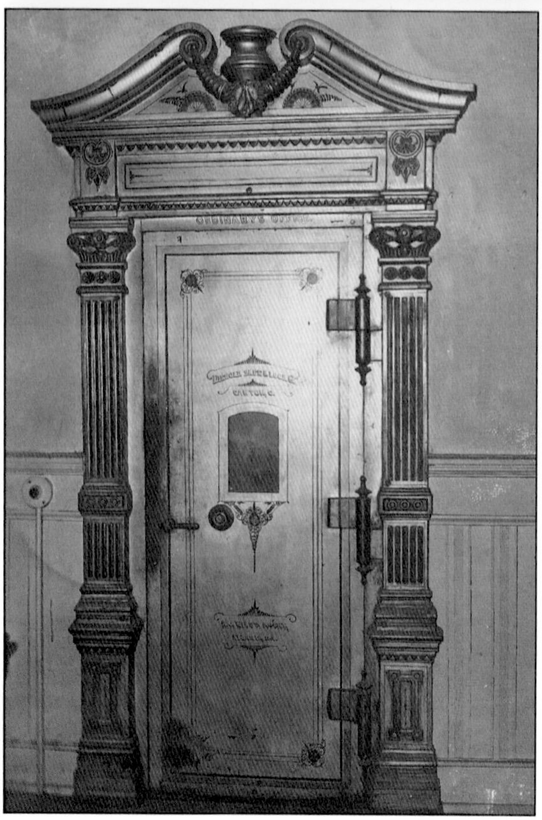

WYNN'S STORE. This photograph, taken during World War I, shows the general store of William Washington Wynn in eastern Laurens County.

KEEPING THE RECORDS SAFE. This 1950s photograph shows the elaborate vault door of the judge of the Ordinary Court, now the Probate Court, which was located in the Laurens County Courthouse. The courthouse was built in 1895 and razed in 1963.

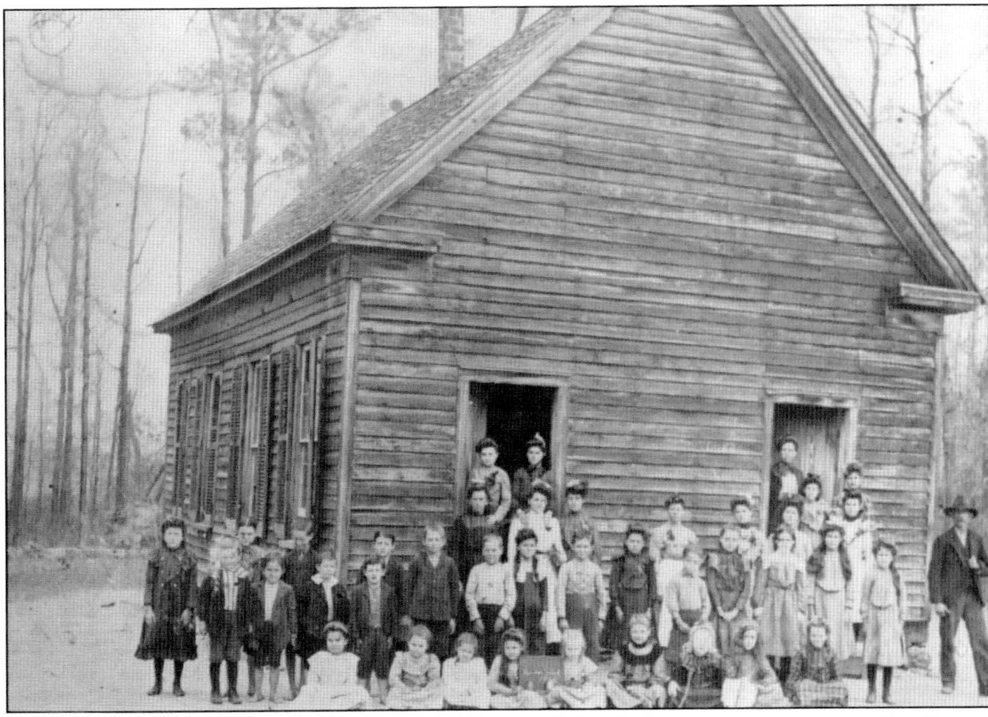

HASKINS CROSSING SCHOOL. Also known as Bender School, this quaint one-room schoolhouse, pictured in 1906, was located on the Macon, Dublin, and Savannah Railroad in the Haskins Crossing community between Dudley and Montrose, near the present intersection of the Georgia Highway 26 and U.S. Highway 80.

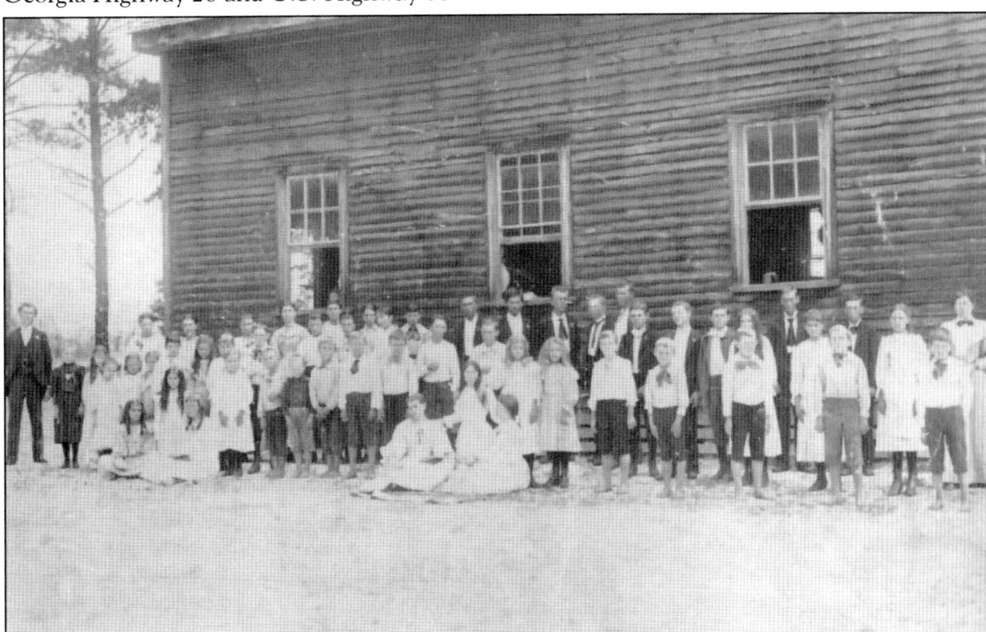

OLD BETHSAIDA SCHOOL. This 1895 photograph shows the school at Bethsaida near Bethsaida Baptist Church on U.S. Highway 80 West, about 2 miles west of Dublin.

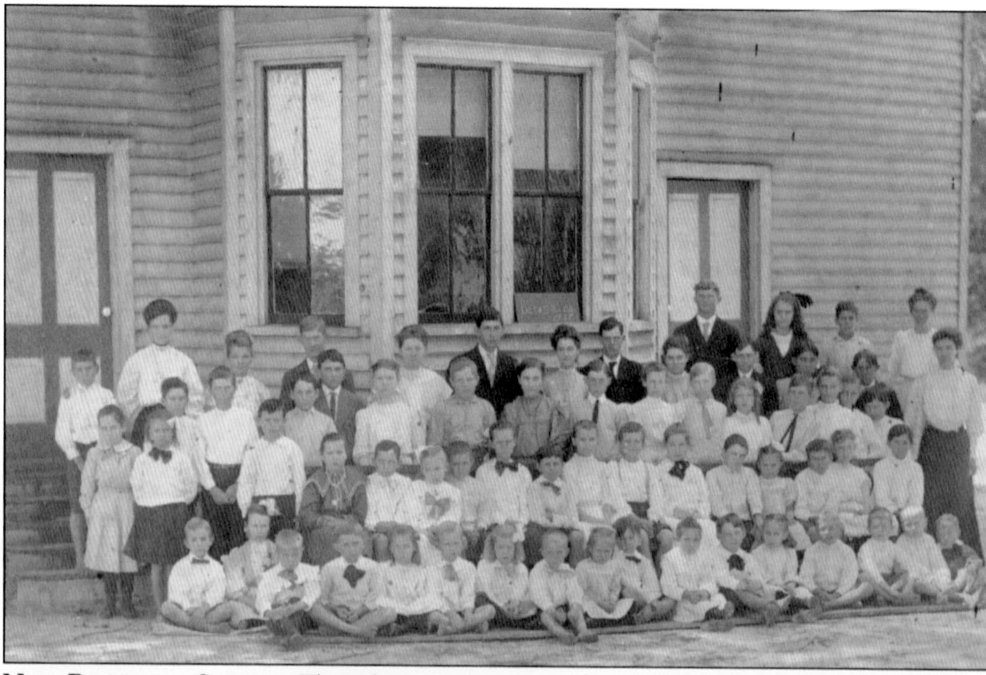

New Bethsaida School. This photograph, taken about 1908, shows the new school at Bethsaida. It was constructed in order to enlarge and improve the school's facilities.

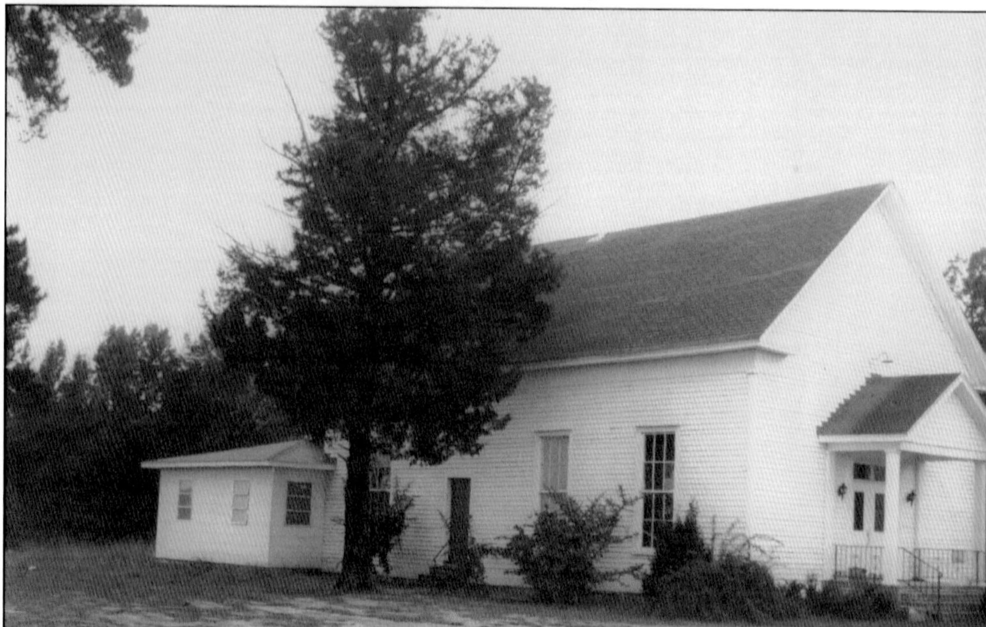

Boiling Springs Methodist Church. Boiling Springs Methodist Church was built in 1851 on land donated by Everard Blackshear. The church was used by both whites and blacks until the Civil War and featured a gallery for slaves who were members of the church. The springs to the north of the church once flowed with a such a powerful force that the name for the place was obvious. The church building is the oldest wooden Methodist church building in the South Georgia Conference.

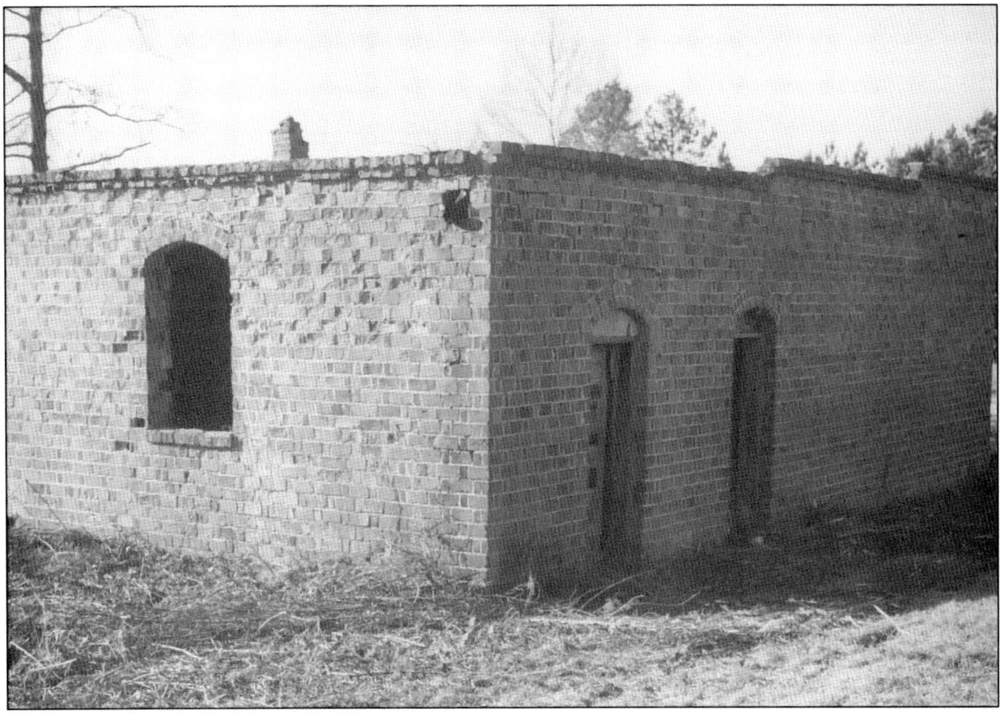

Curl's Store. In its day, Curl's Store occupied the prime commercial corner in the railroad town of Brewton. The store building, which once stood at the corner of Jackson and Peachtree Streets, was recently torn down.

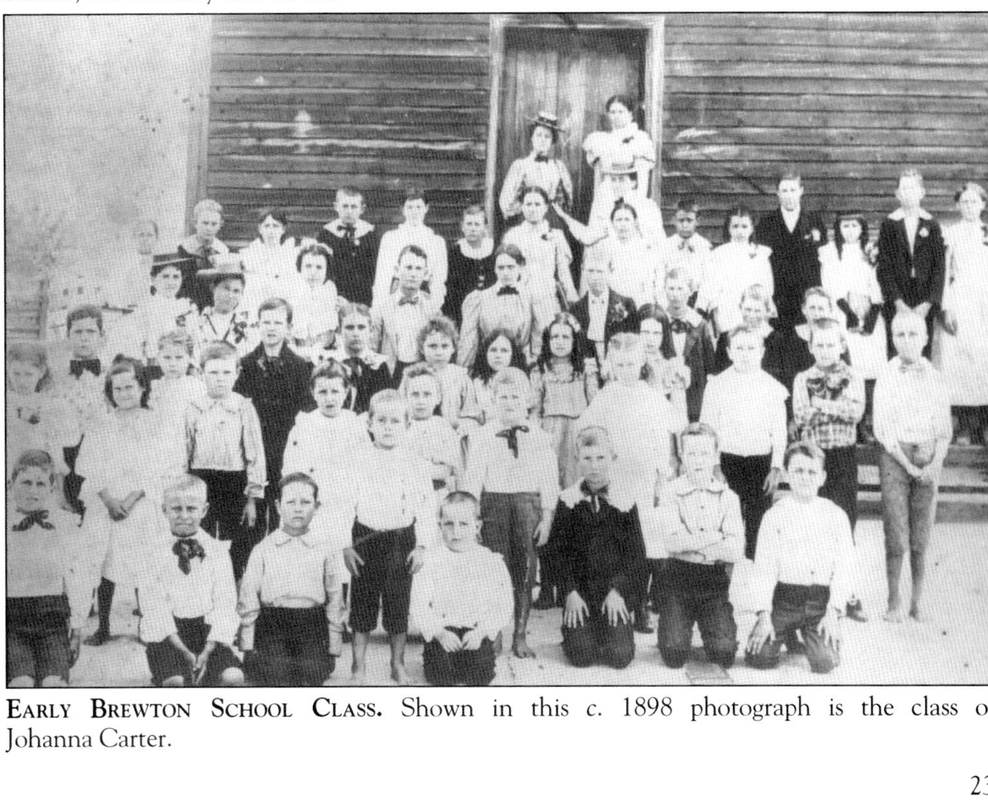

Early Brewton School Class. Shown in this *c.* 1898 photograph is the class of Johanna Carter.

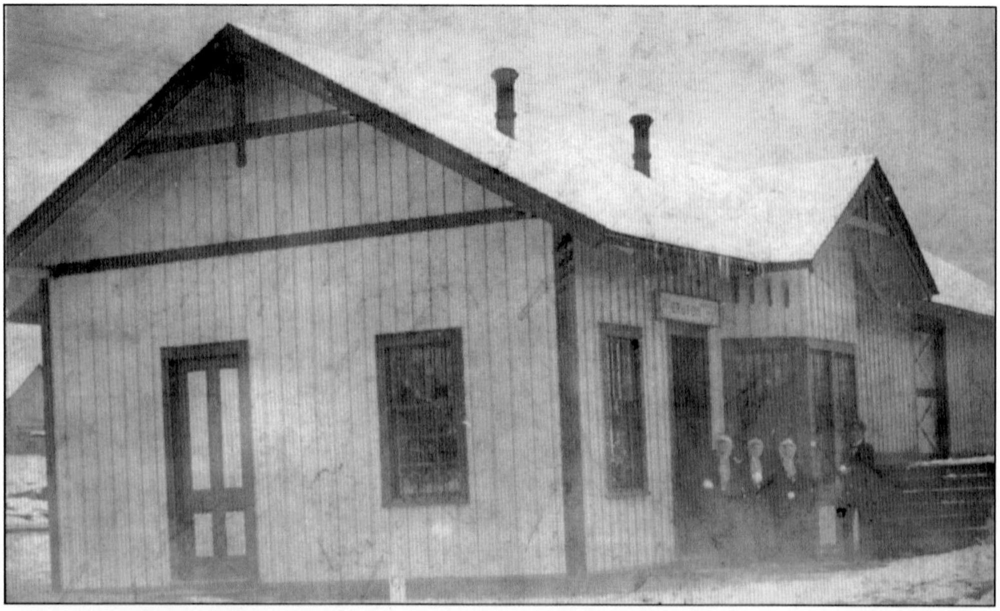

BREWTON DEPOT. This early photograph, taken about 1889, shows four young men with snowballs, following a rare snowfall, standing in front of the Wrightsville and Tennille Railroad Depot at Brewton. A close observation of the sign on the building reveals that the name of the town was spelled "Bruton" before it was officially changed to Brewton. The original post office, founded by Henry T. Jones, was known as "Dodo," until it was changed to Brewton in 1894.

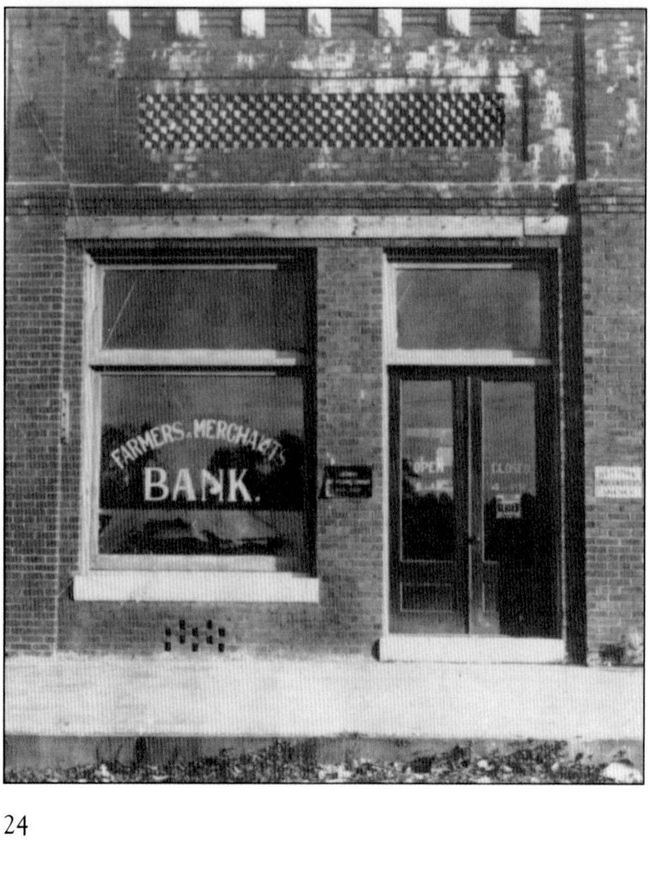

FARMERS AND MERCHANTS BANK. The Farmers and Merchants Bank was founded in Brewton in 1910 by James L. Keen, I.E. Thigpen, J.H. Curl, H.T. Burch, J.M. Lovett, and Lehman Keen. The bank moved to Dublin in the mid-1930s due to security problems and the decline of Brewton during the Depression. Today, the bank is one of the safest banks in the country and one of the largest privately owned small city banks in the state.

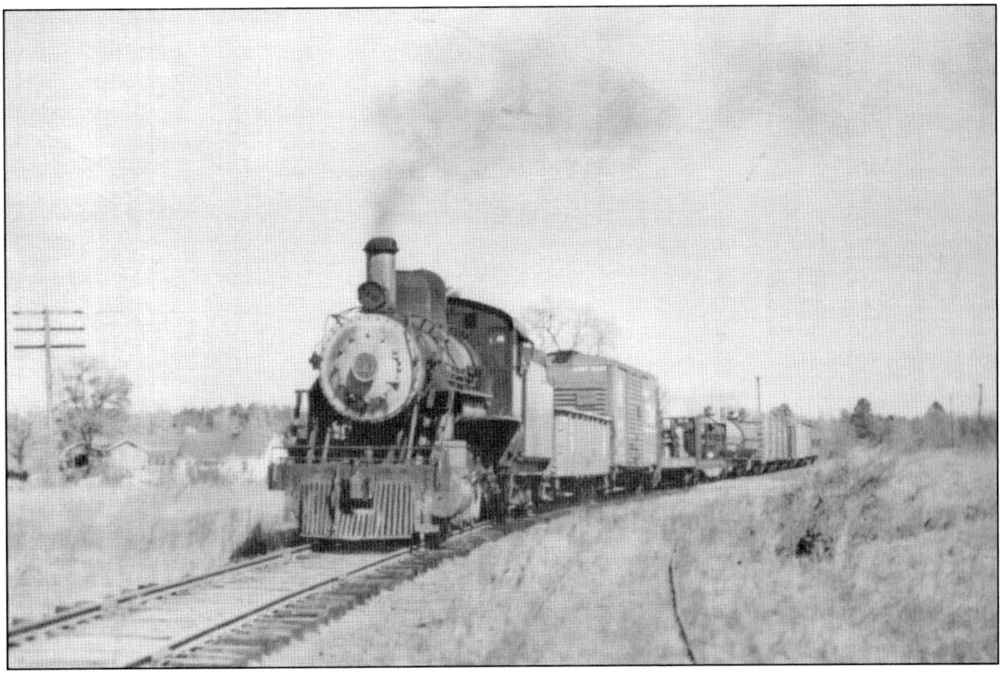

The Wrightsville and Tennille Railroad. This 1954 photograph shows Train No. 1 passing through Brewton. The railroad came to Brewton in 1885 and was an important factor in the town's economy for half a century.

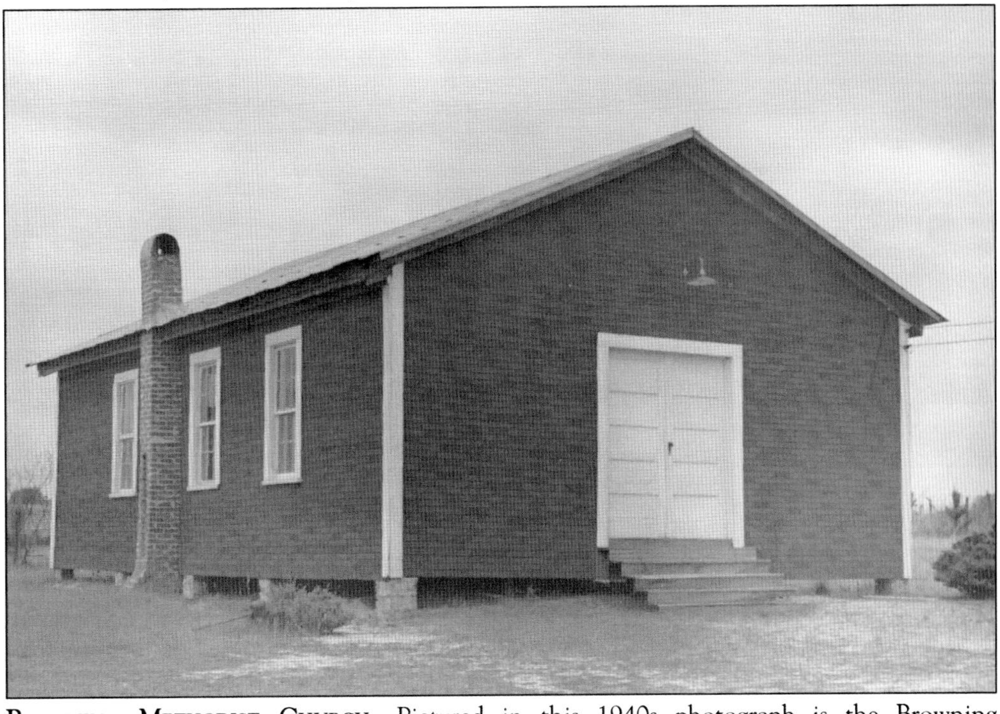

Browning Methodist Church. Pictured in this 1940s photograph is the Browning Methodist Church, which is located a few miles north of Cedar Grove in southern Laurens County.

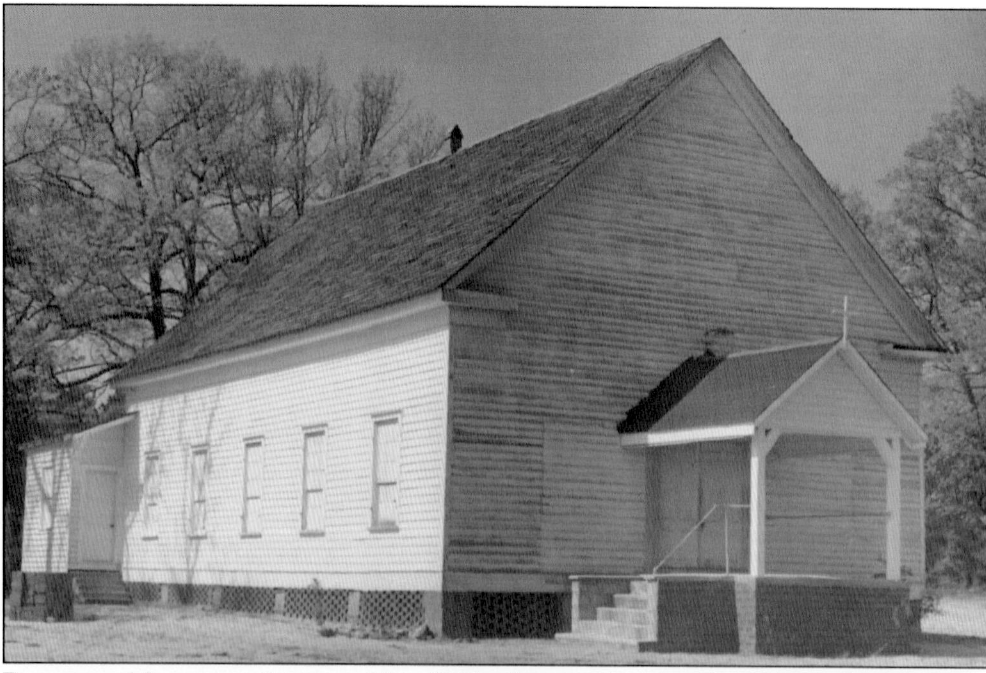

Buckhorn Methodist Church. This 1940s photograph shows the old wooden Methodist Church in the Buckhorn community. The first Methodist Church in Laurens County and the predecessor to Buckhorn Church was Darsey's Meeting House. It was built by Seth Darsey on the old John Lord place, southwest of Dudley on what is known as the "Chicken Road."

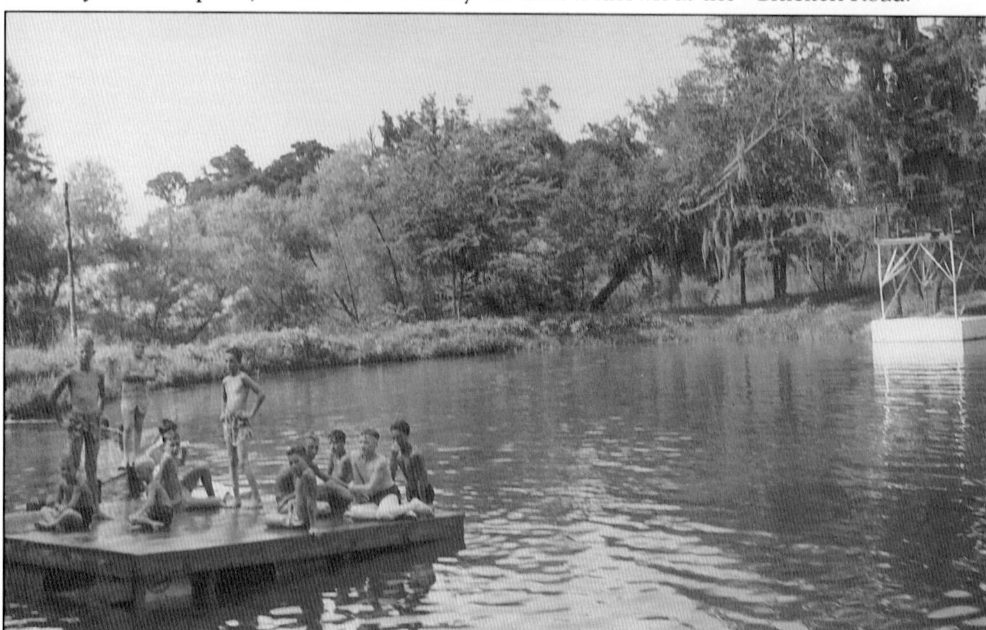

Session's Lake. Session's Lake was one of Laurens County's most popular recreation spots from the 1930s through the 1960s. The lake was located on Country Club Road, just south of the country club. During World War II, the men and boys of the Georgia State Guard Units in Laurens County trained around the lake.

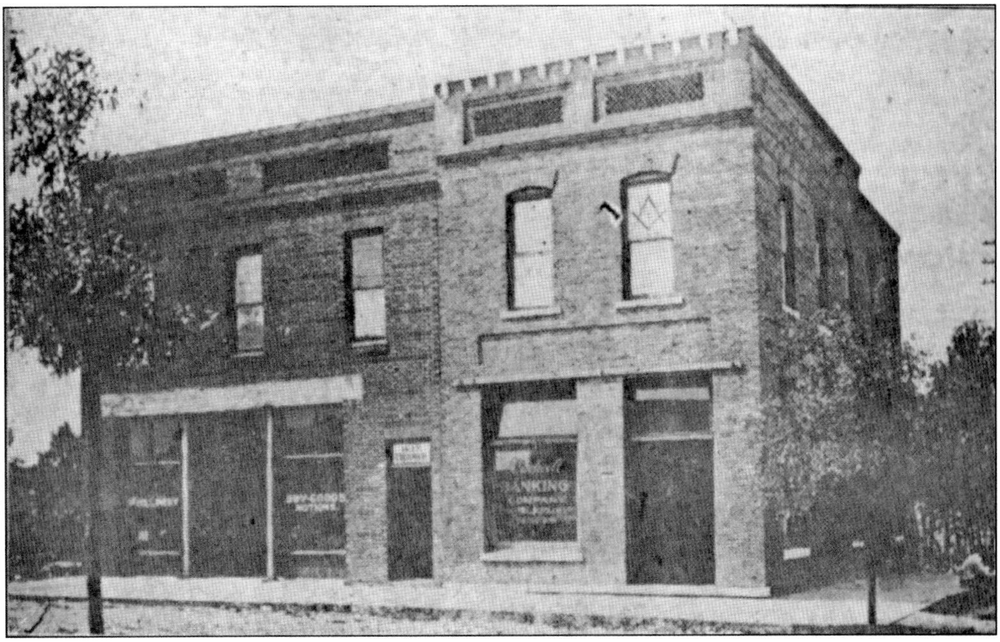

CADWELL BANKING COMPANY. The Cadwell Banking Company, shown in this 1918 photograph, was founded by L.B. Holt, G.C. Wood, H.C. Coleman Jr., W.H. Mullis Sr., J.A. Burch, H.C. Burch, H.R. Bedingfield, A. McCook, H.C. Stonecypher, and W.B. Coleman on January 5, 1910. It was Laurens County's third bank outside of Dublin.

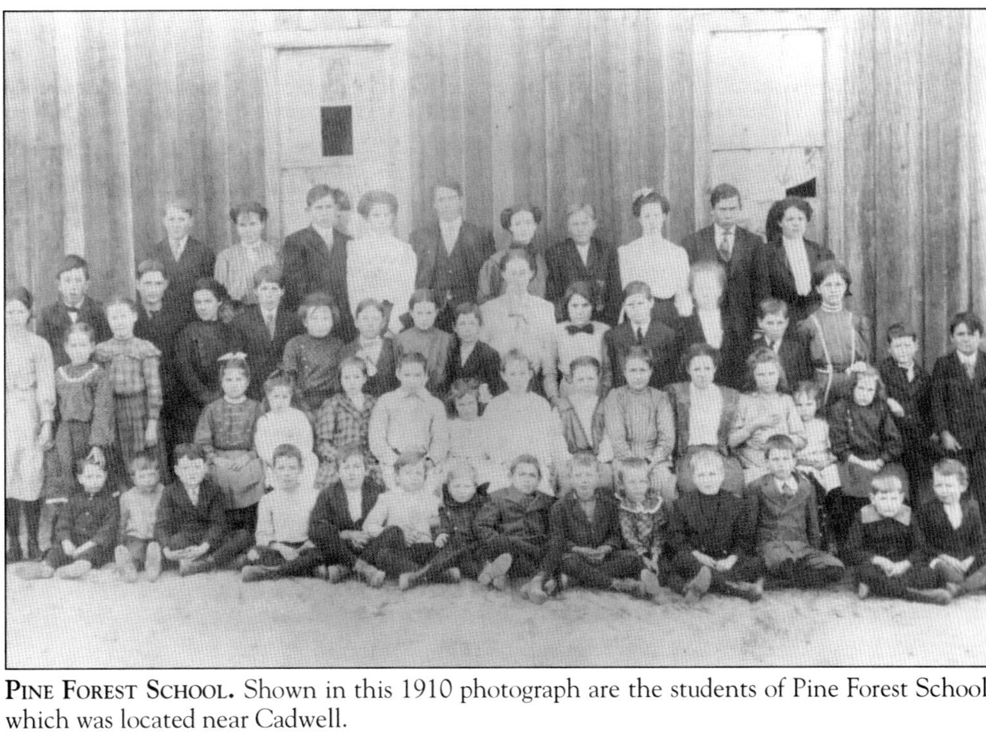

PINE FOREST SCHOOL. Shown in this 1910 photograph are the students of Pine Forest School, which was located near Cadwell.

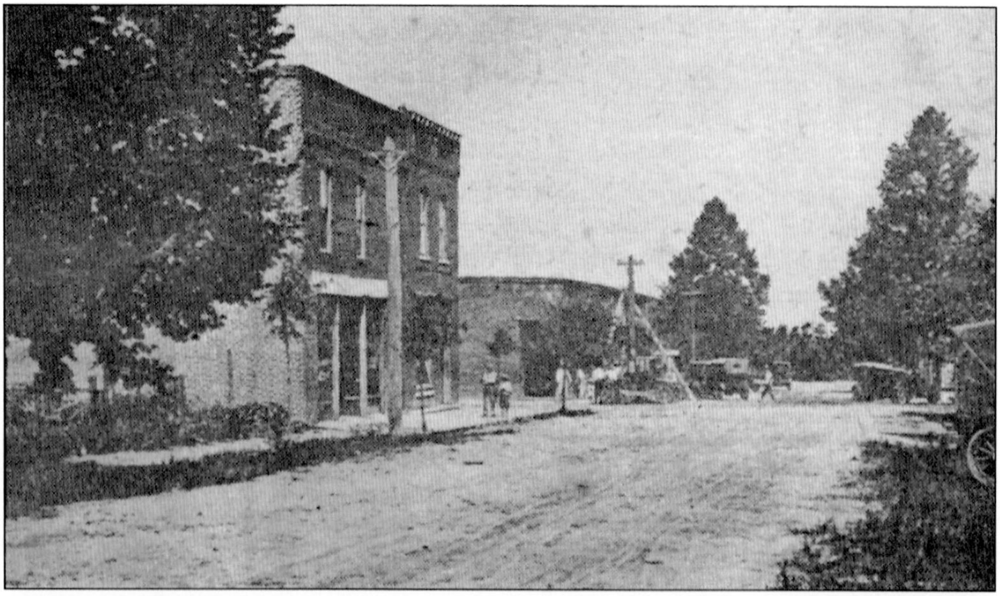

CADWELL IN 1918. This photograph shows the main business street in Cadwell in 1918. The town reached its peak in that year, just before the boll weevil nearly wiped out the cotton crop.

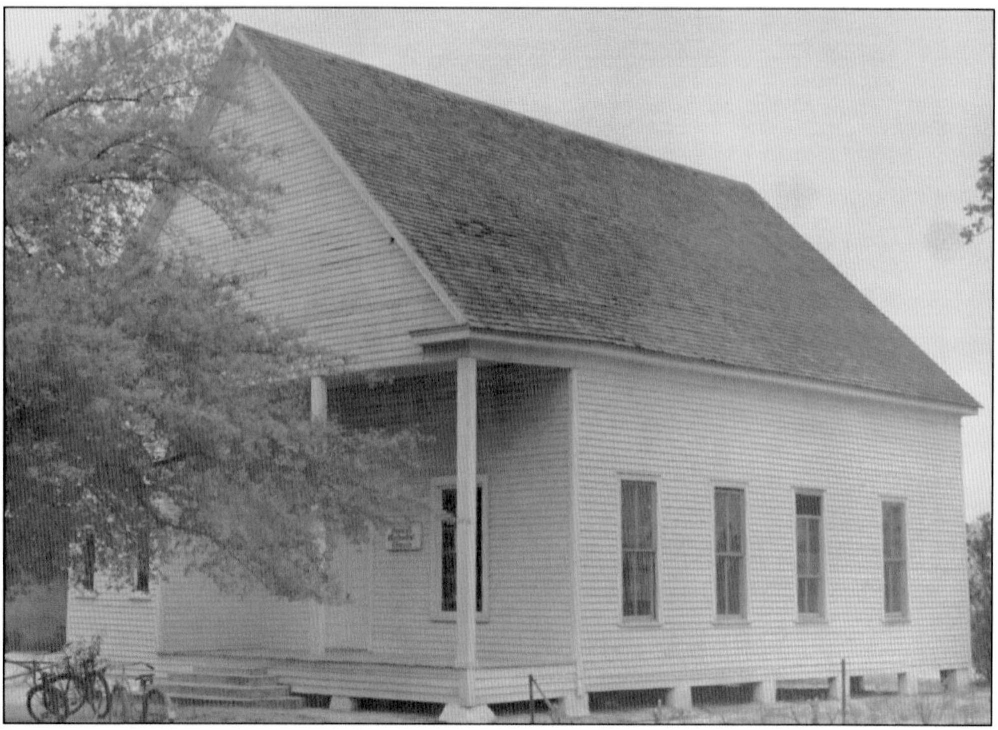

CADWELL METHODIST CHURCH. Shown in this 1940s photograph is the Methodist church at Cadwell located next to the school.

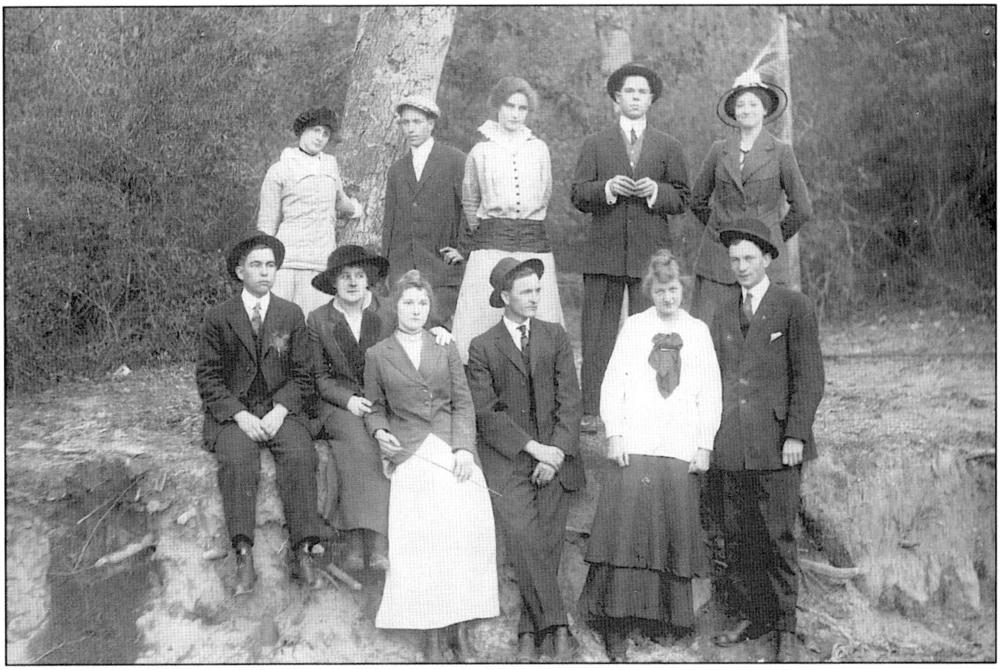

EXCURSIONS. Excursions to recreational areas in Georgia were popular with Laurens Countians in the first quarter of the 20th century. This photograph, taken c. 1920, shows a group at Indian Springs. Mattie Lee Wade is third from the right on the top row, and Marshall Chapman is on the far right on the bottom row. The identities of the other people are unknown.

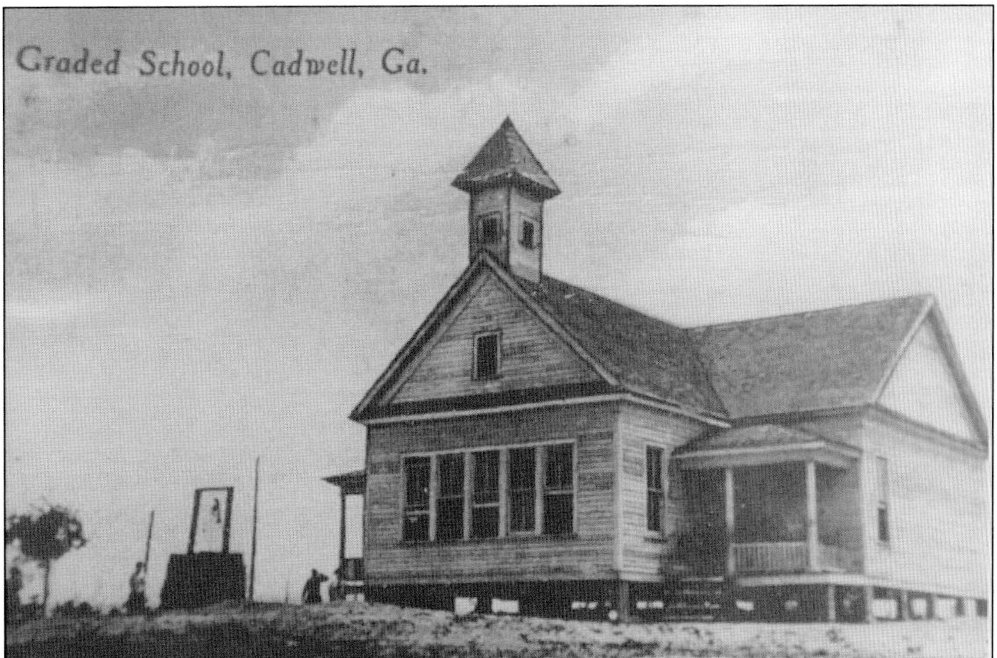

OLD GRADED SCHOOL AT CADWELL. Shown in this early-20th-century photograph is the first school at Cadwell. The school was founded in 1907.

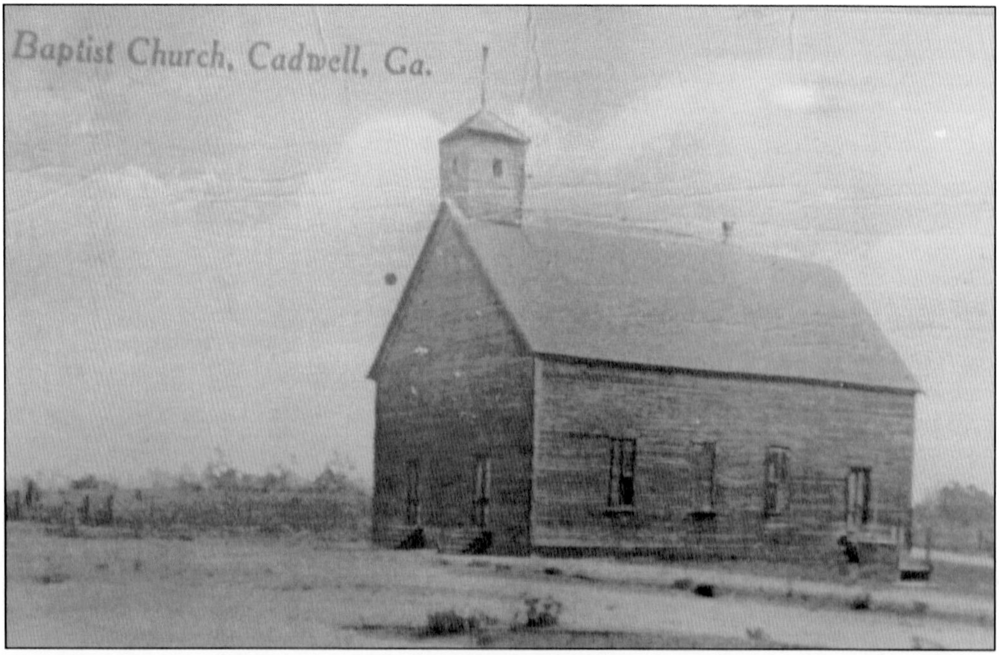

THE FIRST BAPTIST CHURCH AT CADWELL. The first building of the Baptist Church at Cadwell is seen here in the early 20th century. The church was organized in 1909, and the first pastor was Eli Evans.

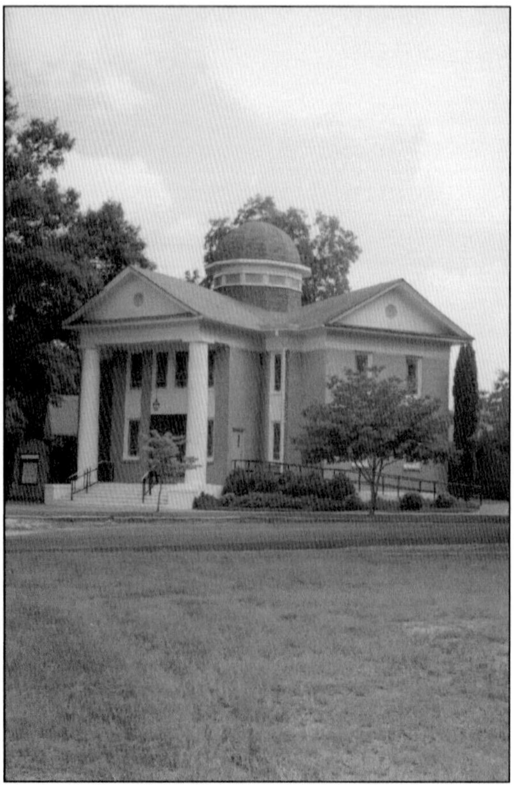

THE FIRST BAPTIST CHURCH AT CADWELL. Shown in this late-20th-century photograph is the second church building of the Baptist Church at Cadwell.

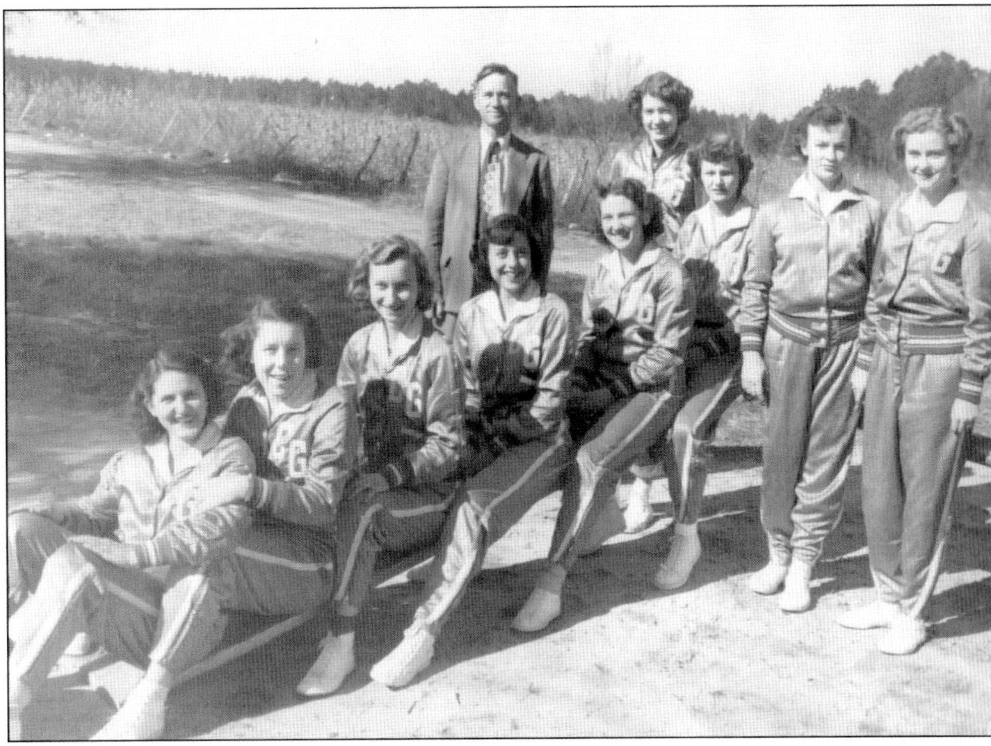

LAURENS COUNTY'S FIRST STATE CHAMPIONS. The girl's basketball team from Cedar Grove High School is pictured in 1951. The team posted a record of 35 and 1 and won the Class C Georgia State Championship. Shown, from left to right, are Ouida Mae Turner, Moena Faulk, Geneva Young, Marilyn Wommack, Ouida Dixon, Edwina Davidson, Alethia Burch (standing), Jackie Gilder, and Hazel Browning. Standing in the back is Coach Lester Farr.

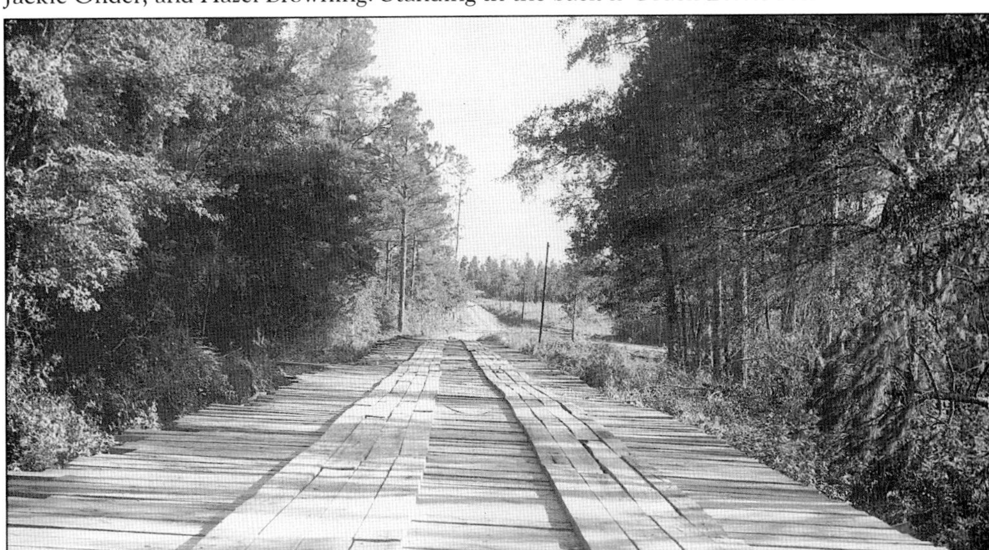

WOODEN BRIDGES. This photograph shows one of the last wooden bridges in Laurens County. Because of their tremendous size, wooden bridges like this one were maintained by Laurens Countians until they were gradually replaced by concrete bridges in the 1960s.

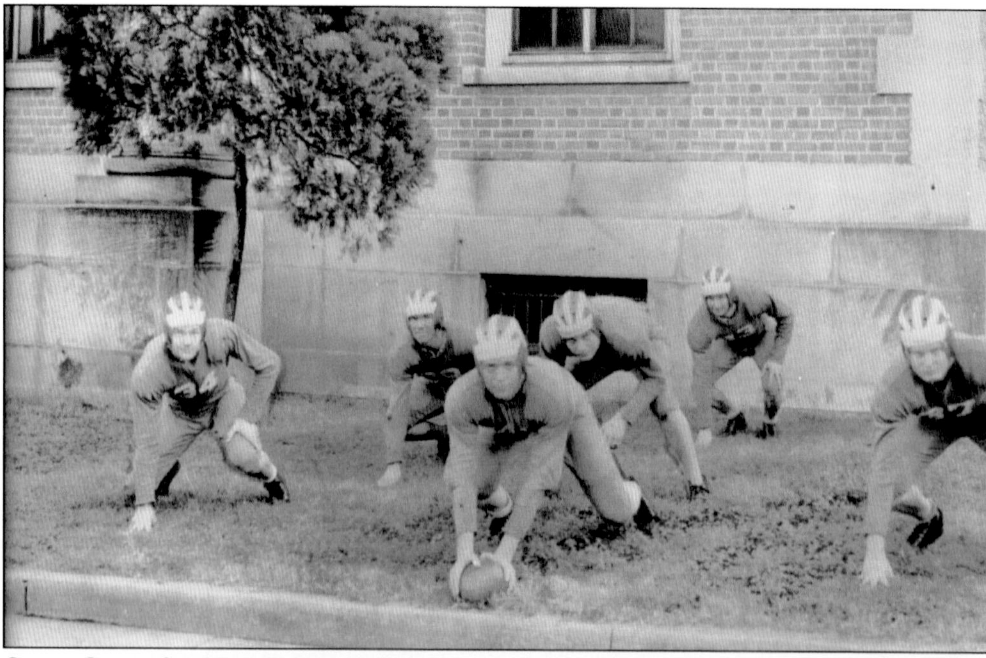

Cedar Grove Six-Man Football Team. Six-man football became popular just before World War II in Laurens County. The Cedar Grove team, including Wallace Lamb (number 39), is shown in this photograph, which was taken at the county office building, formerly the old post office, on Madison Street in Dublin.

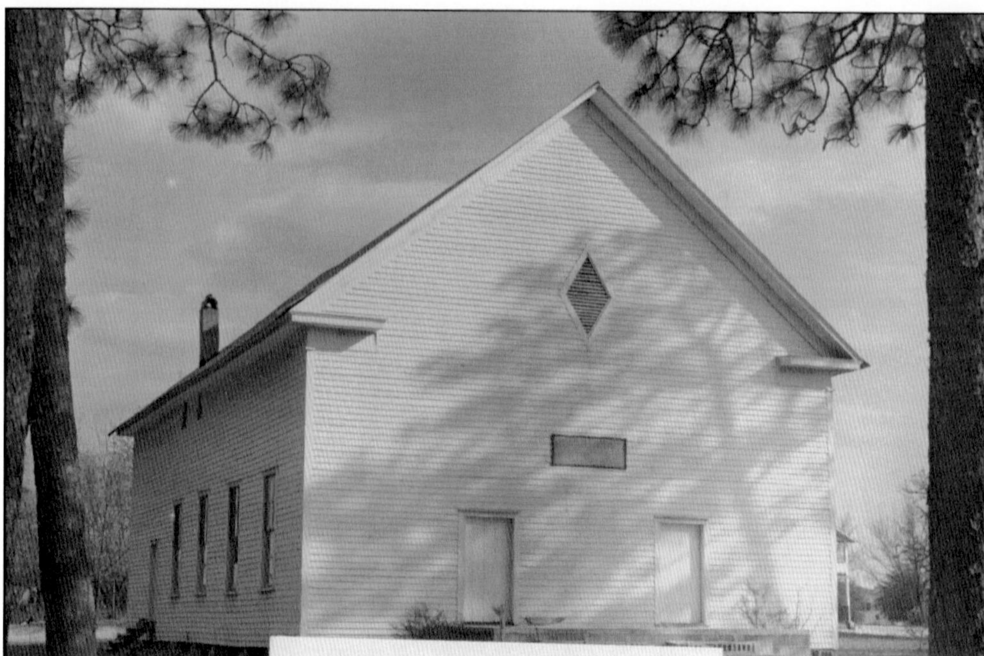

Cedar Grove Methodist Church. Cedar Grove Methodist Church was founded in 1886 by Cornelius Clark. The building shown in the photograph was constructed in 1905 and is still in use today.

Eye Catcher. The owners of the OK Tire Store in Dublin knew that the Paul Bunyan–like tire technician would catch the eyes of many of the county's automobile owners. Notice the dog looking up at the giant.

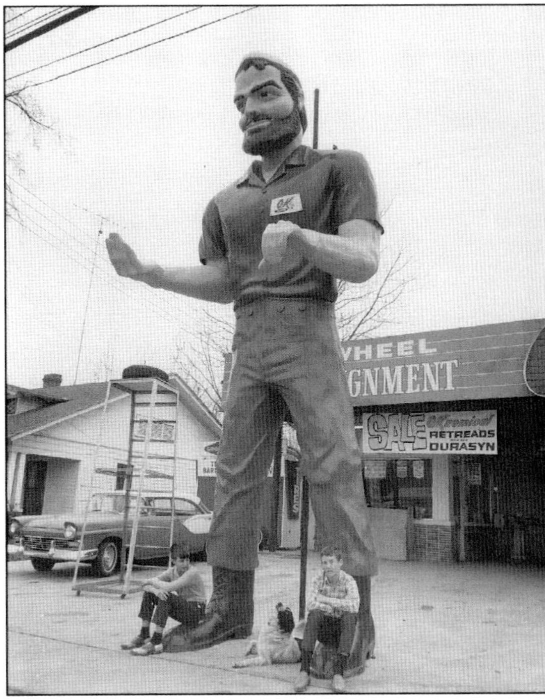

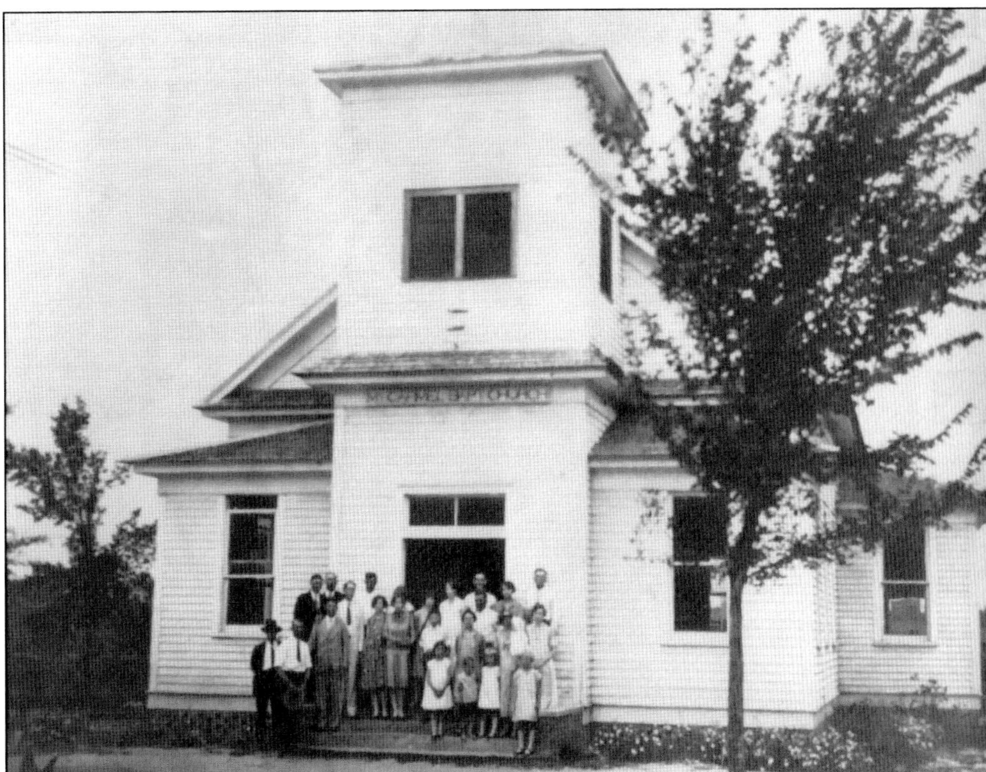

Mt. Carmel Baptist Church. This beautiful wooden church located in the Mt. Carmel community near Dexter was mercilessly destroyed by a tornado on April 25, 1929.

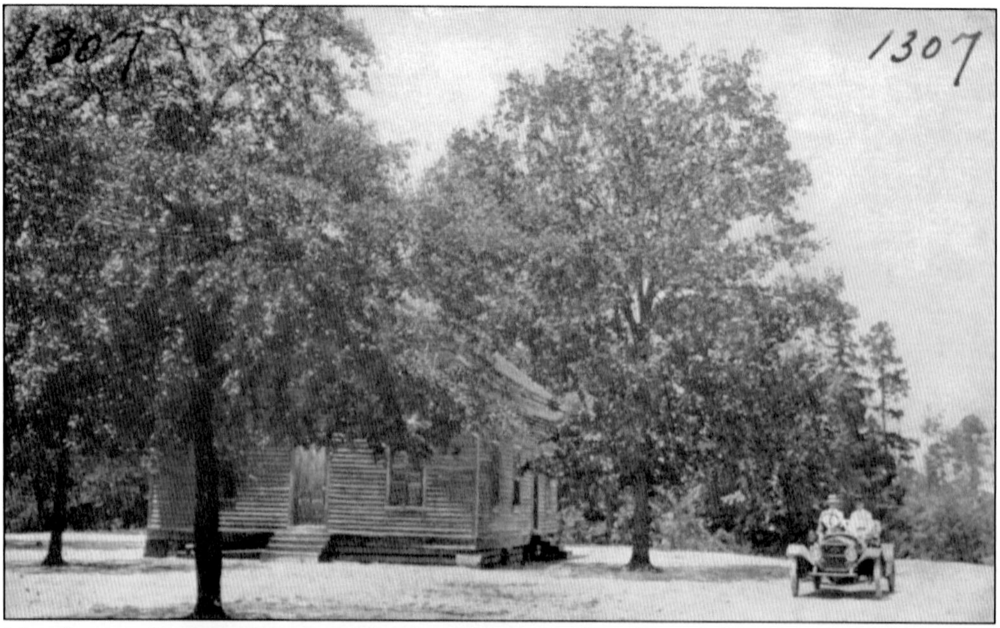

MT. CARMEL BAPTIST CHURCH. Mt. Carmel Baptist Church near Dexter is pictured here in 1909. It was organized in 1857, and Larry Hobbs served as its first pastor. This church was in use until the 1920s.

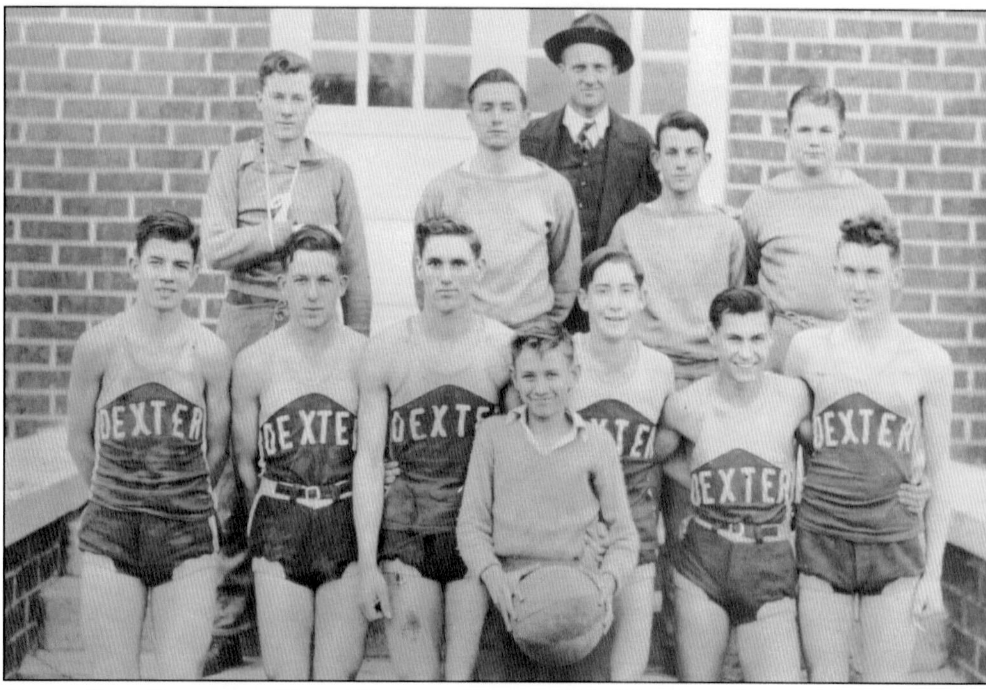

DEXTER BOYS BASKETBALL TEAM. The boys of Dexter High School are shown in this photograph taken just after World War II. Shown, from left to right, are (first row) Phil Gilbert; (second row) Jack Gilbert, Clifford Davidson, Lester Patisual, Earl Thomas, Tommy Funderburke, and Howard Warren; (third row) Aaron Hobbs, Farrell Williamson, James Brown, and Gerald Collins; (fourth row) Oscar Adams, coach and principal.

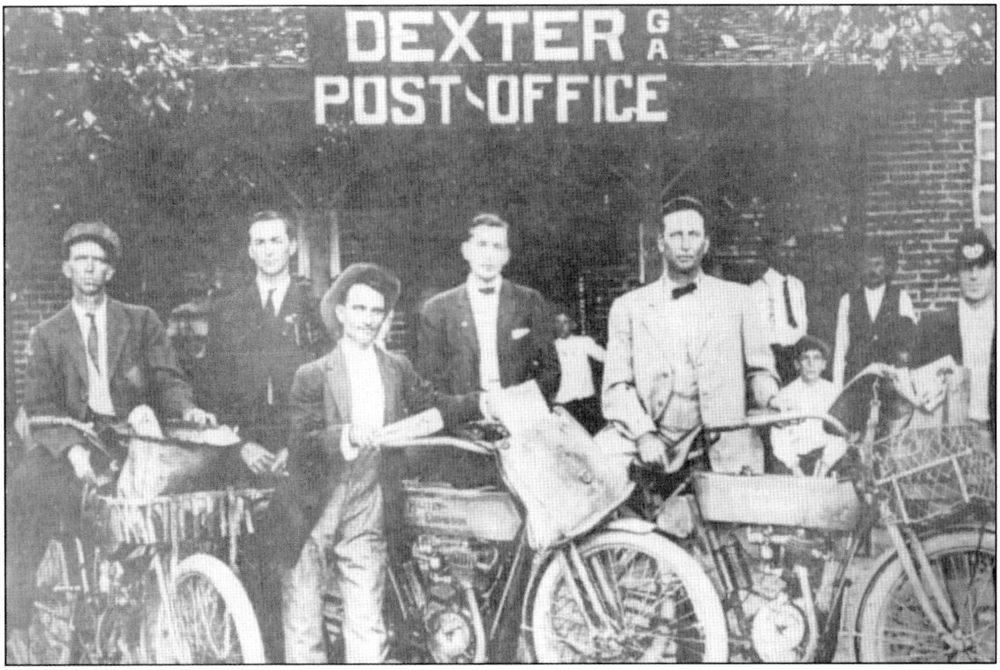

DEXTER POST OFFICE. Shown in this early 1900s photograph are, from left ro right, mail carriers G.H. Green, W.P. English, H.I. King (postmaster), G.F. Shepard, and J.T. Register. The post office was founded in 1890, and J.H. Witherington was the first postmaster.

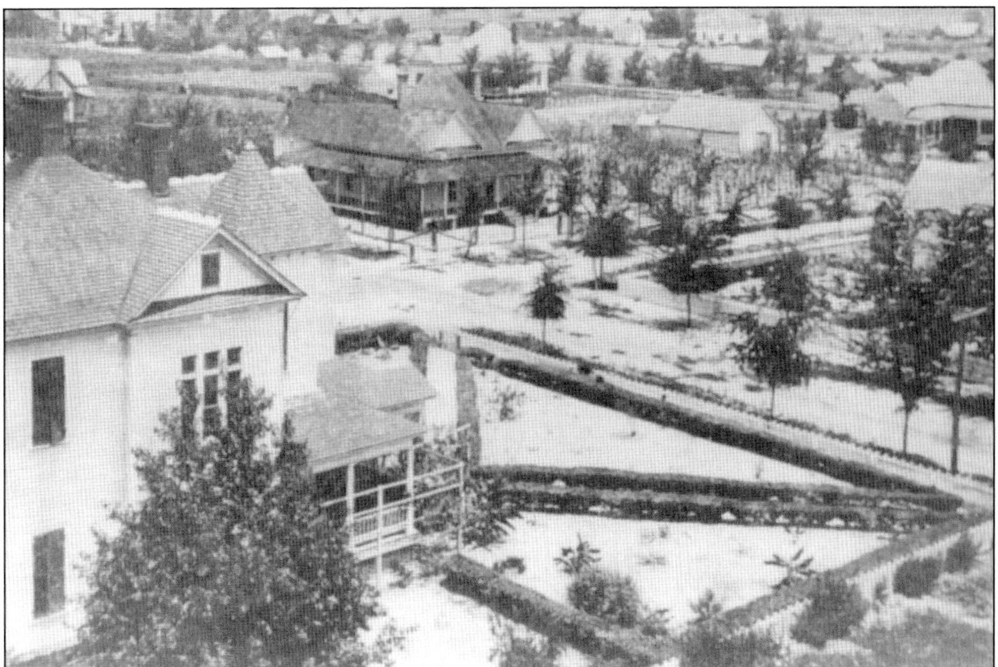

BIRD'S-EYE VIEW OF DEXTER. This photograph, taken about 1911, was taken from the top of the town water tank. The R.C. Hogan house is shown on the left. The Methodist church can been seen in the upper left corner.

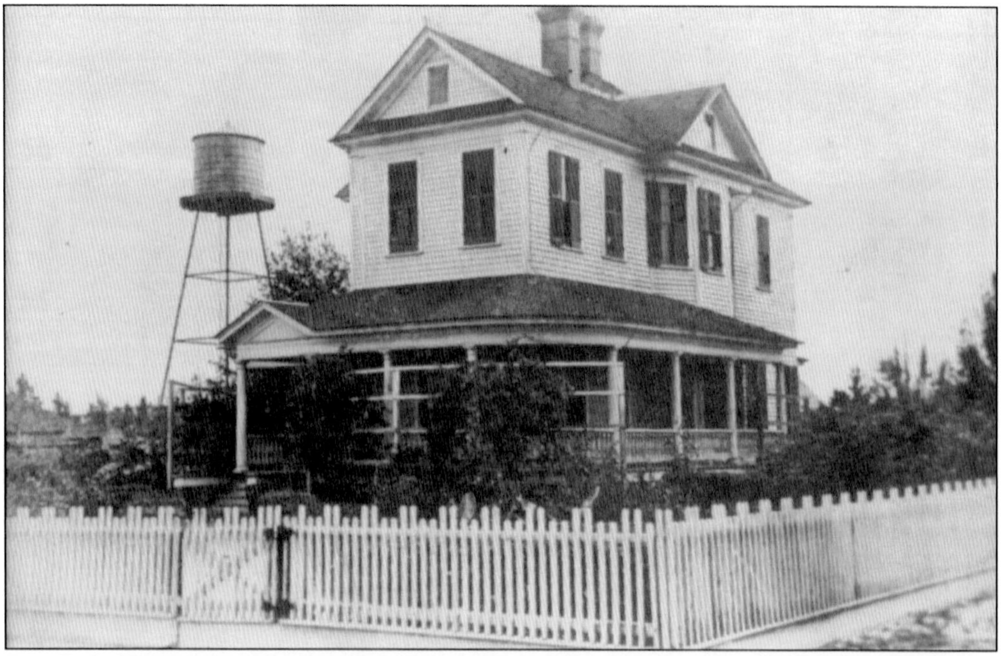

THE R.C. HOGAN HOUSE. This handsome home of Mr. and Mrs. R.C. Hogan was located on the corner of King and Alpha Streets in Dexter.

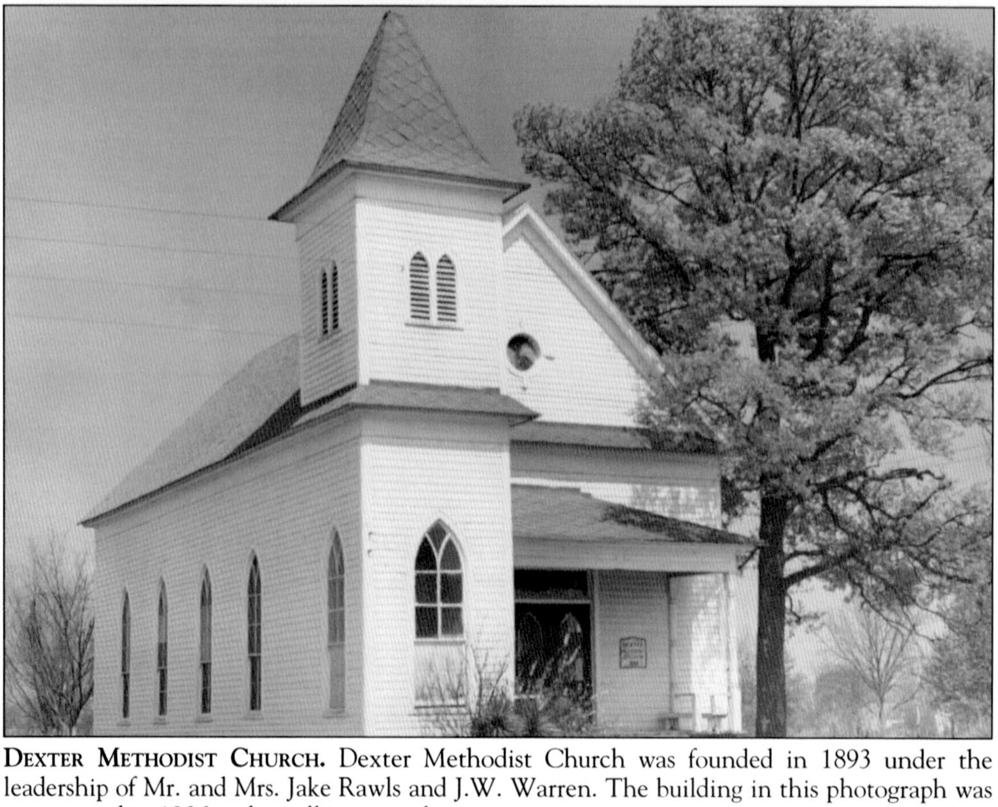

DEXTER METHODIST CHURCH. Dexter Methodist Church was founded in 1893 under the leadership of Mr. and Mrs. Jake Rawls and J.W. Warren. The building in this photograph was constructed in 1906 and is still in use today.

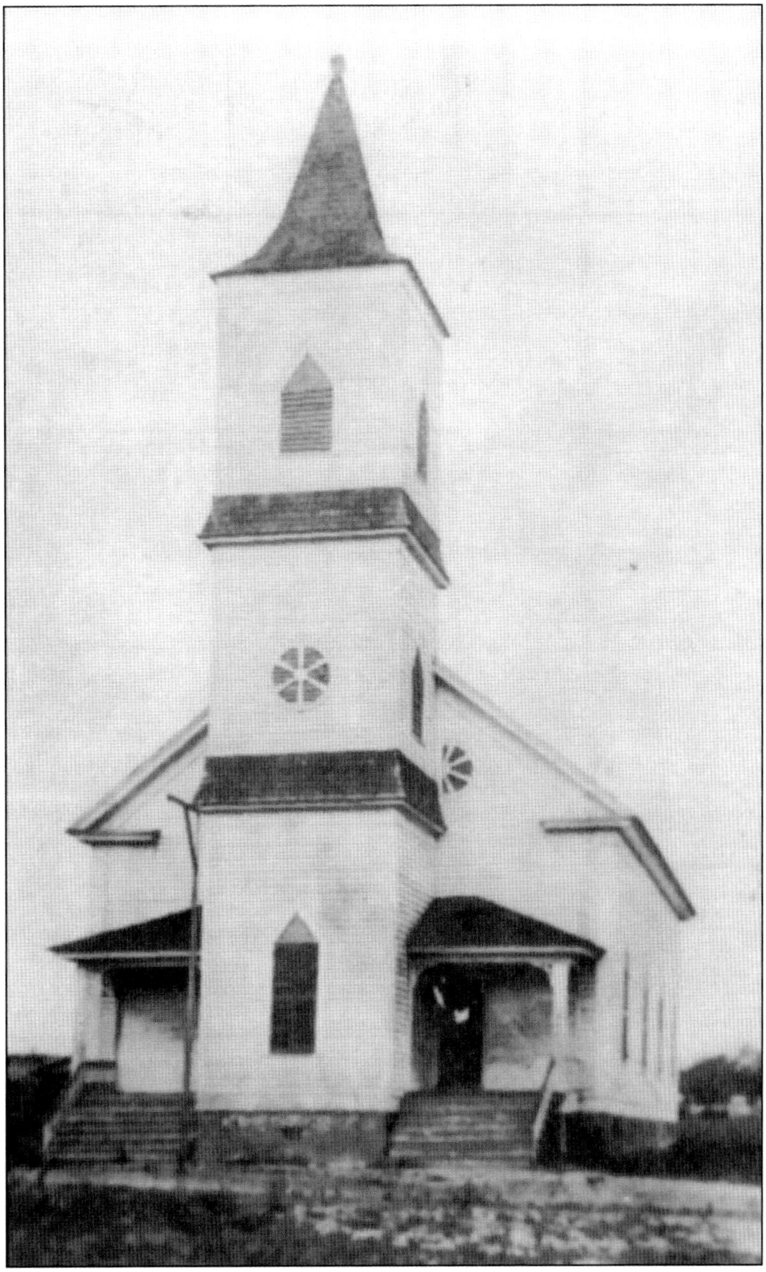

Dexter Baptist Church. Dexter Baptist Church, seen here *c.* 1911, was founded in 1893. The first minister was Rev. P.A. Jessup.

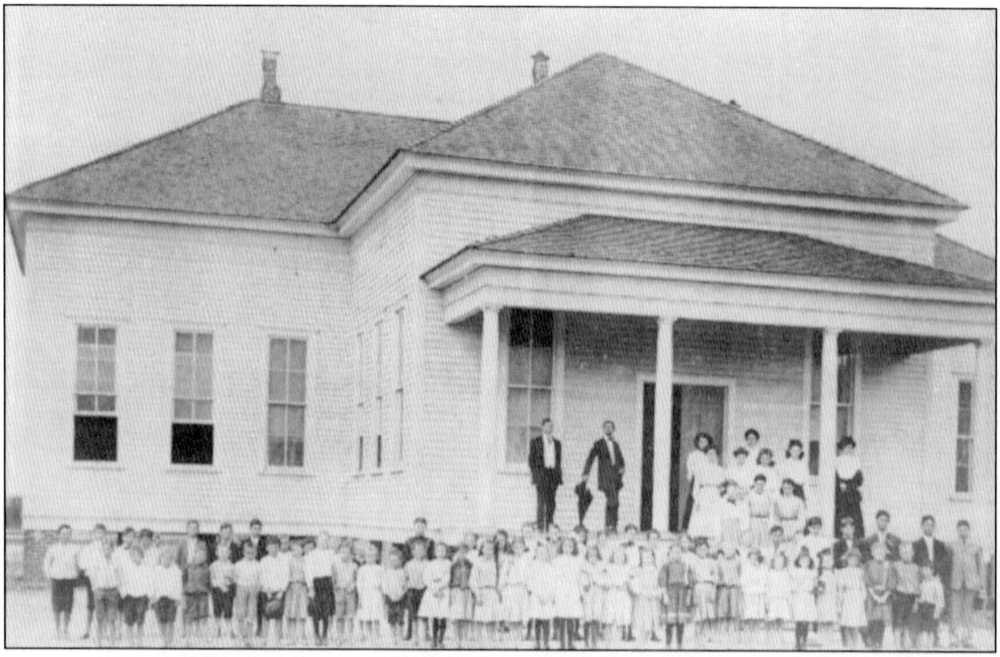

DEXTER SCHOOL. Dexter's school building was one of the finest and one of the largest in Laurens County in the early 1900s.

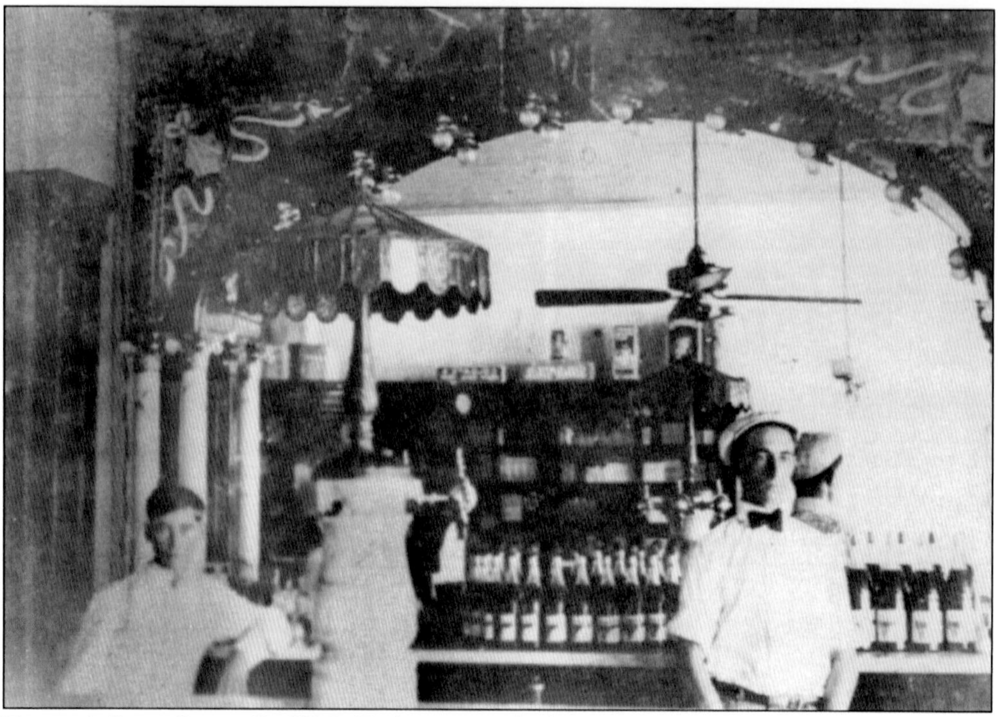

TAYLOR'S DRUG STORE. Dr. W.C. Taylor operated a drug store in Dexter at the corner of Omega and South Main Streets. This 1914 photograph shows, from left to right, Henry F. Thomas and James Thomas by the soda fountain.

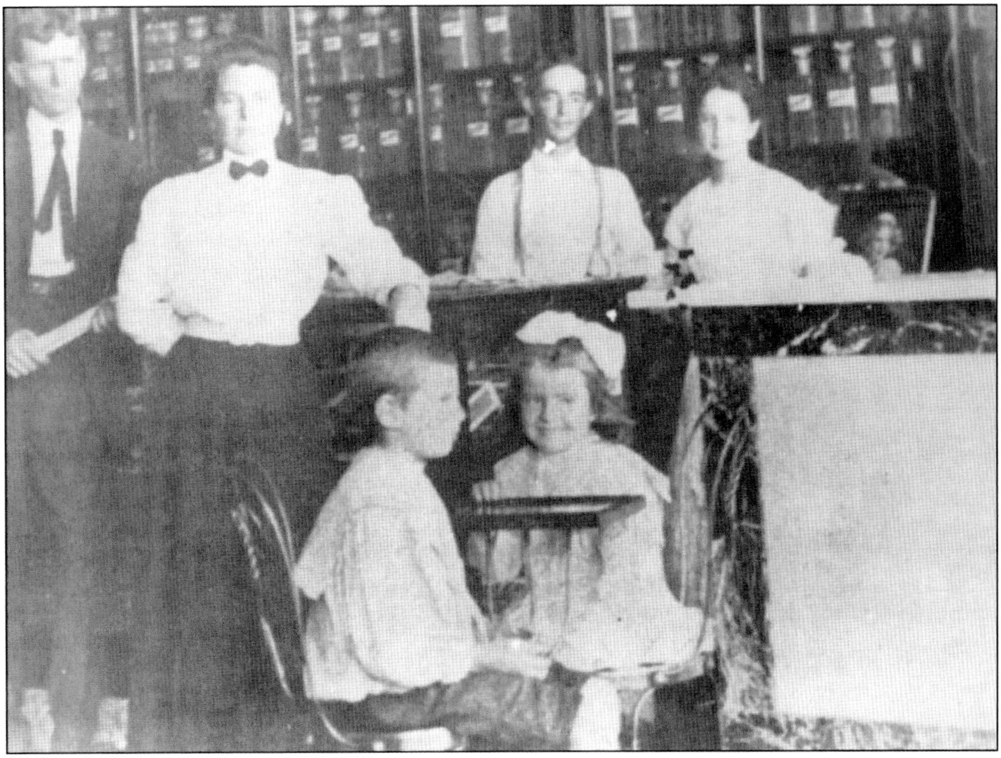

WIGGINS' DRUG STORE. Dr. L.W. Wiggins and his wife operated a drug store where the present office is now located. Shown in the photograph, from left to right, are Dr. Wiggins, Mrs. Wiggins, Lee Wiggins (seated), and Eleanor Wiggins (seated). The names of the two clerks behind the counter are unknown.

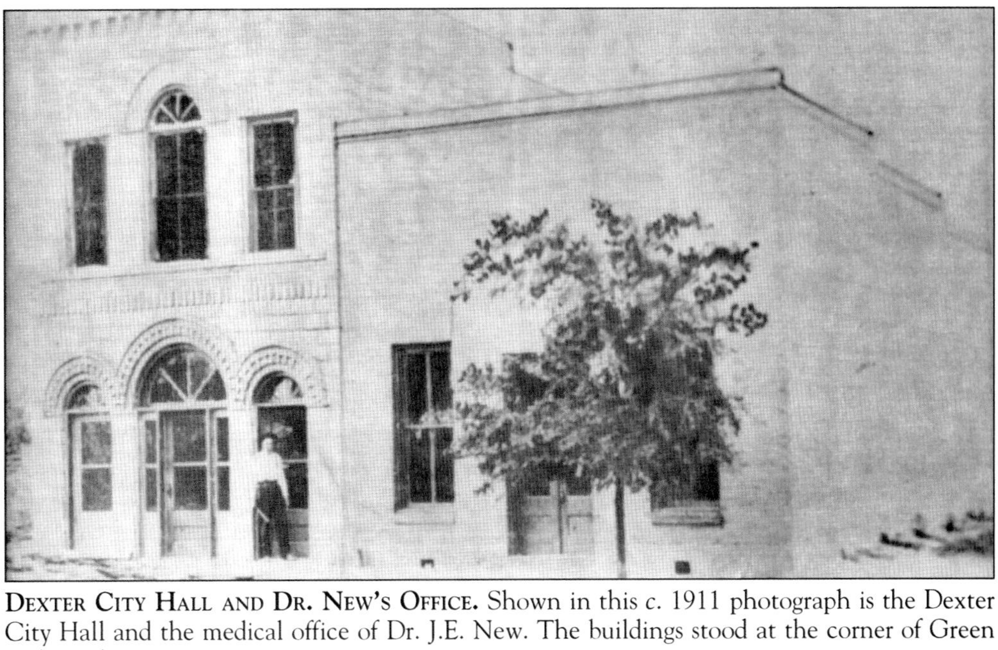

DEXTER CITY HALL AND DR. NEW'S OFFICE. Shown in this *c.* 1911 photograph is the Dexter City Hall and the medical office of Dr. J.E. New. The buildings stood at the corner of Green and South Main Streets.

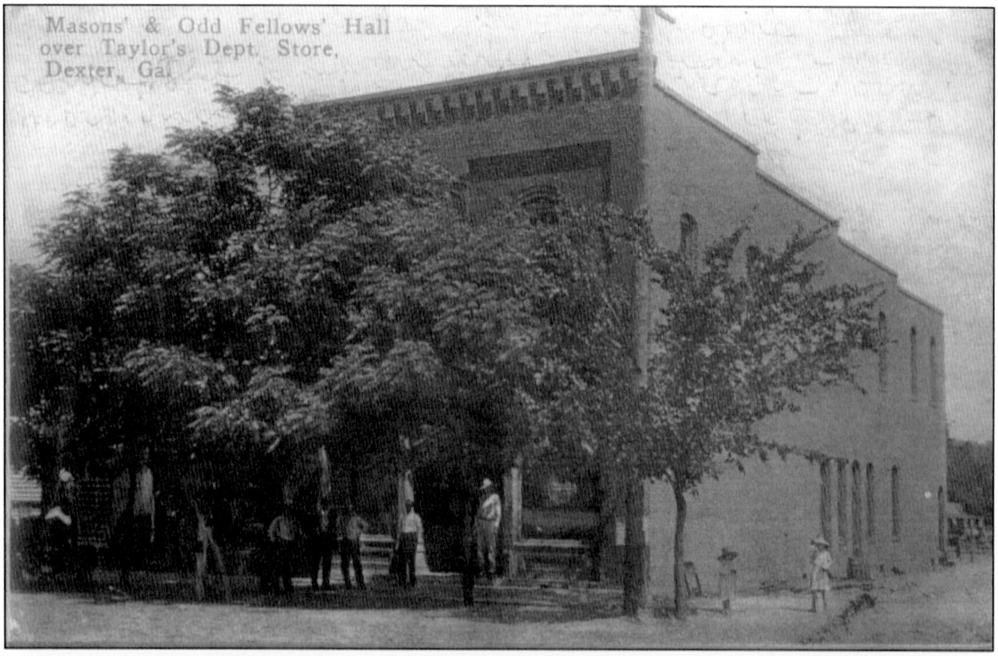

MASONIC AND ODD FELLOWS HALL. The Dexter lodges of the Masons and the Odd Fellows were located in the second floor of Taylor's Department Store, seen in this 1910 photograph.

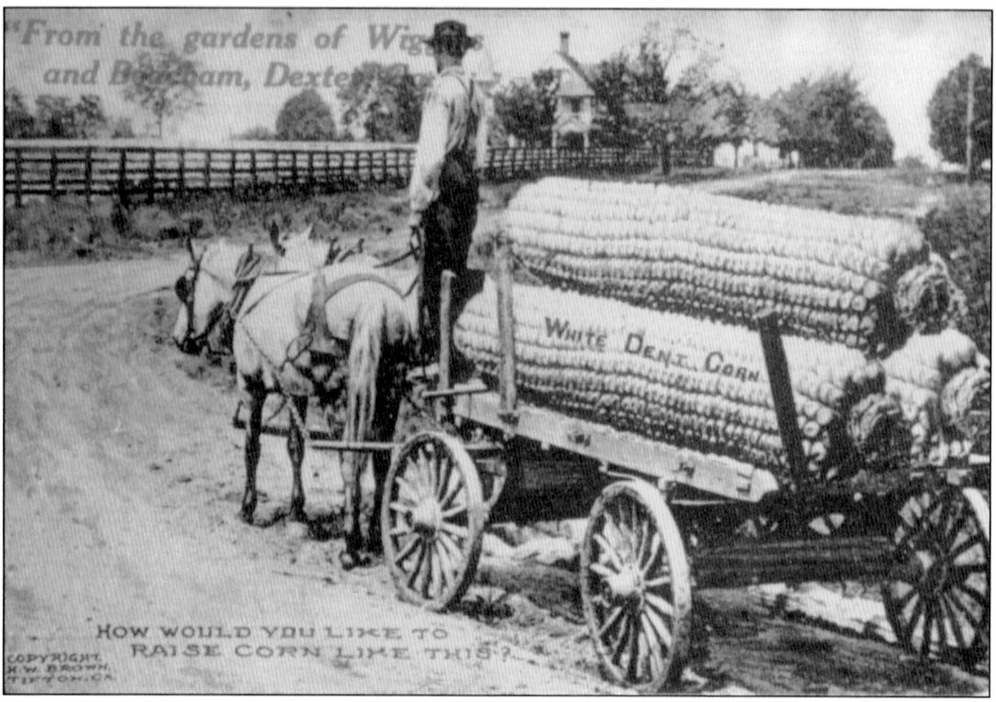

GOOD CORN CROP. This exaggerated postcard was used to advertise the White Dent corn grown in the Wiggins and Beacham gardens in Dexter.

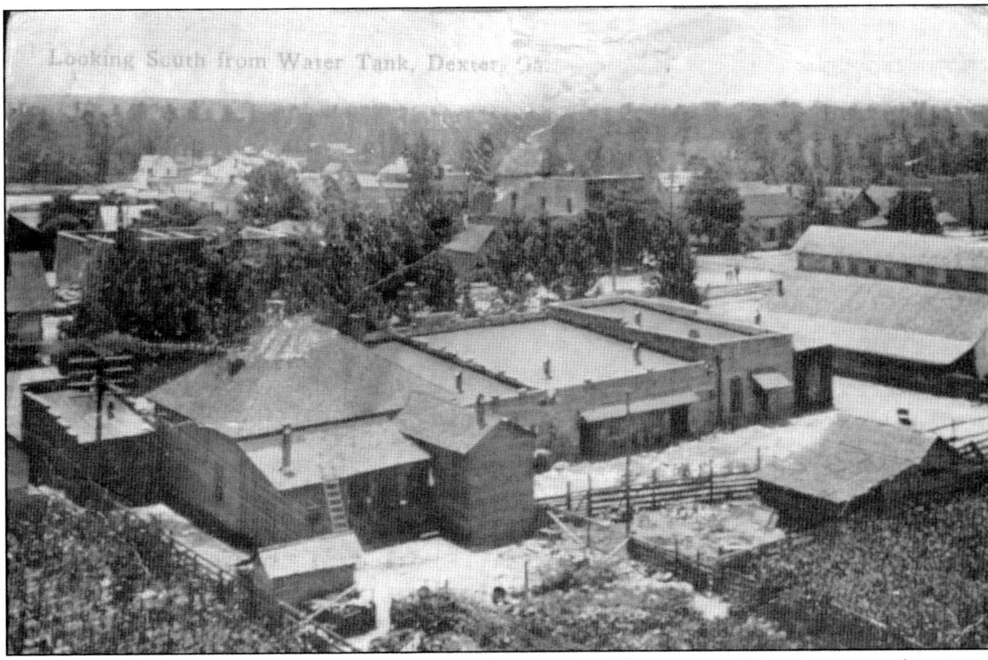

Bird's-Eye View of the Dexter Business District. This view of the business district of Dexter was taken from the water tower looking south about 1910.

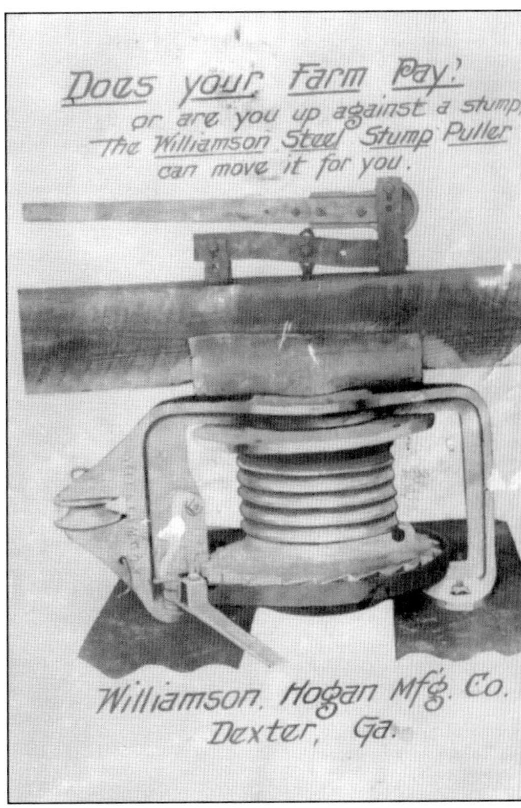

Tired of Those Aggravating Stumps. This early advertising card promoted the quality of the Williamson Steel Stump Puller, which was sold by Williamson Hogan Manufacturing Company of Dexter.

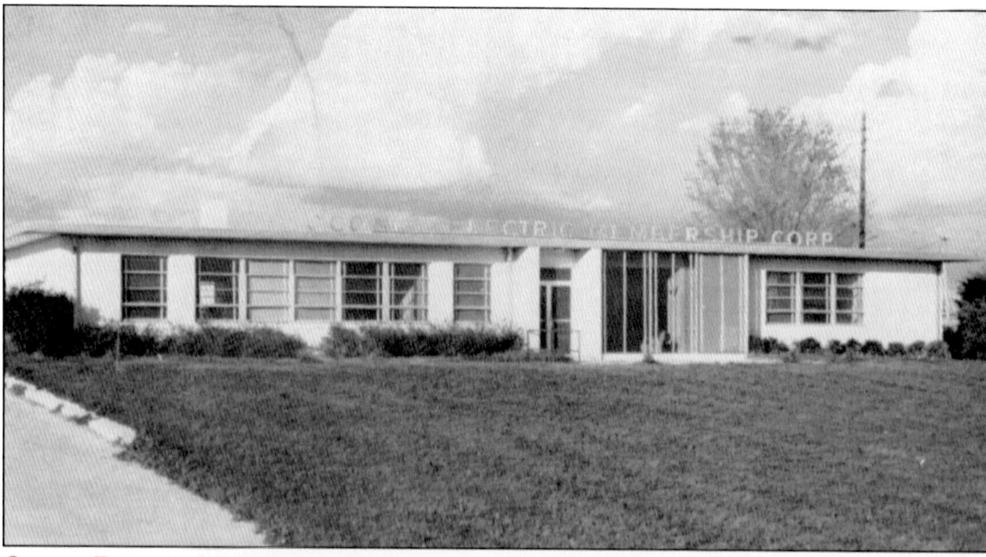

Oconee Electric Membership Corporation. This photograph taken in the 1950s shows the Dudley office of Oconee Electric Membership Corporation, which was chartered on November 18, 1938. The first board of directors was composed of J.L. Allen, T.C. Waldrep, J.L. Whitaker, Paul J. Jones Sr., M.B. Bell, Joseph R. Lord, and G.C. Ingram. The electric membership corporations brought the first electric service to rural homes in the late 1930s and throughout the 1940s and 1950s.

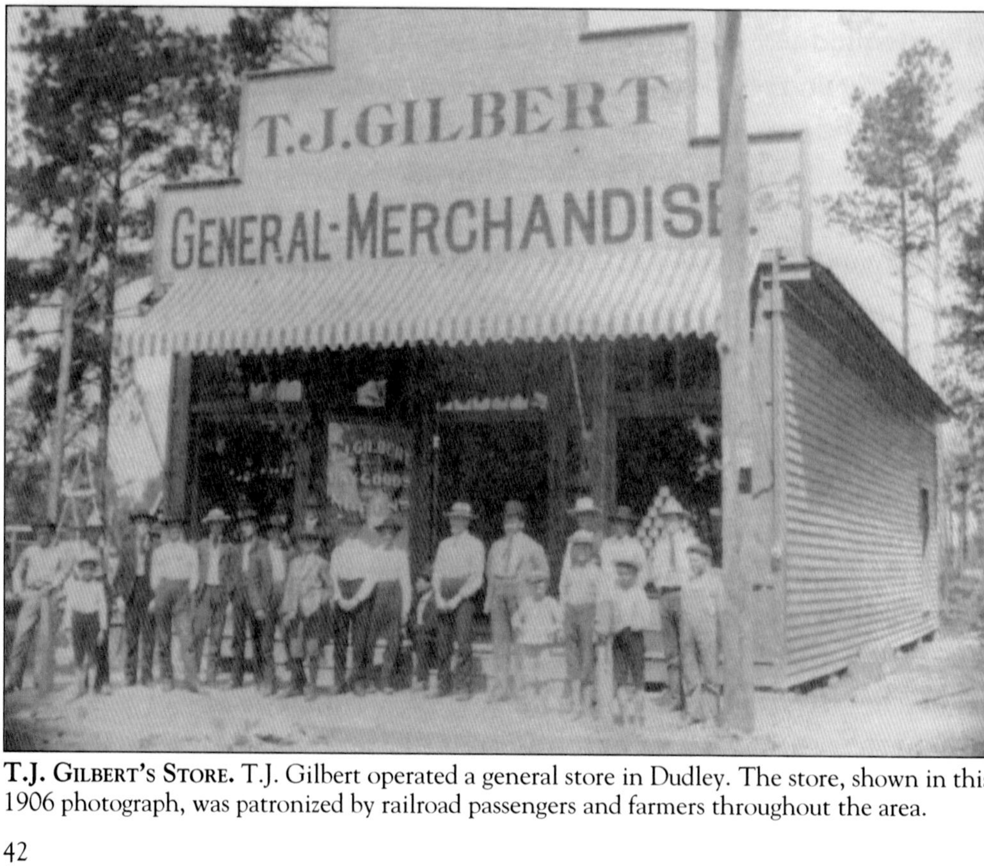

T.J. Gilbert's Store. T.J. Gilbert operated a general store in Dudley. The store, shown in this 1906 photograph, was patronized by railroad passengers and farmers throughout the area.

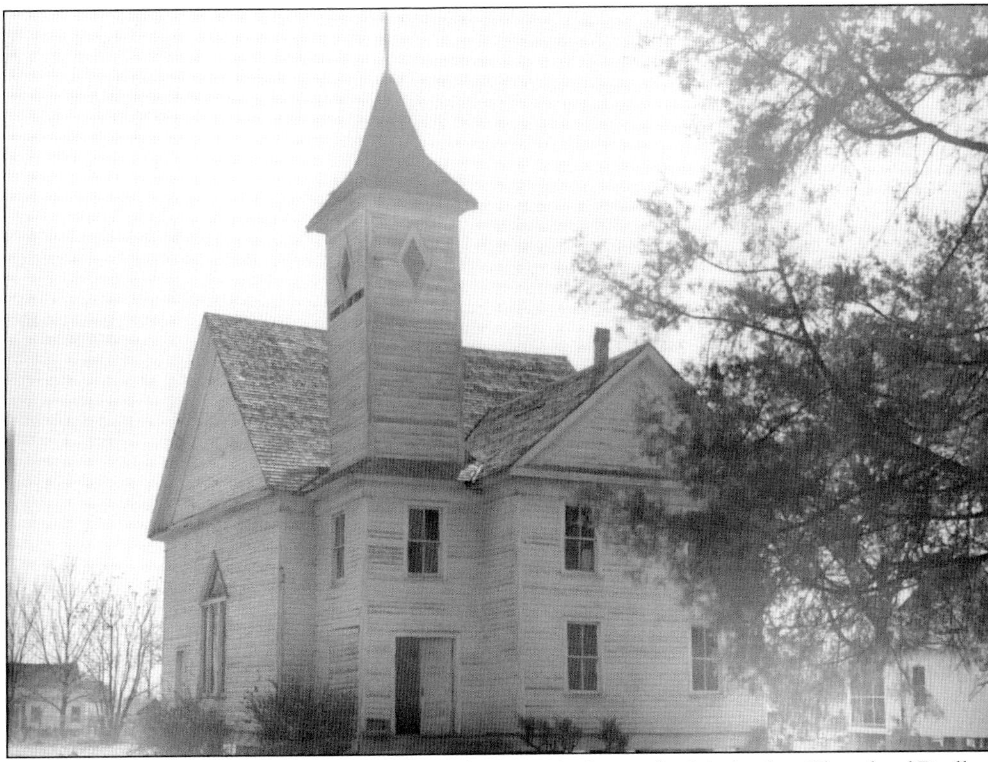

DUDLEY METHODIST CHURCH. This 1940s photograph shows the Methodist Church of Dudley, which was founded in 1897 at Haskins Crossing by Rev. C.A. Moore. The church in this photograph was built in 1902 and was used until the middle of the 20th century.

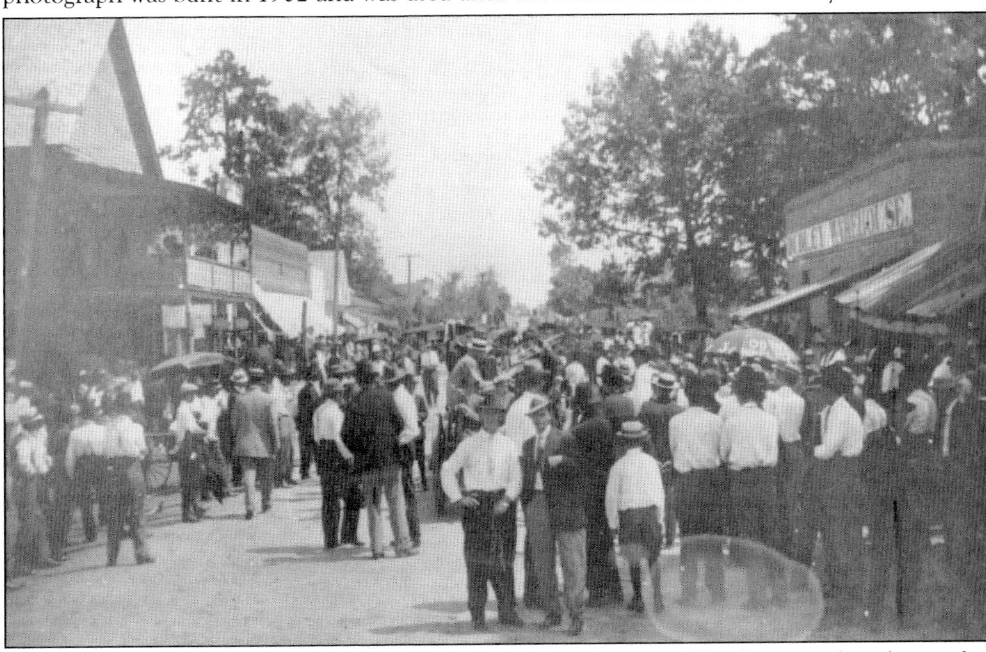

BIG DAY IN DUDLEY. This 1915 photograph of the main street of Dudley is said to show a free barbecue for the residents of the town.

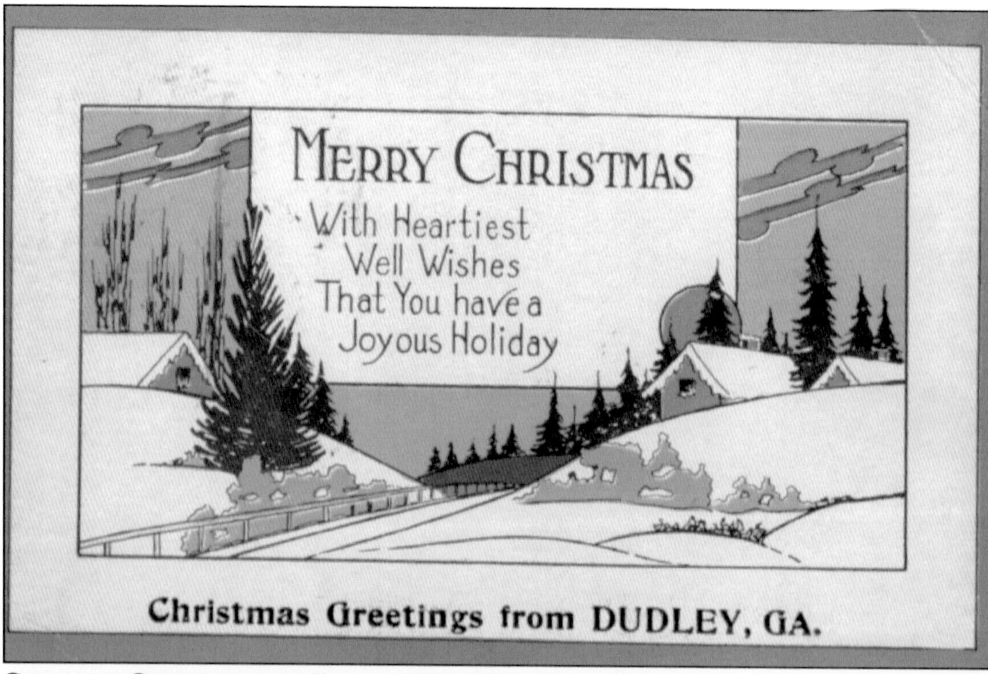

CHRISTMAS GREETINGS FROM DUDLEY. This 1910 postcard relayed Christmas greetings from a resident of Dudley.

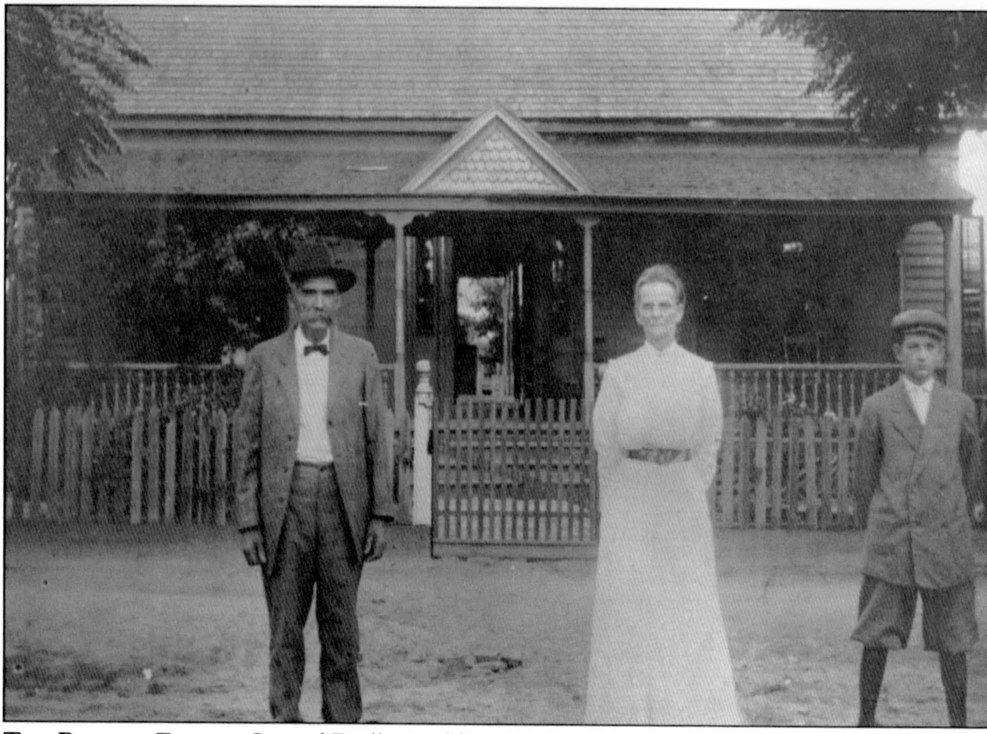

THE BOBBITT FAMILY. One of Dudley's oldest families was the Felix Bobbitt family. Shown in this 1911 photograph in front of their home on Second Street, from left to right, are Felix Bobbitt, Emma Carroll Bobbitt, and Thomas Clarence "Dolly" Bobbitt.

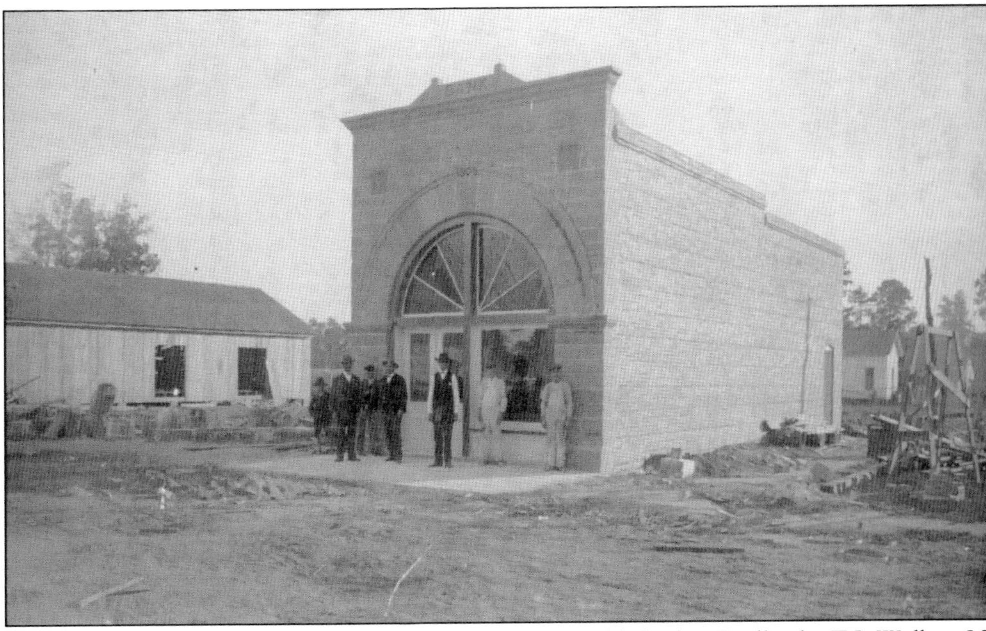

Bank of Dudley. Laurens County's oldest bank was established in Dudley by T.J. Walker, I.J. Duggan, W.J. Gilbert, R.J. Chappell, and B.S. Russell on October 2, 1905. The bank was one of only two banks to keep their doors open throughout the Great Depression.

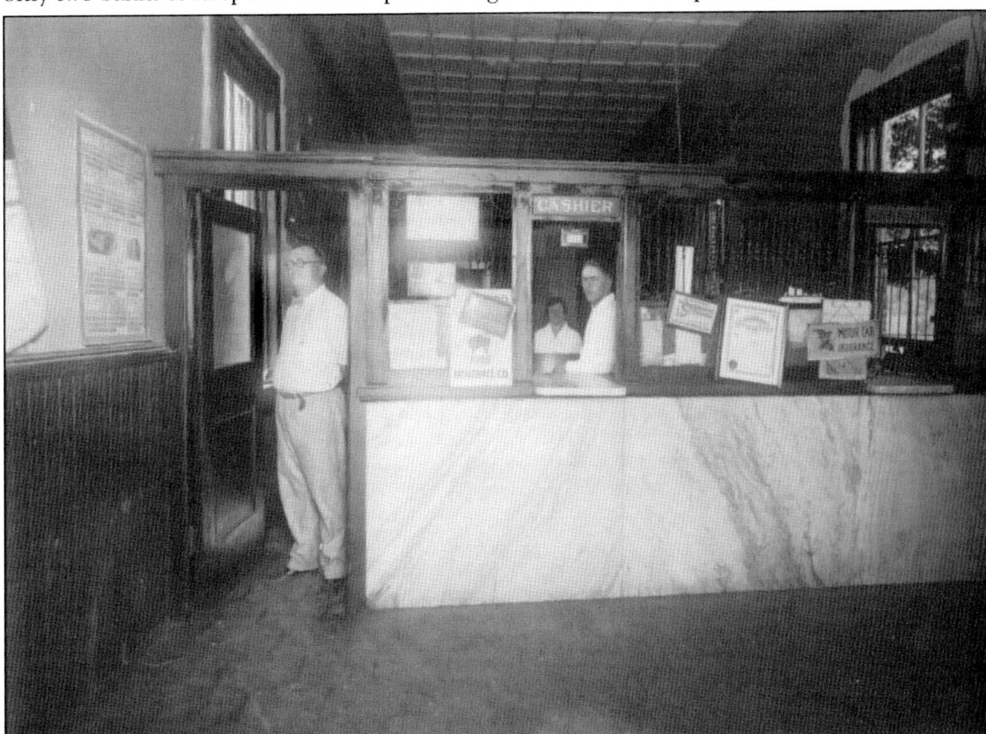

Bank of Dudley. Shown in this early photograph of the interior of the Bank of Dudley is Rupert Hogan (behind the teller's window) and a man thought to be Warthen Chappell standing in the doorway.

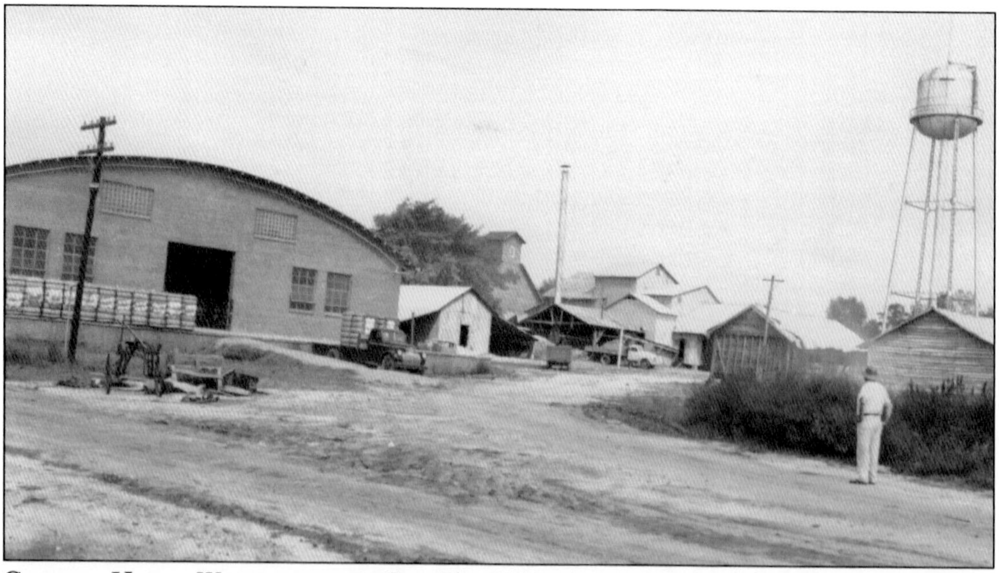

CHAPPELL HOGAN WAREHOUSE AND GIN. This 1950s photograph shows the gin and warehouses of Chappell and Hogan in Dudley. The massive operation was Dudley's largest employer for a time.

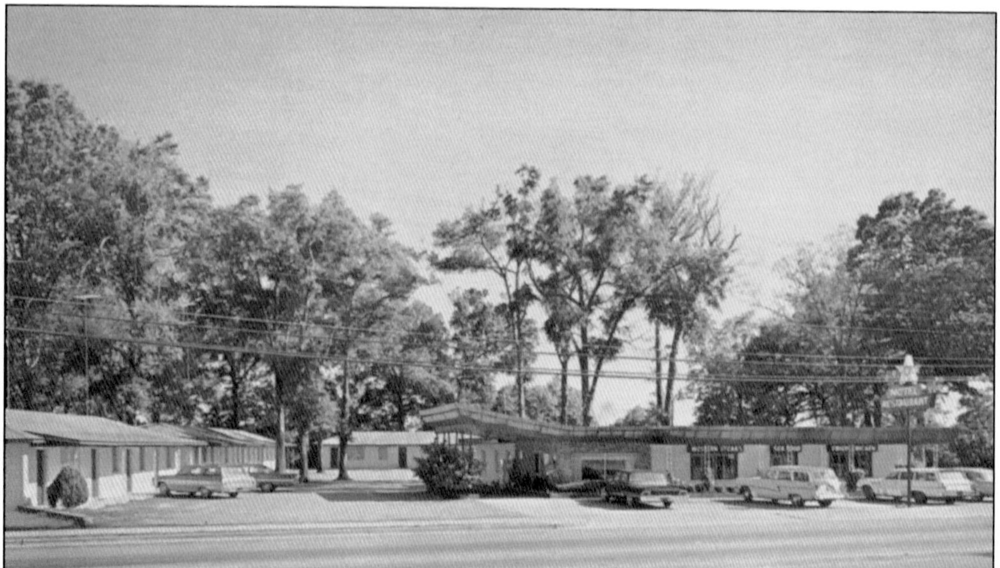

CANADY PLAZA MOTEL. This typical 1950s motel was established by J.N. Canady to capitalize on the huge number of travelers who passed through East Dublin along U.S. Highway 80. The motel featured one of East Dublin's most popular restaurants.

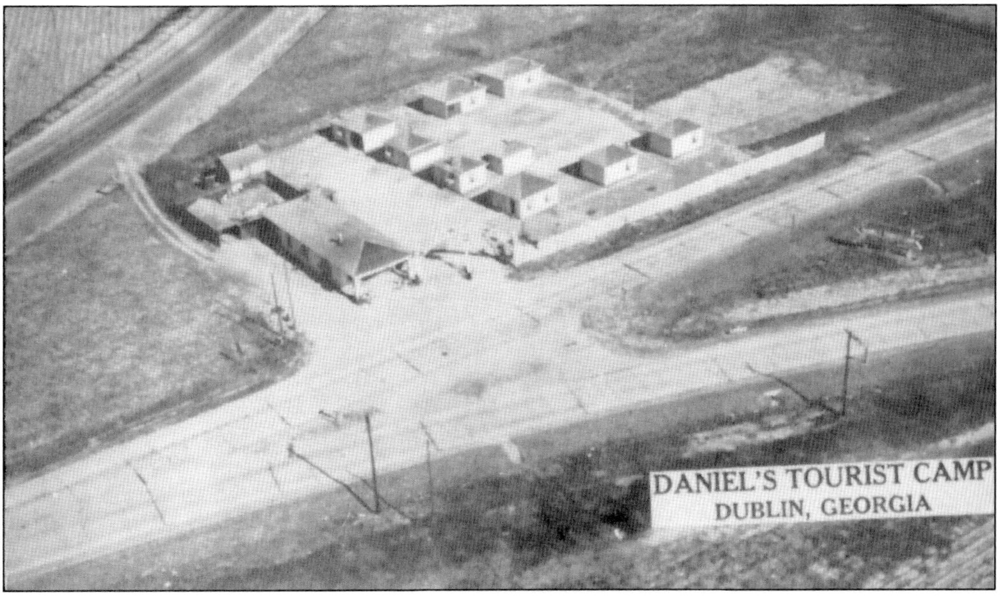

DANIEL'S TOURIST CAMP. Tourist camps were popular in the second quarter of the 20th century. This camp was located in East Dublin near the point where Highways 80, 319, and 29 split.

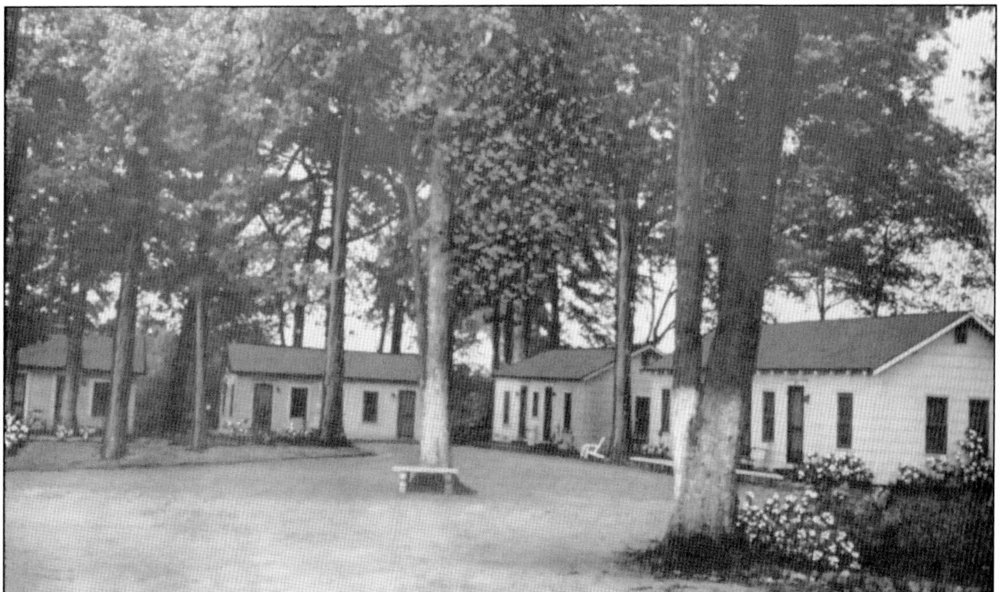

TANNER'S COURT. In the 1950s, B.B. Tanner established this neat group of tourist cabins at the bend in Central Drive in East Dublin.

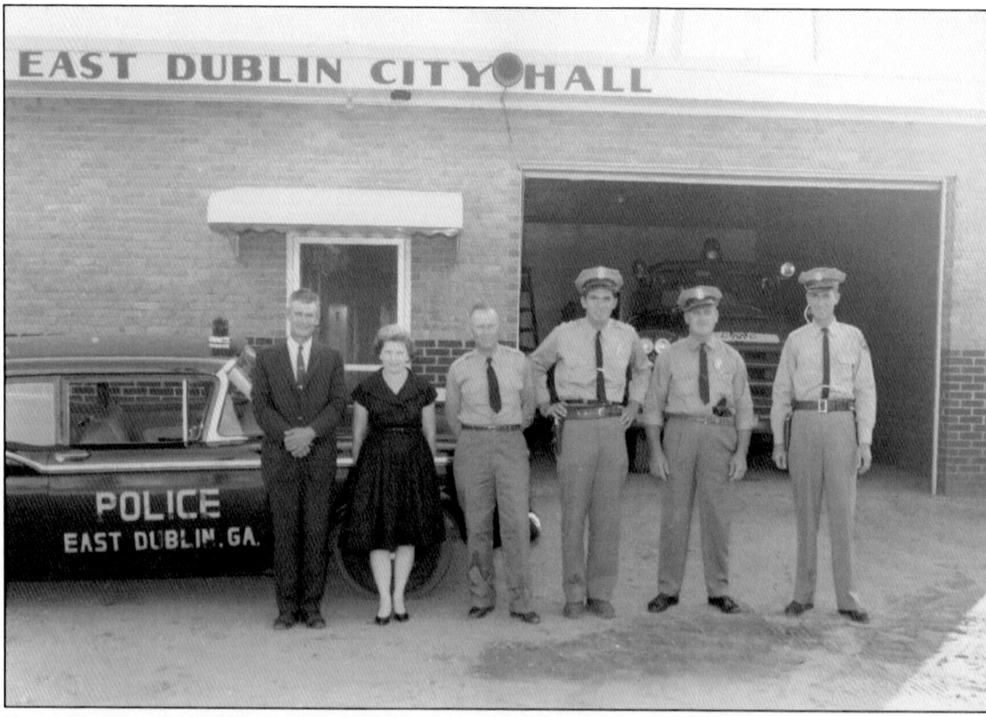

EAST DUBLIN CITY HALL. East Dublin was officially chartered on February 1, 1952, but the city hall was erected later in the 1950s. The city's first mayor was E.B. Warnock, and its first councilmen included J.T. Braddy, W.L. Lake, J.E. Sammons, H.D. Keen, and O.D. Cullens.

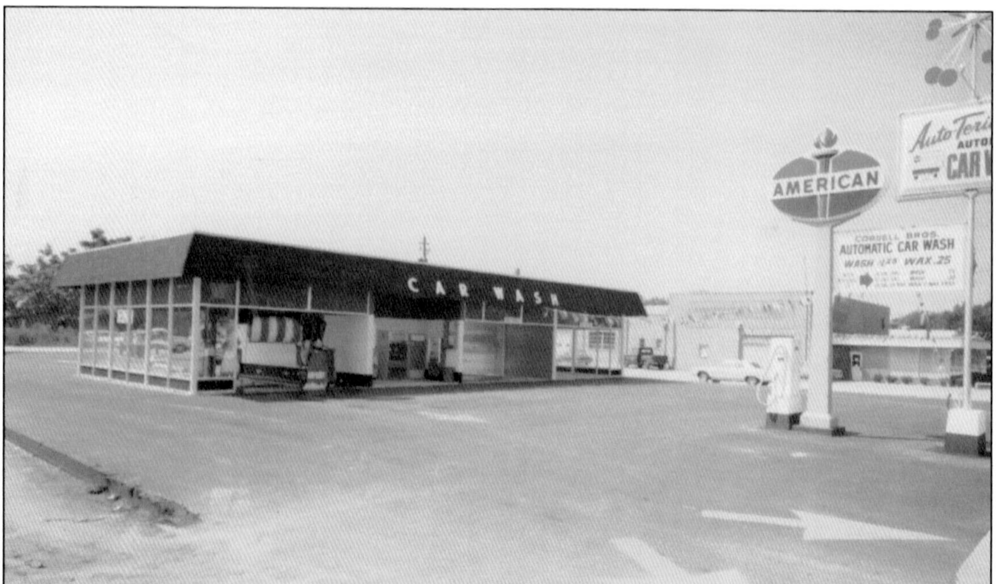

THE FIRST AUTOMATIC CAR WASH. The first electro-mechanical car wash in Laurens County opened on August 16, 1969, on Central Drive in East Dublin. The Auto-Teria, owned by Howard L. Cordell Sr. and his brother Clayton Cordell, could wash a car in 2 minutes. The first car to be washed was that of East Dublin mayor Hugh Wood.

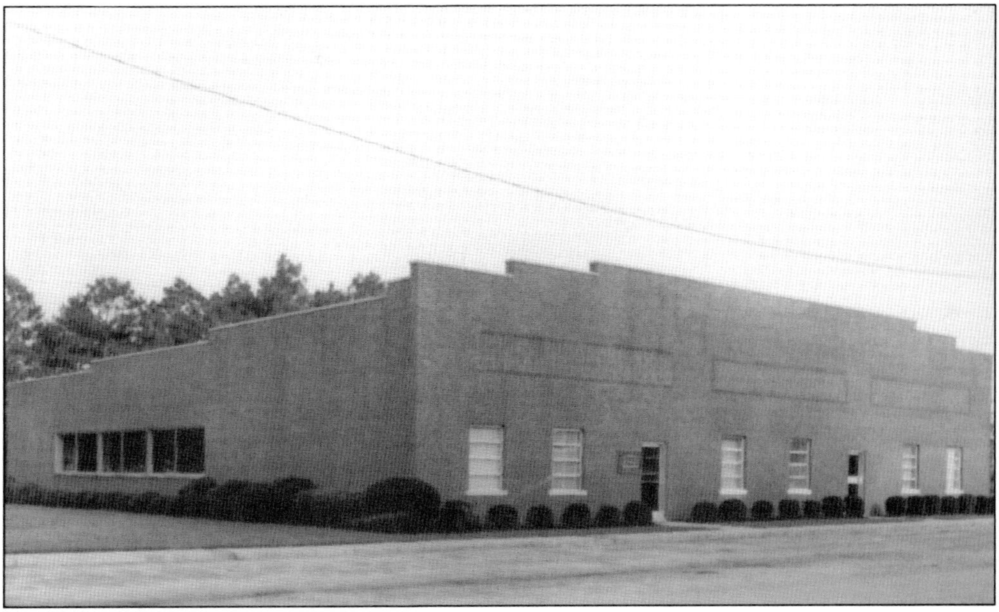

TEXTILE-ANALINE DERBY NYANZA CHEMICAL COMPANY. This chemical company was established in 1950 to make dyes for the cloth that was being made across town in East Dublin at J.P. Stevens and Company.

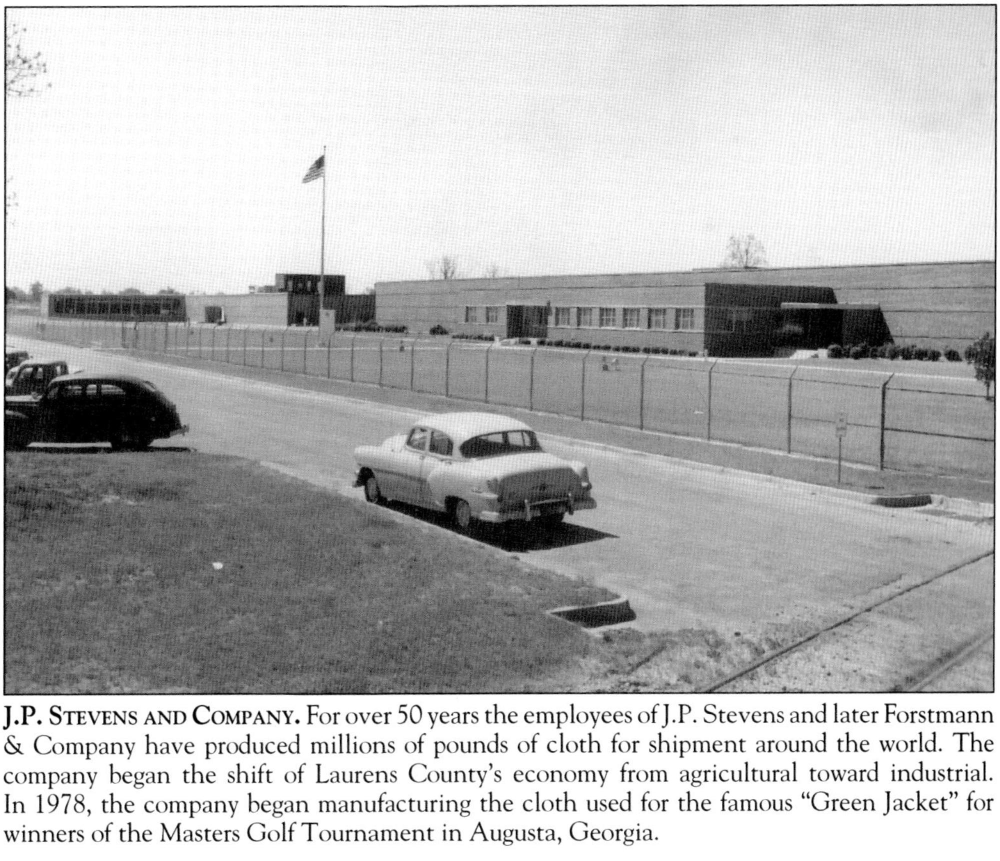

J.P. STEVENS AND COMPANY. For over 50 years the employees of J.P. Stevens and later Forstmann & Company have produced millions of pounds of cloth for shipment around the world. The company began the shift of Laurens County's economy from agricultural toward industrial. In 1978, the company began manufacturing the cloth used for the famous "Green Jacket" for winners of the Masters Golf Tournament in Augusta, Georgia.

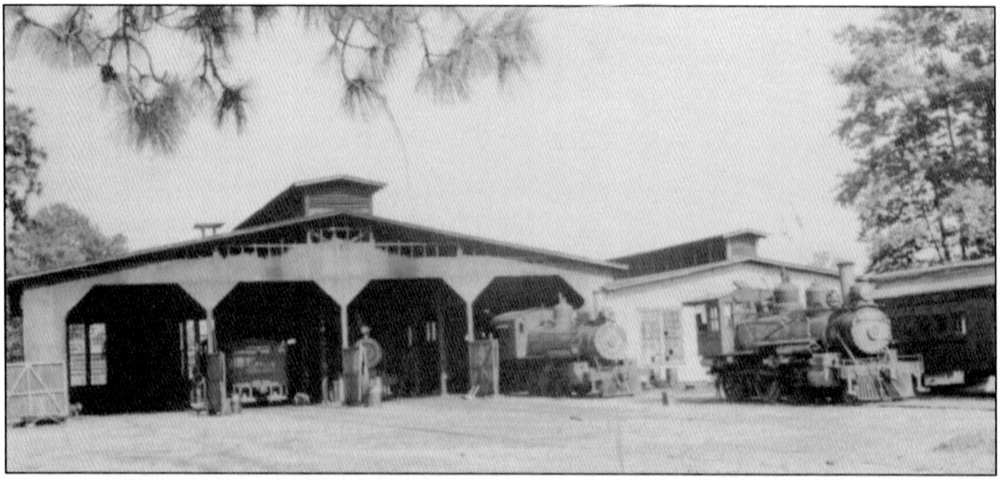

The North Dublin Shops. This 1947 photograph shows the shop buildings of the Wrightsville and Tennille Railroad in what was then called North Dublin and later East Dublin.

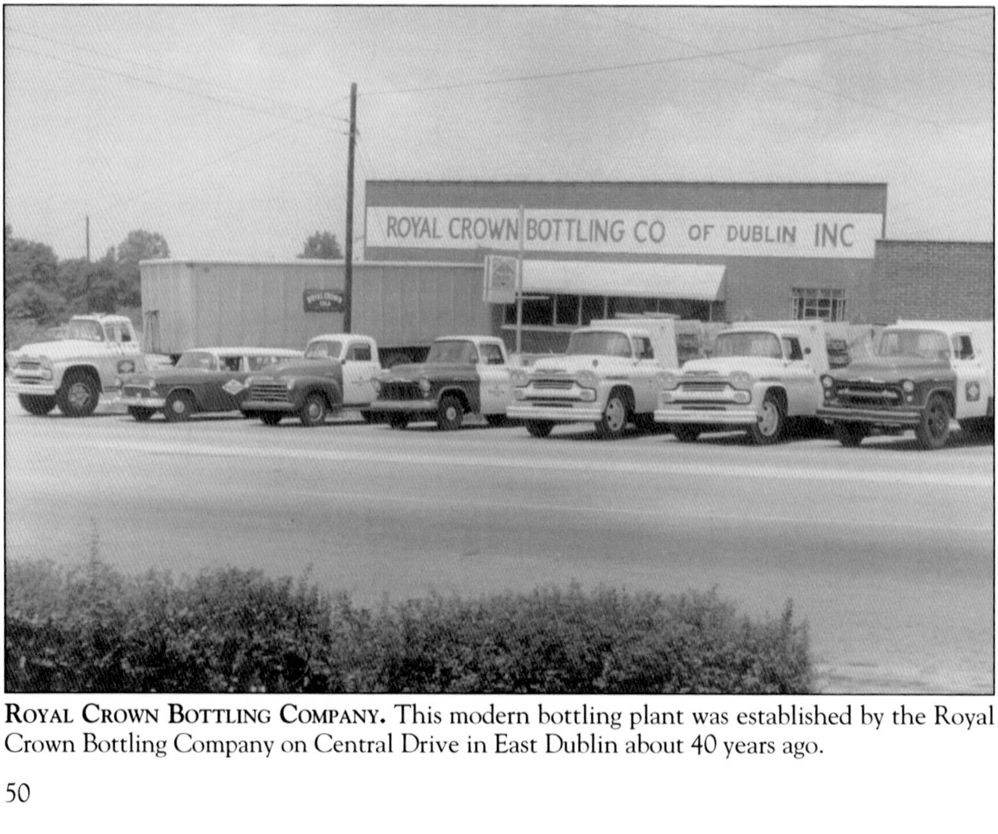

Royal Crown Bottling Company. This modern bottling plant was established by the Royal Crown Bottling Company on Central Drive in East Dublin about 40 years ago.

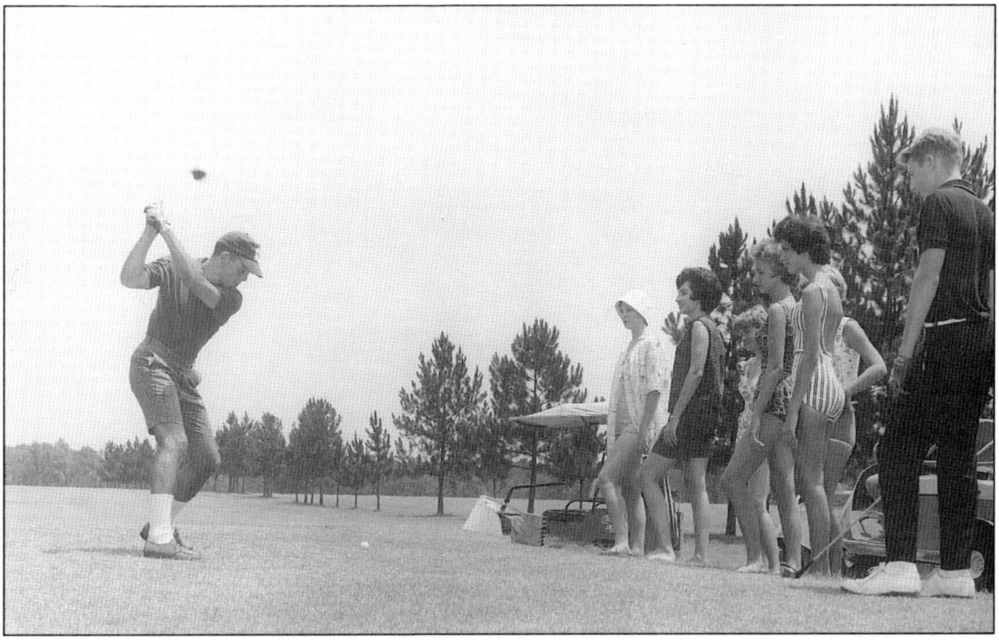

Dublin Country Club. This early 1960s photograph shows a group of bathing beauties watching a golfer tee off at the Dublin Country Club, which was reorganized in 1947. The course is located near the end of Country Club Road, formerly Blackshear's Ferry Road, north of Dublin. For over 50 years, the course here has been played by tens of thousands of golfers. Bert Greene, who played on the Professional Golfers' Association tour, played on the course in the early 1950s, while his father was the club pro.

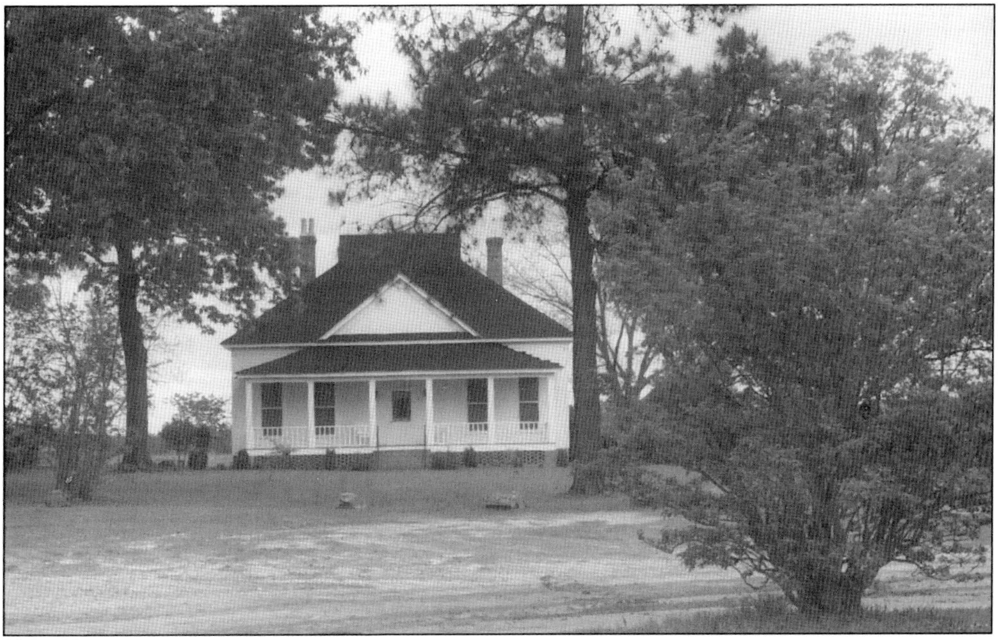

The T.E. Kellam Home. One of Laurens County's finest remaining examples of a turn-of-the-century farmhouse, this home was owned by T.E. Kellam, who maintained a large farm on Claxton Diary Road.

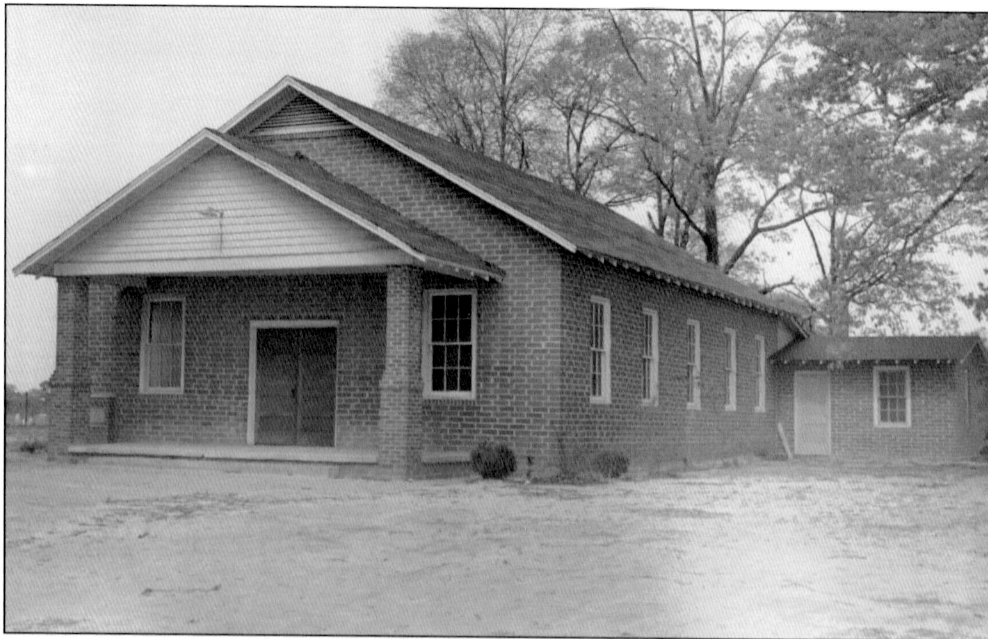

Evergreen Methodist Church. This church was founded in the 1880s at a brush arbor at Old Evergreen School. The building was erected in 1945.

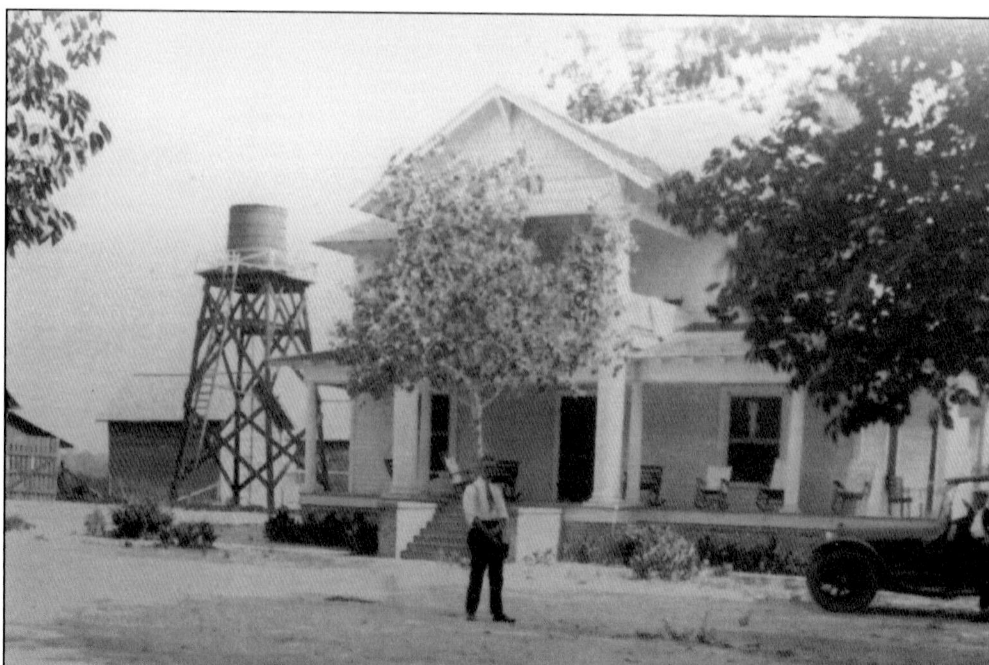

Garretta Farm. This photograph shows the farm house of Dublin banker and businessman A.W. Garrett. Garretta was a small community located on Turkey Creek at the Dublin and Southwestern Railroad about 3 miles south of Interstate 16.

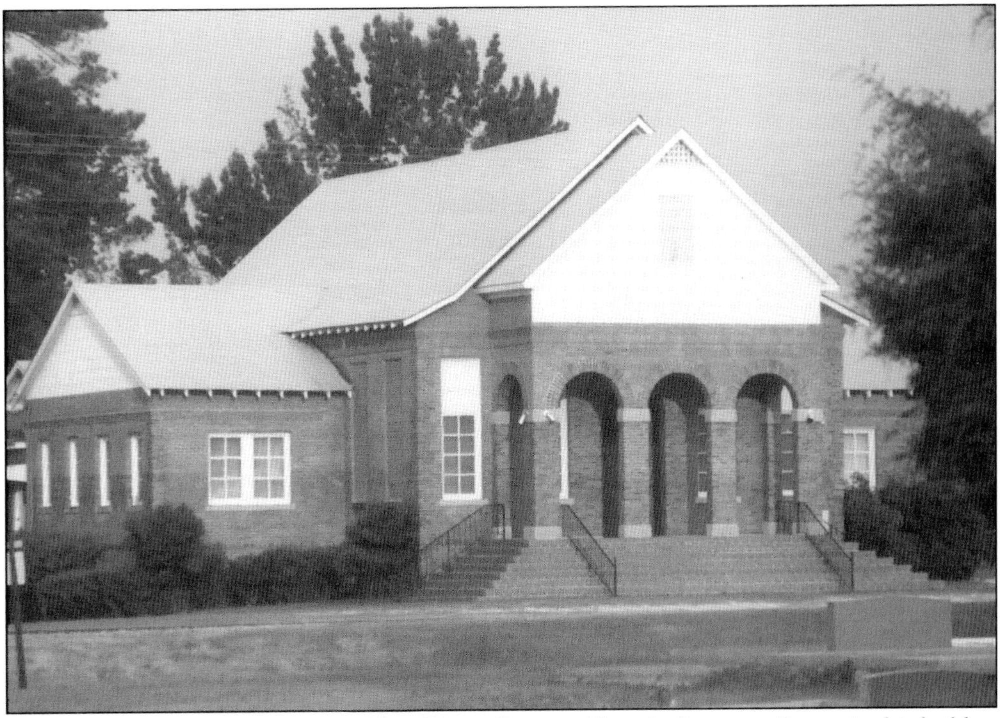

Blue Water Baptist Church. Blue Water Baptist Church, Laurens County's third oldest church, was founded in 1838. The first services were held in a small log cabin located on the banks of Blue Water Creek. The present church, which was completed in 1922 under the leadership of Rev. T.E. Toole, is located on U.S. Highway 441, south of Dublin.

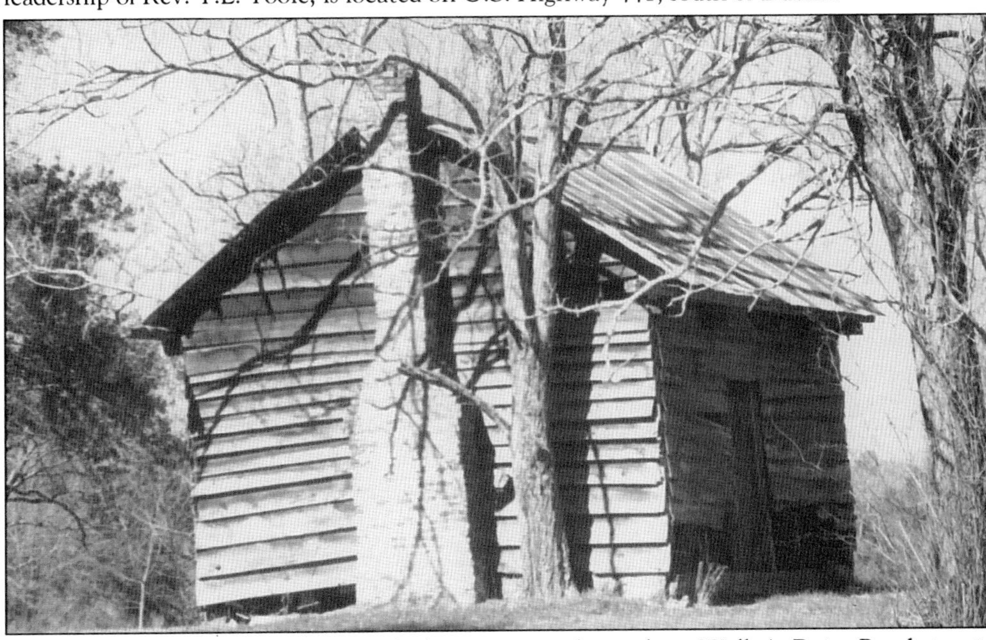

The First Courthouse. This simple log structure, located on Walke's Dairy Road, is said to have been the first Laurens County Courthouse when the county seat was located at Sumpterville in 1810.

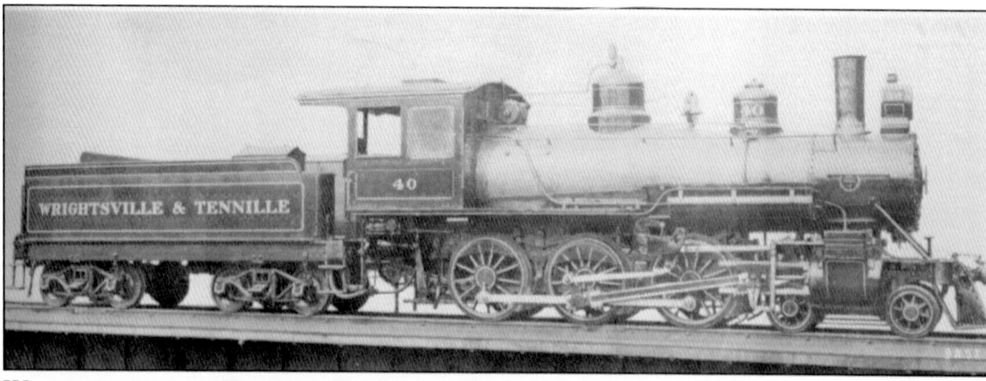

Wrightsville and Tennille Railroad. The town of Lovett was born in 1884 when the Wrightsville and Tennille Railroad came to the community in northeastern Laurens County. Shown in this builder's photo is Baldwin Locomotive Engine No. 40.

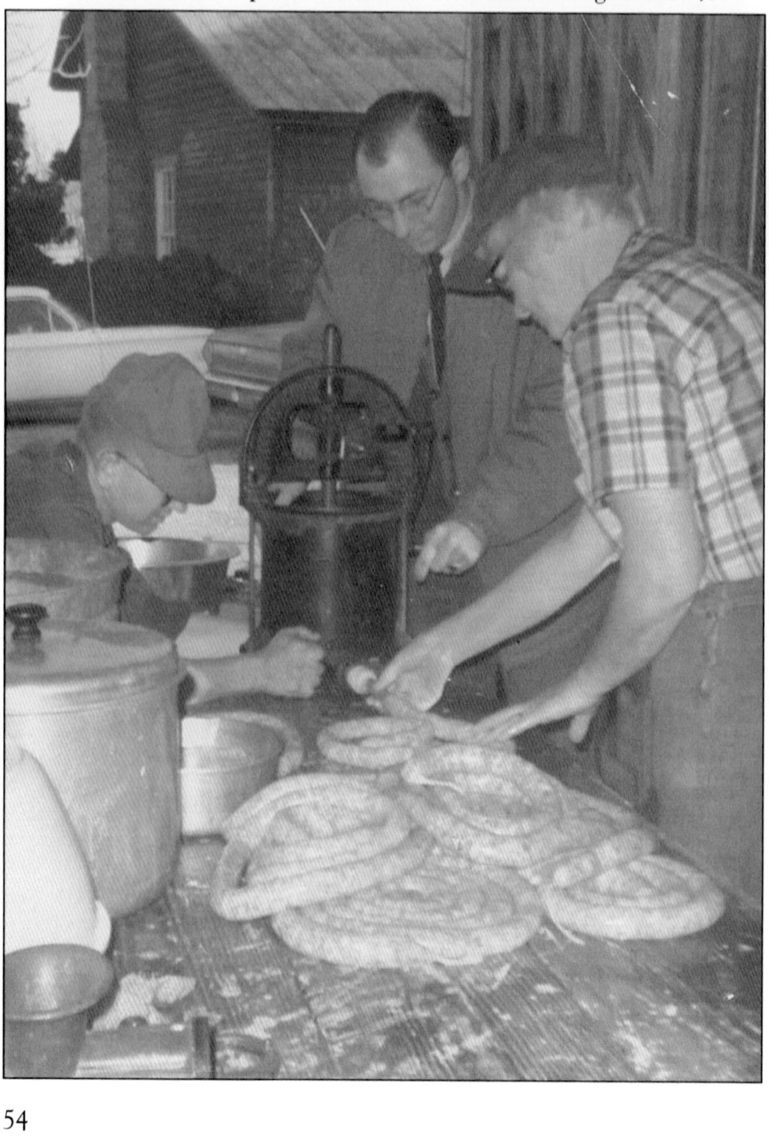

Making Sausages. A favorite staple of Laurens Countians' diets was homemade sausage. In this 1968 photograph, Curtis Evans (left) and Paulis Evans show Brother Dan Mahoney (center) the fine art of sausage making.

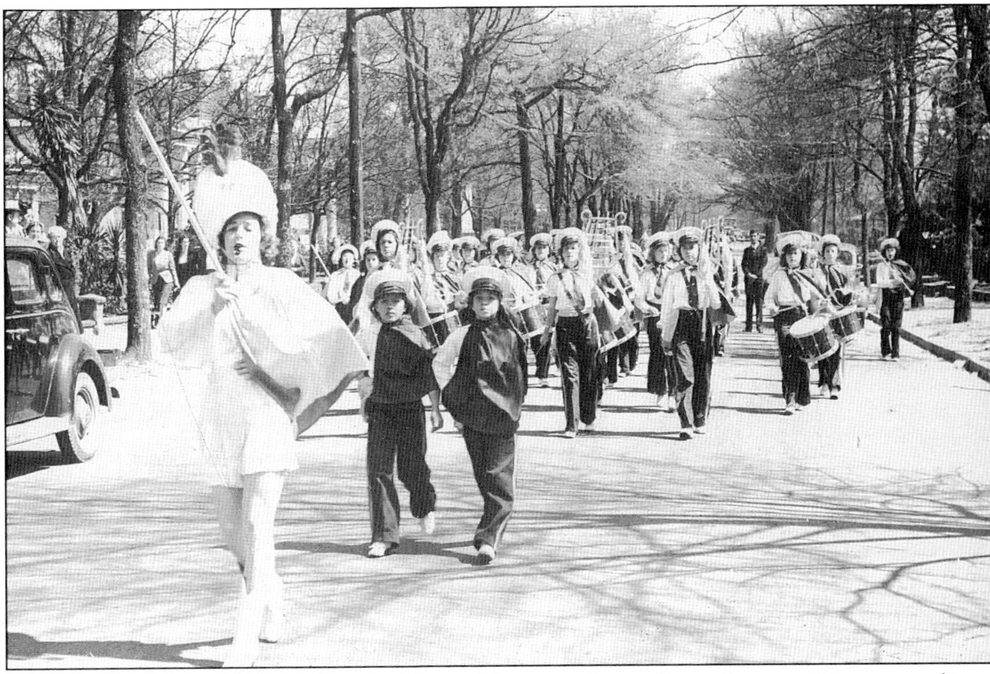

The Laurens County High School Band. Musicians from all over Laurens County combined their talents to form a county-wide marching band. This photograph, taken c. 1940, shows a parade down Bellevue Avenue.

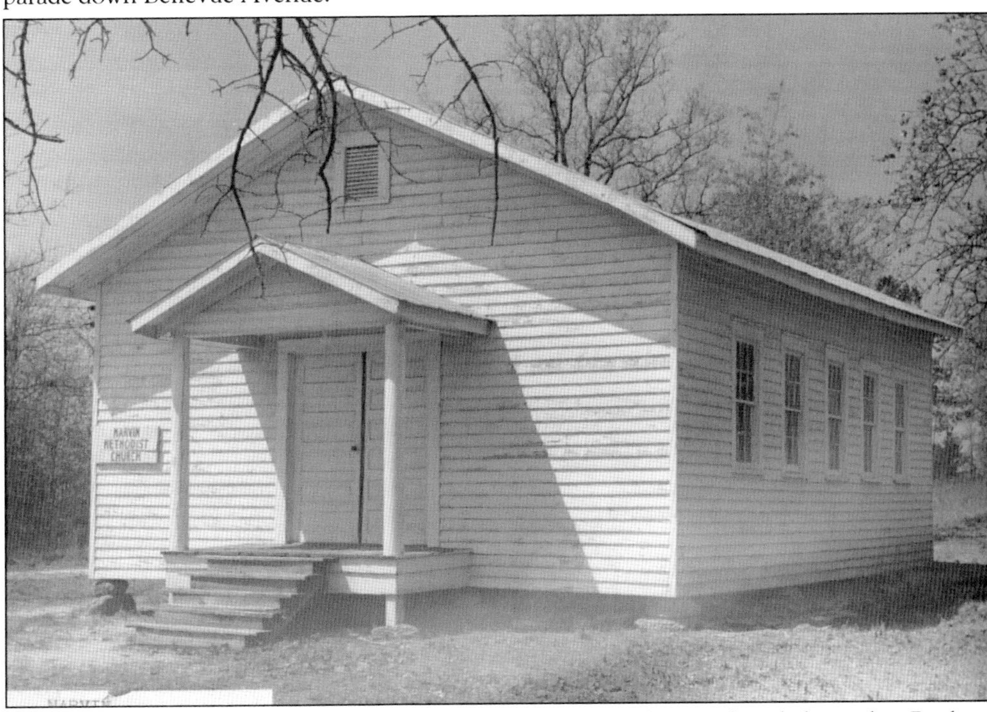

Marvin Methodist Church. Marvin Methodist Church was founded in the Buckeye community in 1868 by David S. Blackshear and A.L. Morgan. The building was moved to Dublin and is now part of Centenary Methodist Church on Telfair Street.

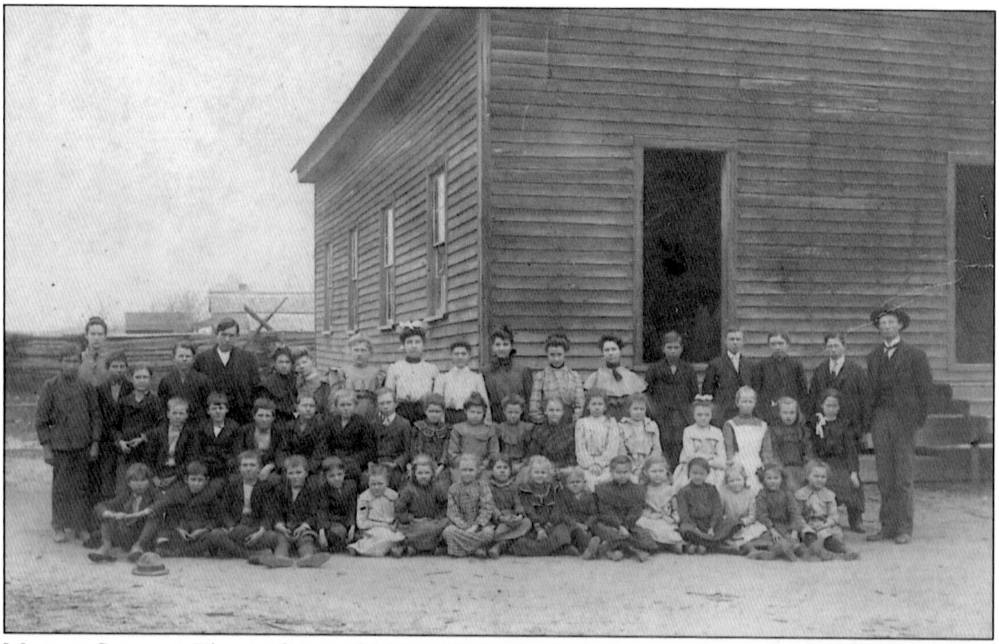

MINTER SCHOOL. The students of Minter School are shown in this early 1900s photograph. Minter was incorporated as a town in 1906, and was located in southeastern Laurens County along the Macon, Dublin, and Savannah Railroad.

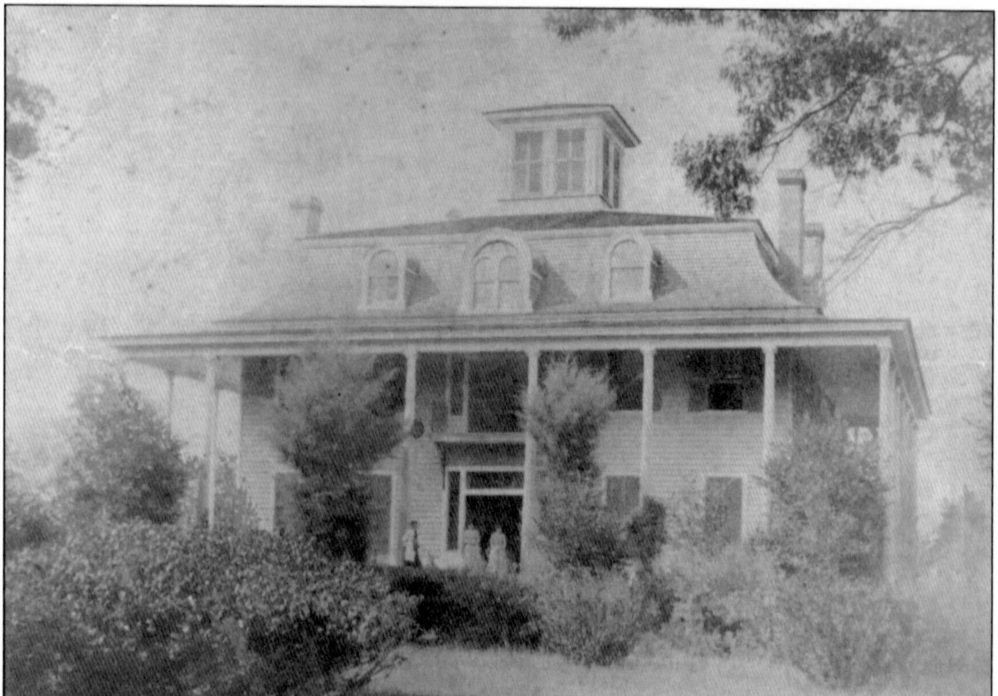

THE VICKERS HOUSE. This remarkable three-story antebellum house was built by planter Ashley Vickers north of Montrose. The house, which featured two-story columns around its perimeter, burned in 1891.

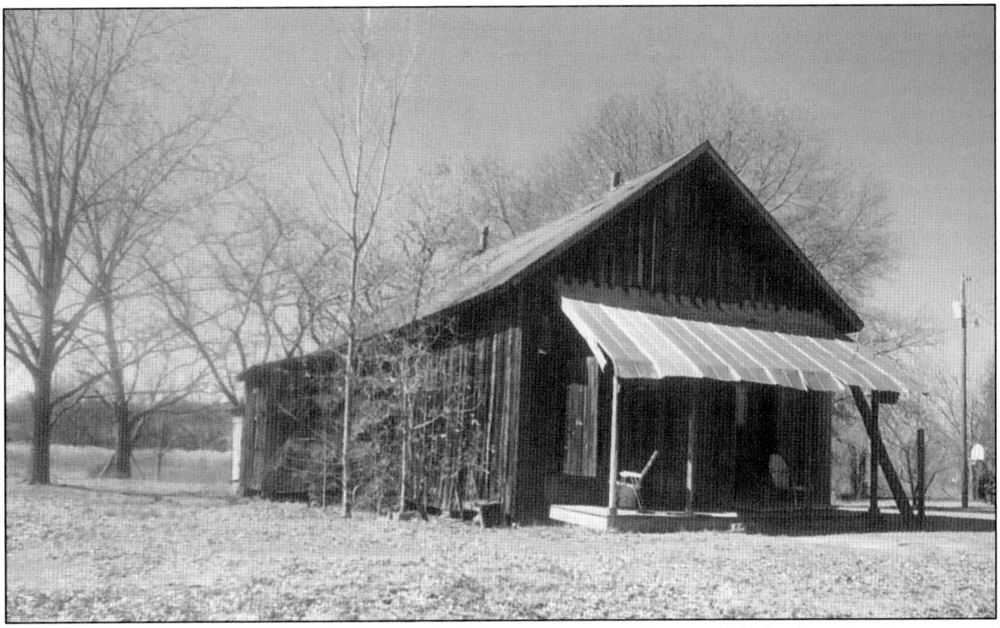

VALAMBROSA POST OFFICE. The Valambrosa Post Office was first established under the name of Picciola in 1879 with Jeremiah H. Yopp as its first postmaster. In 1889, the name was changed to Valambrosa. The post office, which closed in 1899, was located in this store building in the Moore Station community on the Macon, Dublin, and Savannah Railroad, west of Dublin.

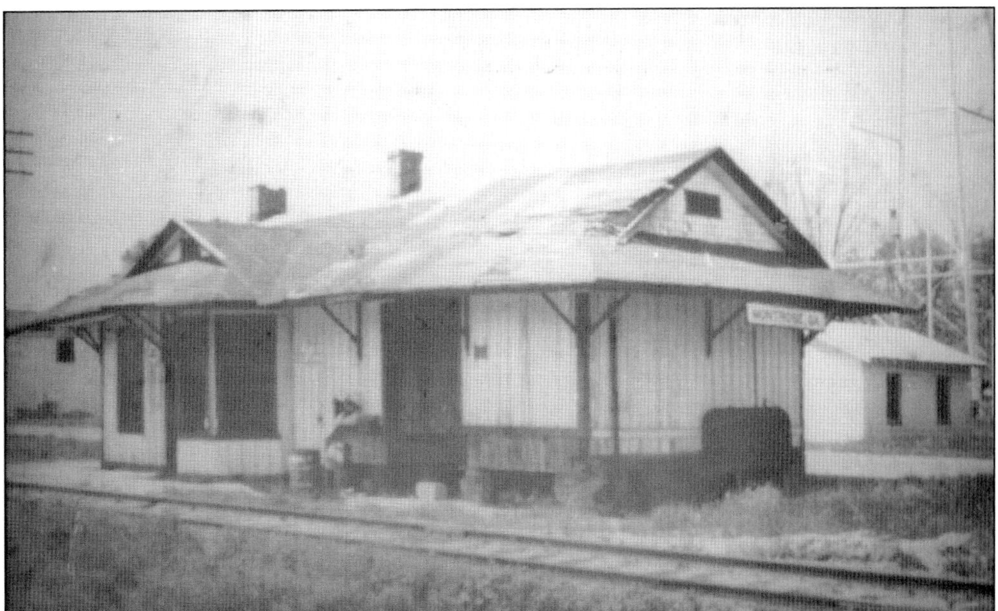

MONTROSE DEPOT. Montrose was the first depot on the rail line of the Macon, Dublin, and Savannah Railroad as it entered Laurens County from the northwest. The town of Montrose, which was incorporated in 1919, was once proposed to be the county seat of Hughes County, which was to be named in honor of Congressman Dudley Mays Hughes, the founder of the railroad and a local property owner.

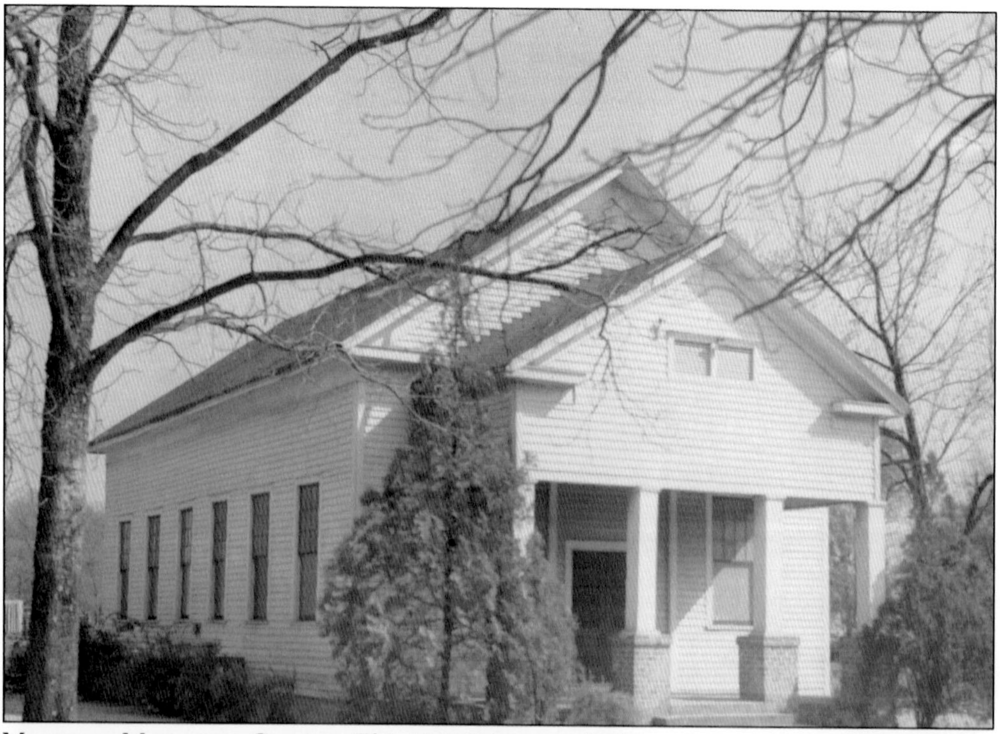

Montrose Methodist Church. This 1940s photograph shows the second church building of the Montrose Methodist Church, which was organized in 1905.

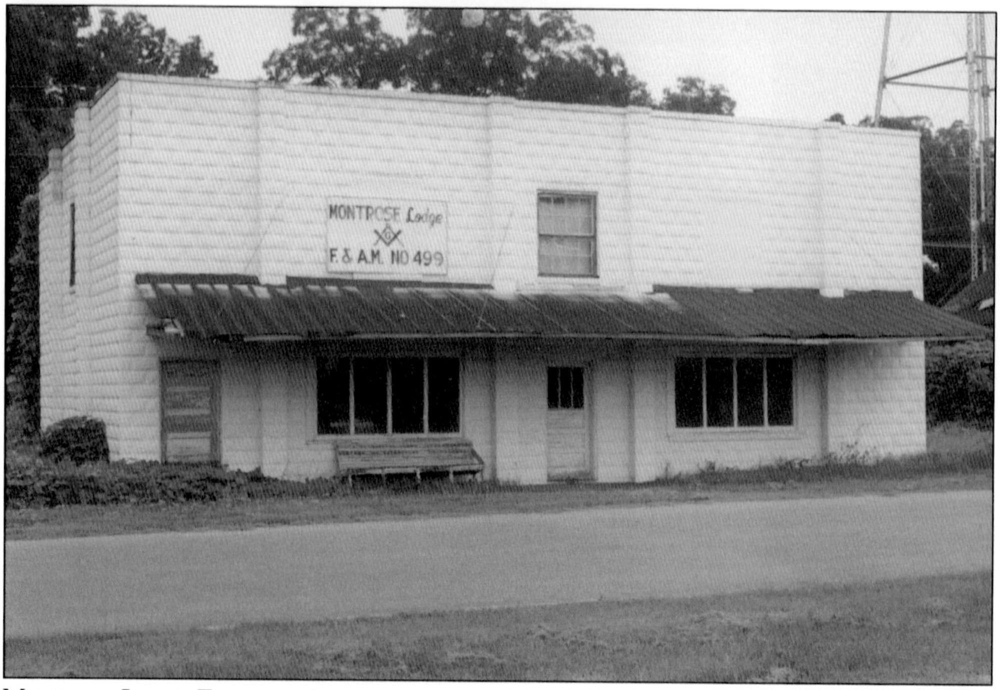

Montrose Lodge Free and Accepted Masons No. 499. Shown in this photograph is a store building that was home to the Masons of Montrose.

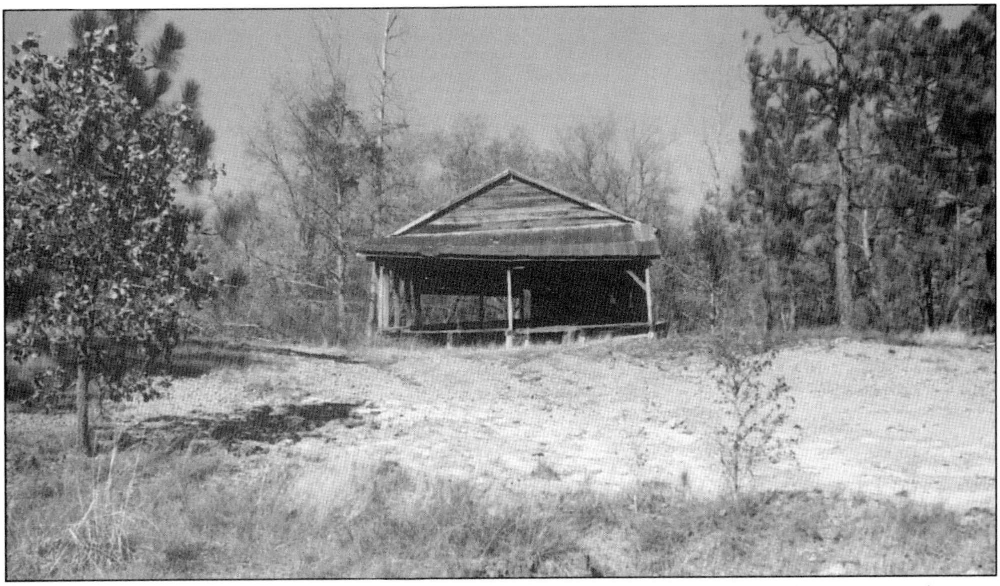

J. Tom Wilkes Turpentine Still. The pine trees of southeastern Laurens County were known for their ability to produce a top grade of turpentine. J. Tom Wilkes, who formed Minter Naval Stores in 1926, built this turpentine still in the Flatrock community south of Minter on the Soperton Highway to produce the naval stores product. Now one of Laurens County's oldest companies, Minter Naval Stores was acquired by Billy Belote and is now operated by his grandson Michael Belote.

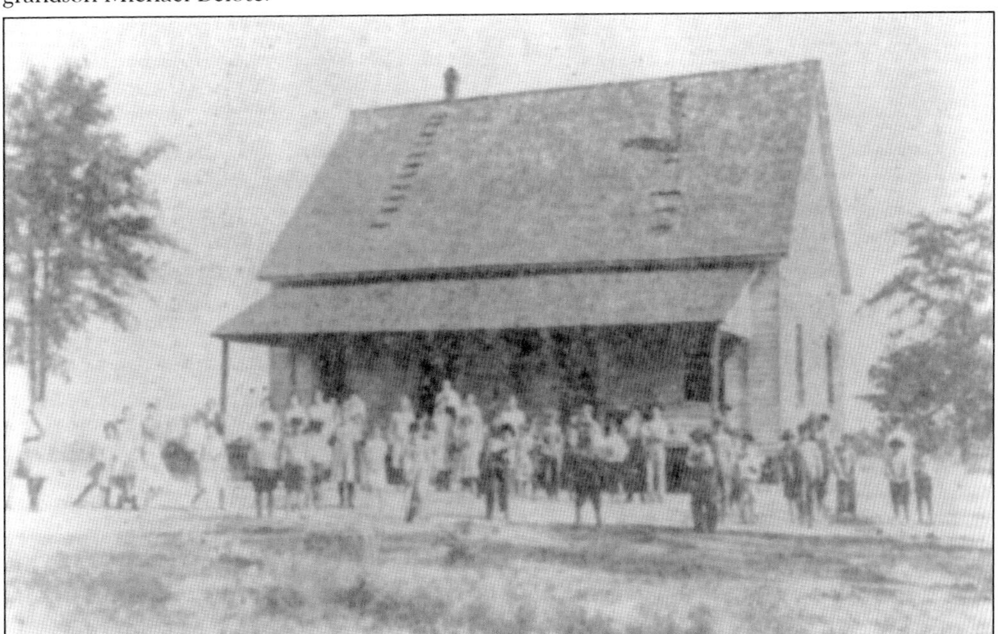

Nameless School. This 1920 school got its name from the community in which it was located. In 1886, James R. Shepard made an application to the federal government for the establishment of a post office south of Dexter. He could not decide on a name for the post office and wrote "Nameless" on the application. The bureaucrats in Washington thought he really meant it and gave the new post office its unusual name.

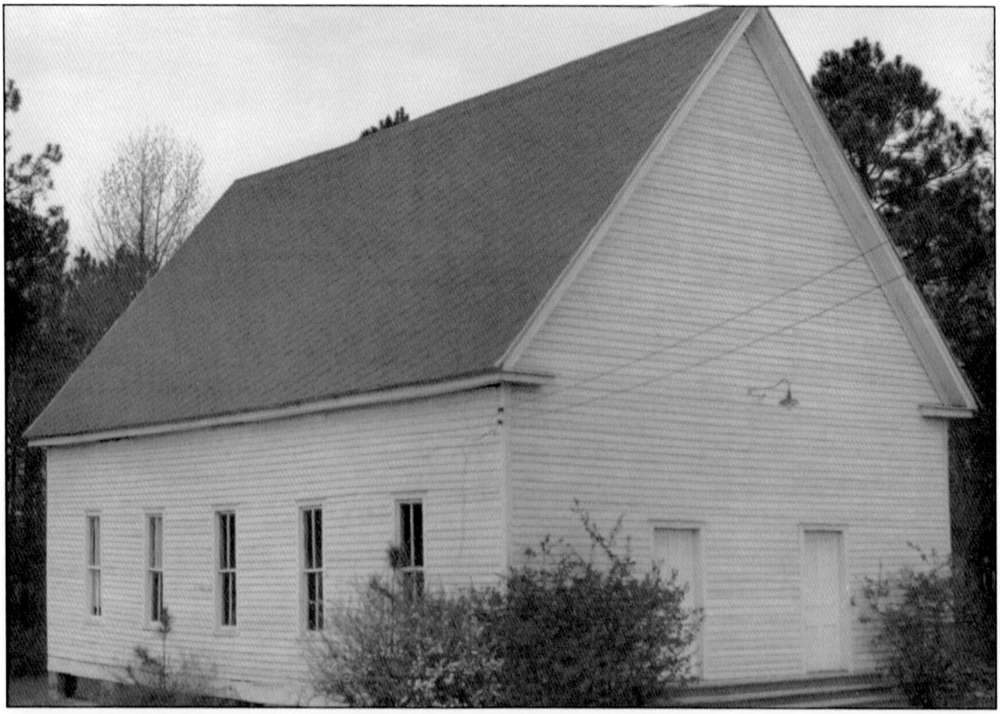

ORIANNA METHODIST CHURCH. The town of Orianna is what they used call a "line town." The county line between Laurens and Montgomery, later Treutlen, Counties ran through the center of town. The Orianna Methodist Church was established in the early 1900s and has not been in existence for several decades.

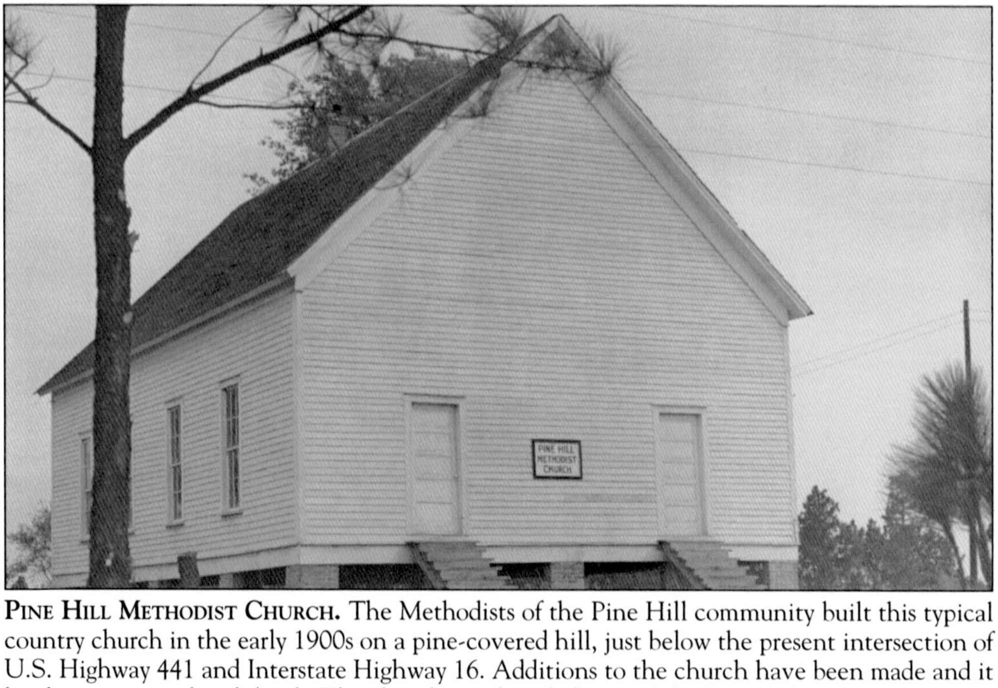

PINE HILL METHODIST CHURCH. The Methodists of the Pine Hill community built this typical country church in the early 1900s on a pine-covered hill, just below the present intersection of U.S. Highway 441 and Interstate Highway 16. Additions to the church have been made and it has been veneered with brick. The church was founded in 1897 by Rev. C.A. Moore.

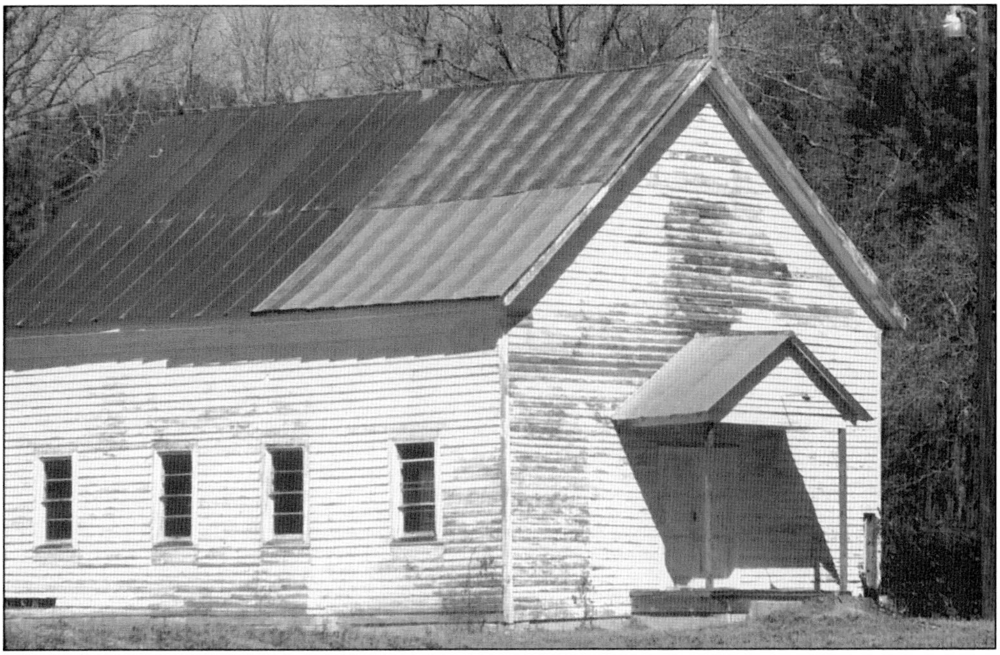

Strawberry AME Church. Strawberry AME Church was founded in 1857 by the Reverend George Linder. This church, which was the first known Laurens County church founded by African Americans, was located on Country Club Road. The building, which was completed about 1900, was recently replaced by a modern church and moved to another site.

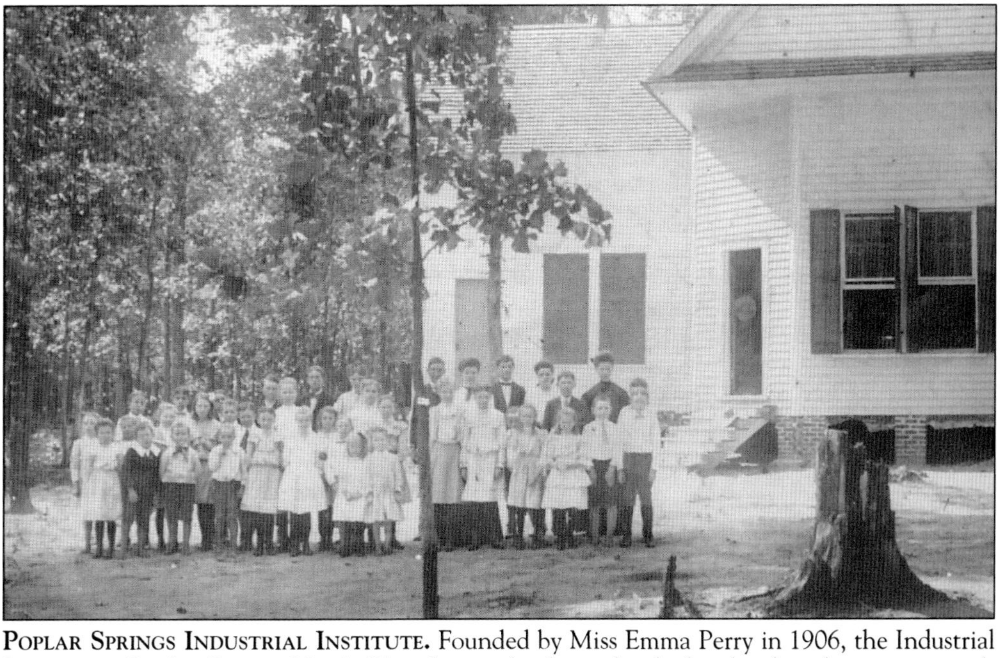

Poplar Springs Industrial Institute. Founded by Miss Emma Perry in 1906, the Industrial Institute at Poplar Springs North Church was the first school of its kind in the area to teach students the industrial and homemaking arts. The school was sponsored mainly by members of Poplar Springs North Church, which was established in 1807 and is the oldest church congregation west of the Oconee River still in existence.

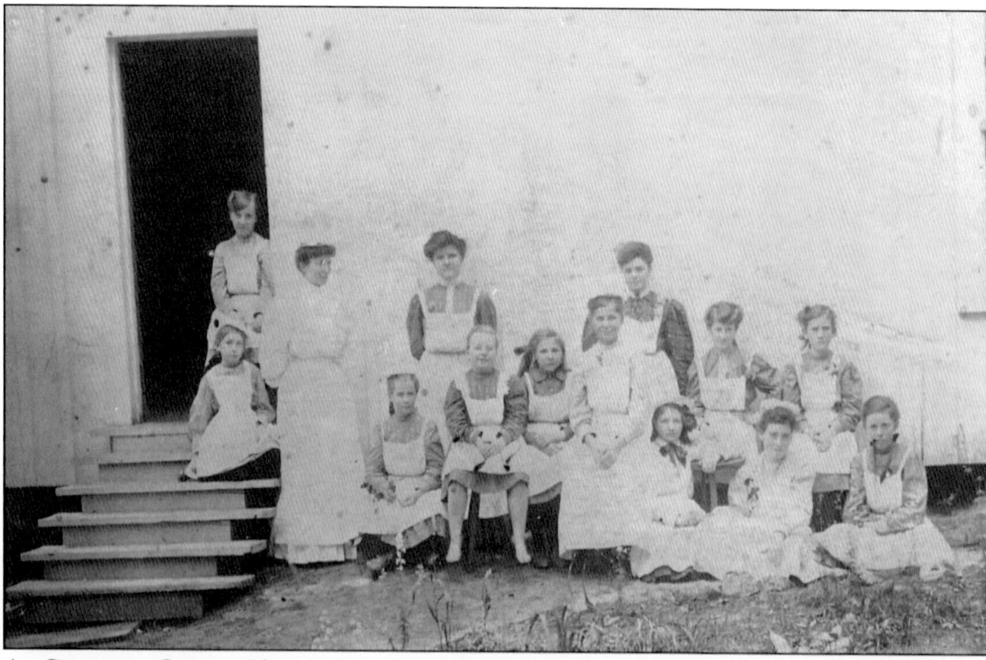

A Cooking Class. This 1910 photograph shows a cooking class at Poplar Springs Industrial Institute.

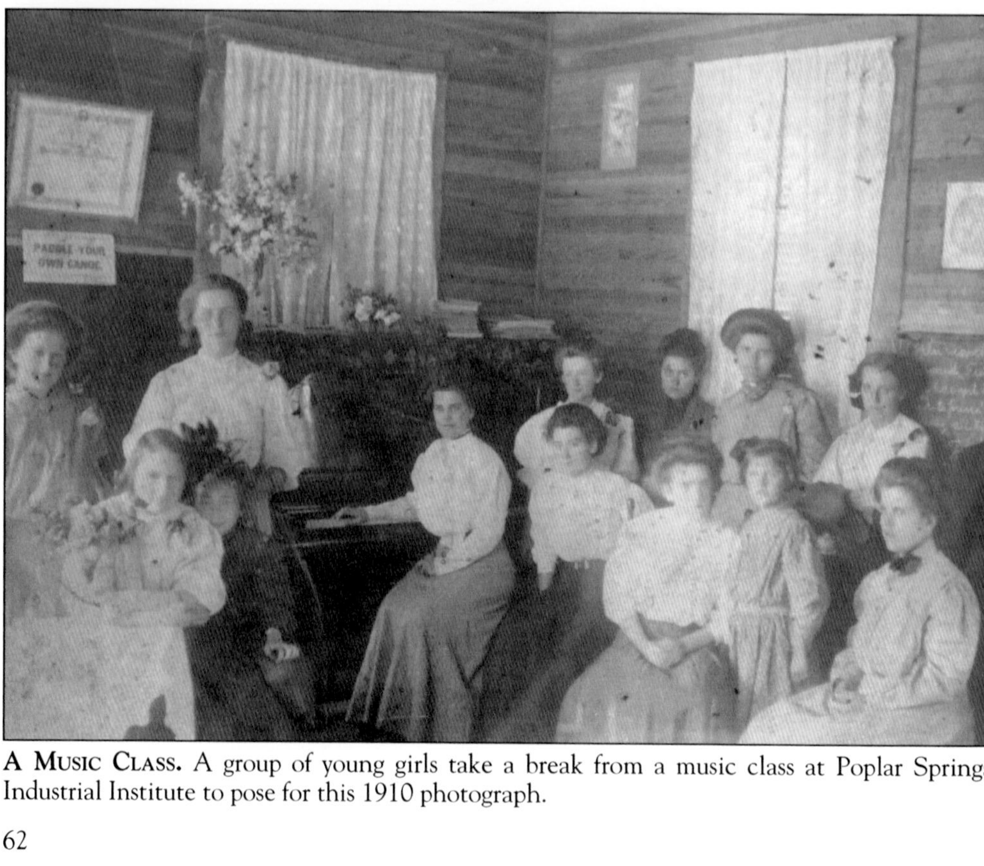

A Music Class. A group of young girls take a break from a music class at Poplar Springs Industrial Institute to pose for this 1910 photograph.

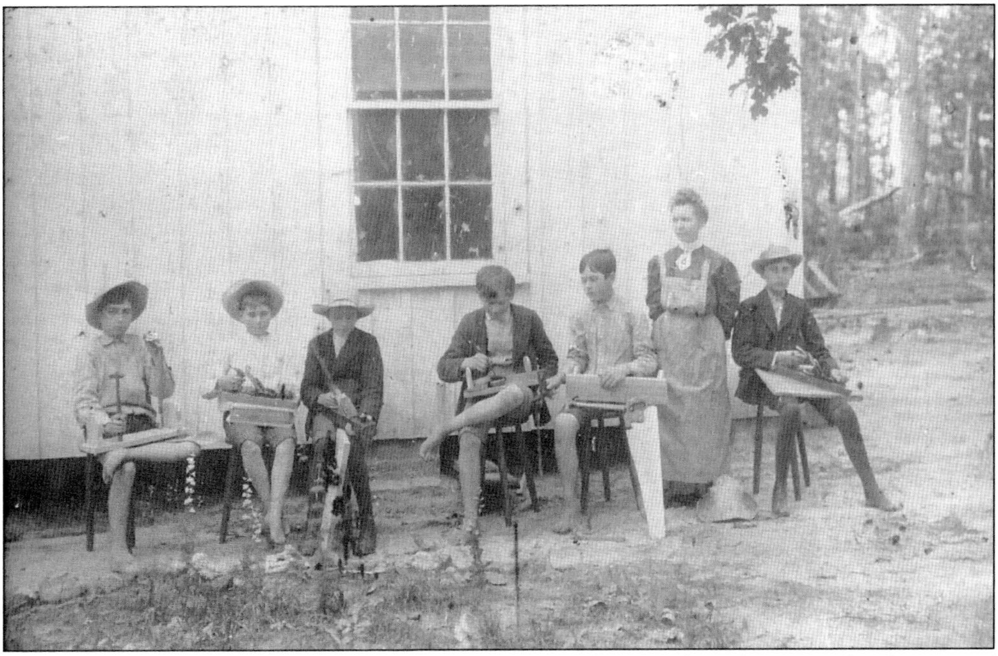

SHOP CLASS. This 1908 photograph shows a group of young boys learning the fine art of woodworking outside the shop building at the Poplar Springs Industrial Institute.

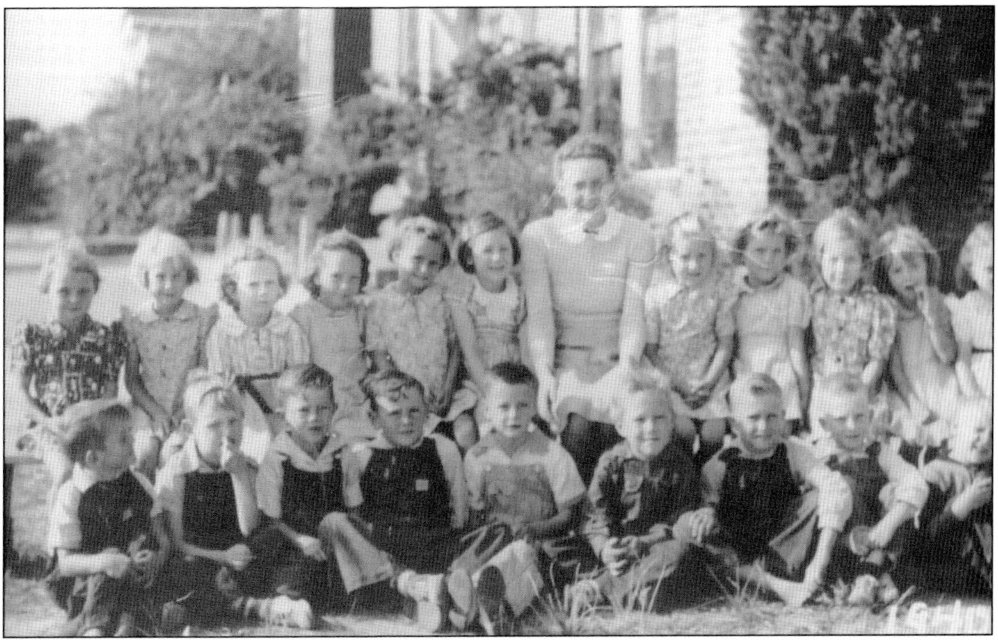

FIRST GRADE AT RENTZ. This photograph, which was taken about 1940, shows the first grade class of Miss Grace Bush at Rentz School.

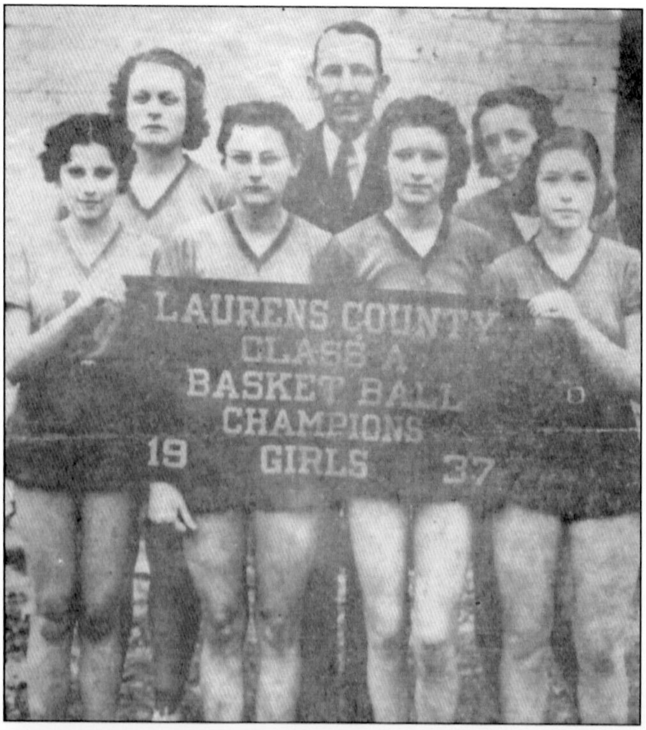

COUNTY CHAMPIONS. Before the consolidation of smaller county schools and before the establishment of statewide basketball tournaments, championship of the county was the goal of every school. Here are the 1937 Laurens County girls champions from Rentz High. From left to right are Dorothy Register, Hattie Flury, Clara Brown, Coach L.H. Cook, Mable Lindsey, Mildred Flury, and Ferralyn Davidson.

RENTZ METHODIST CHURCH. The Methodists at Rentz established a church in 1905, seen here in 1948. The church is no longer in service but is owned by the members of the Baptist Church, whose church stands across the street.

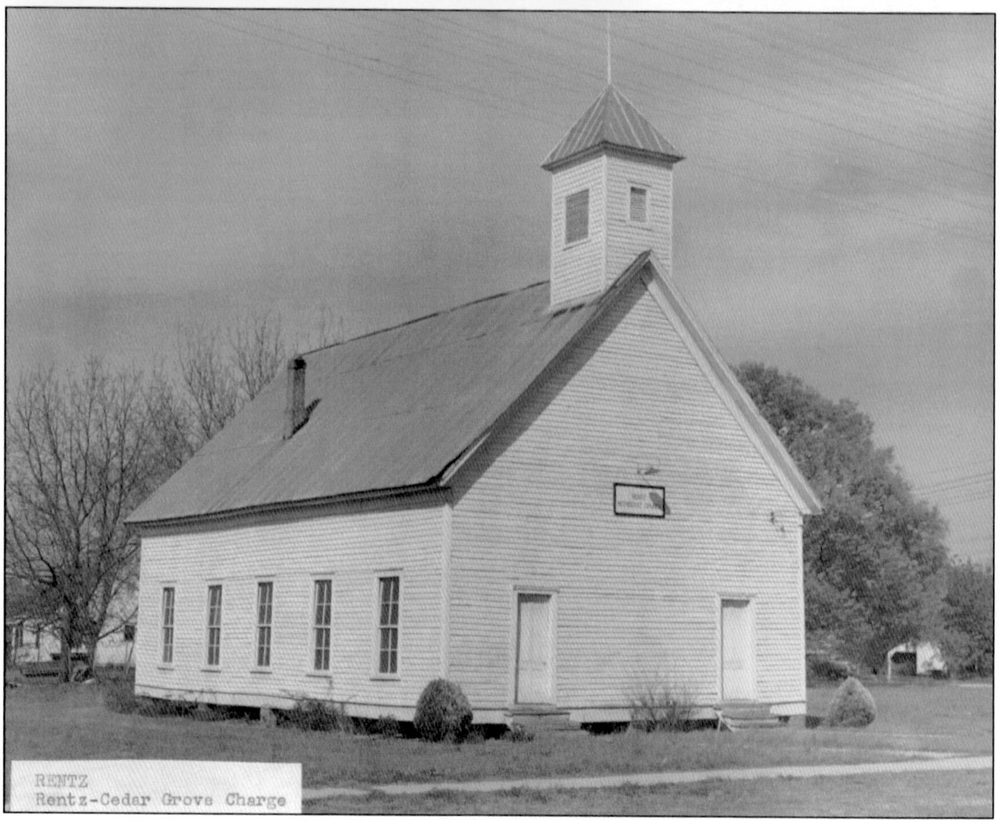

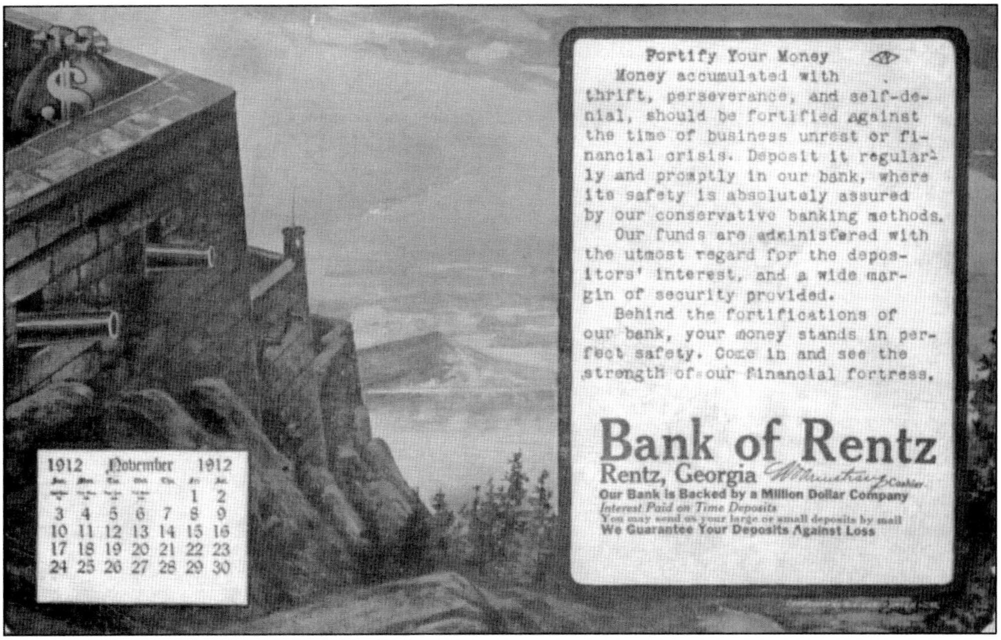

THE BANK OF RENTZ. The Bank of Rentz was founded around 1910. After it failed, a new bank, the Rentz Banking Company, began business in the sawmill town of Rentz on the Dublin & Southwestern Railroad. The Rentz Banking company operated successfully for six decades before it was purchased by the Citizens and Southern Bank.

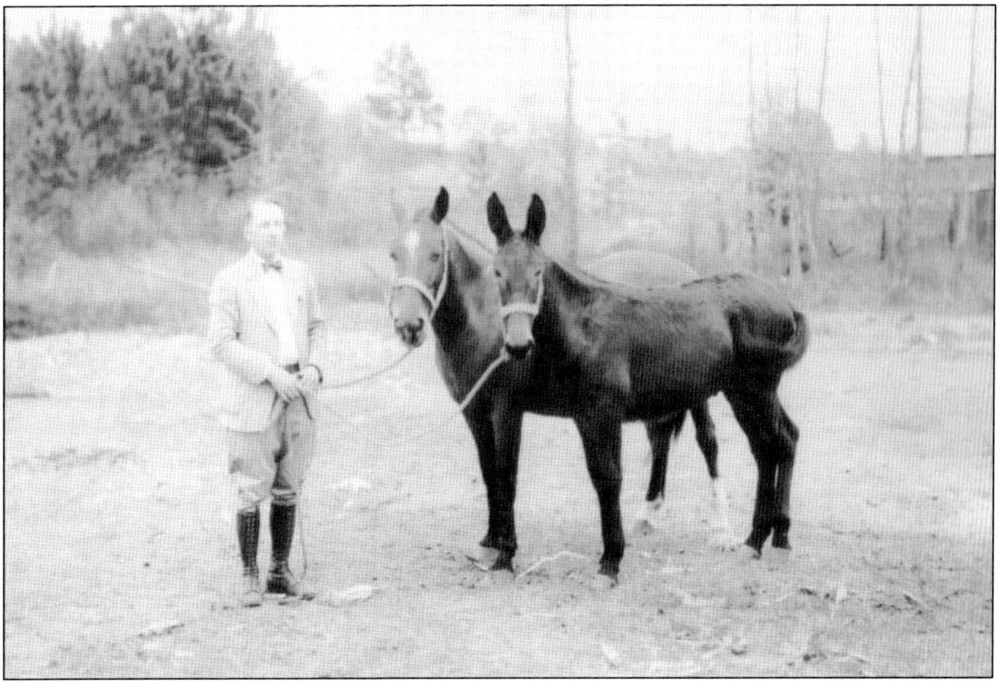

A PRIZE PAIR. Professor L.H. Cook of Rentz shows off a mare and her mule colt, which won a Future Farmers of America competition in 1939.

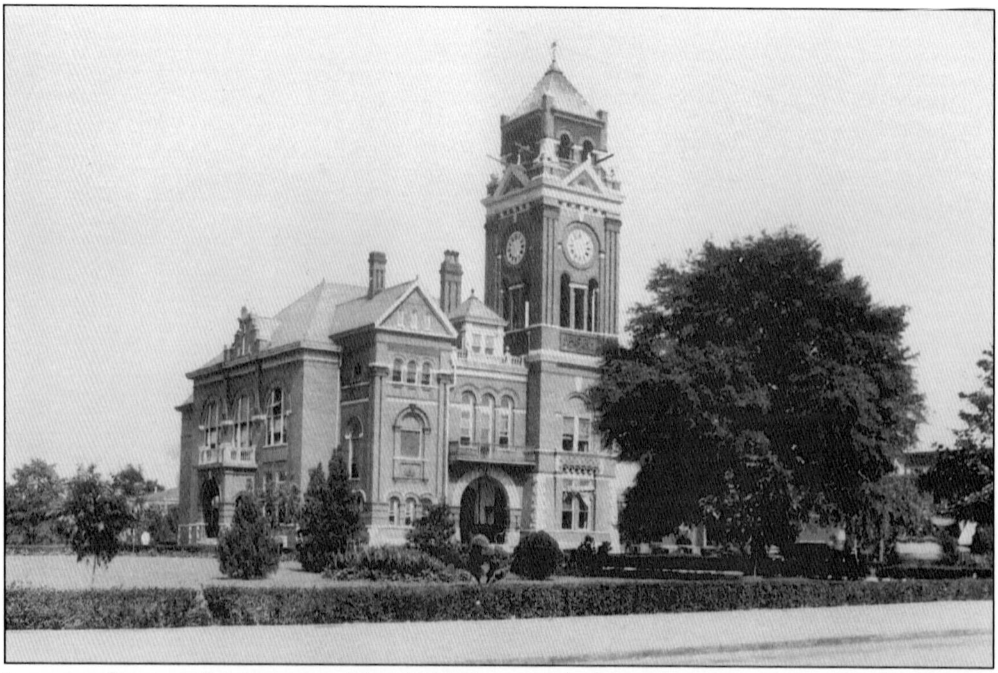

LAURENS COUNTY COURTHOUSE. This 1918 photograph shows the Laurens County Courthouse, which was constructed in 1895. For nearly 70 years, this building was the center of governmental, political, and social events for the county. The building was razed in 1963 to make room for a modern courthouse.

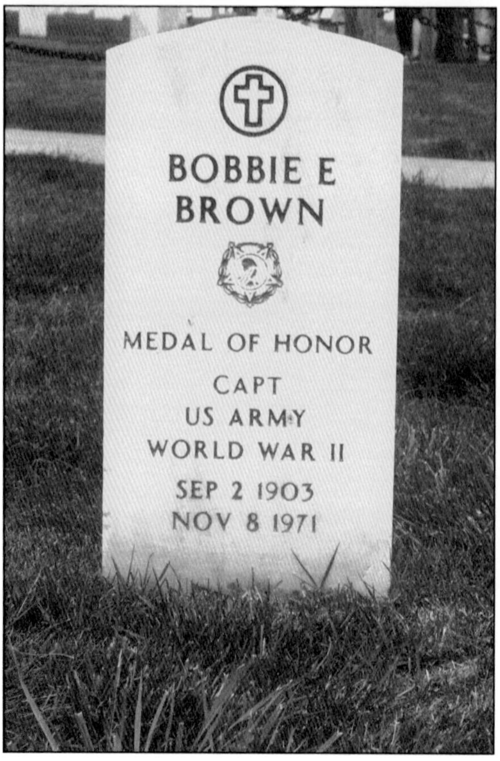

CAPT. BOBBIE E. BROWN. The body of Captain Brown lies in Section 46, a special section of Arlington National Cemetery dedicated to the greatest heroes of our country, in Grave #1021-1F. Captain Brown, a native of Laurens County, was awarded the Congressional Medal of Honor for his heroism at the Battle of Crucifix Hill in 1944. The State of Georgia has renamed Georgia Highway 19, which passes through Captain Brown's home community, the Capt. Bobbie E. Brown Highway in honor of this true American hero.

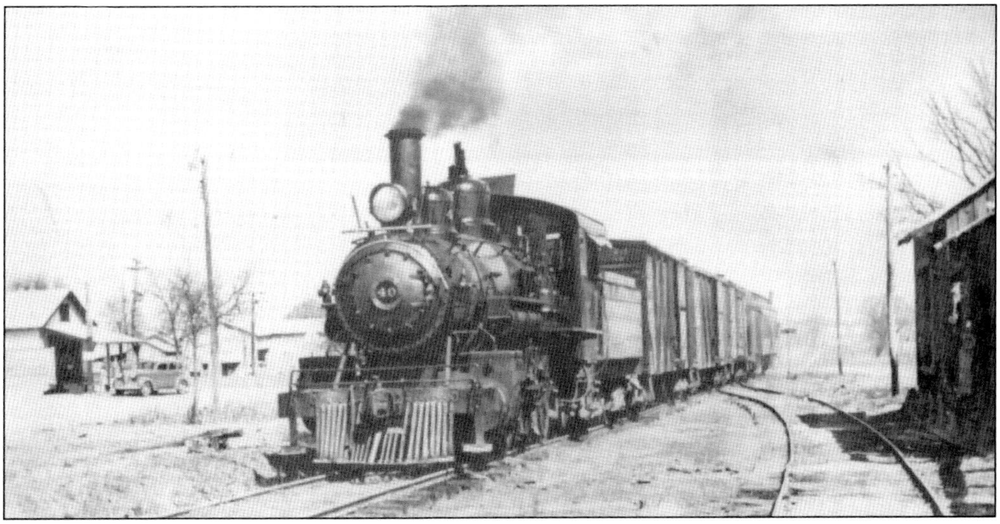

THE LAST TRAIN. This 1941 photograph shows one of the last trains of the Dublin-Eastman leg of the Wrightsville and Tennille Railroad to run into Rentz. In 1905, the Dublin & Southwestern Railroad began its operations from Dublin to Rentz, the site of the former sawmill of E.P. Rentz.

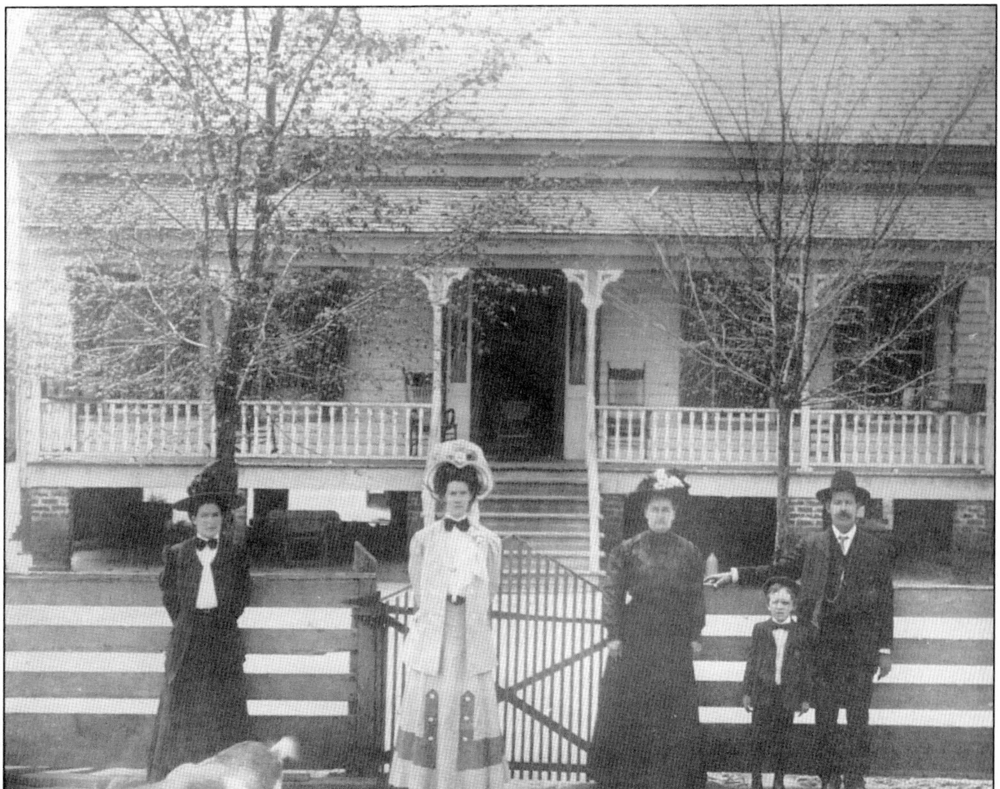

THE HOLMES HOUSE. This was the home of Margaret Stevens Holmes, and this estate adjoined "Valdosta," the home of Governor George M. Troup on the old River Road. This photograph was taken in 1915.

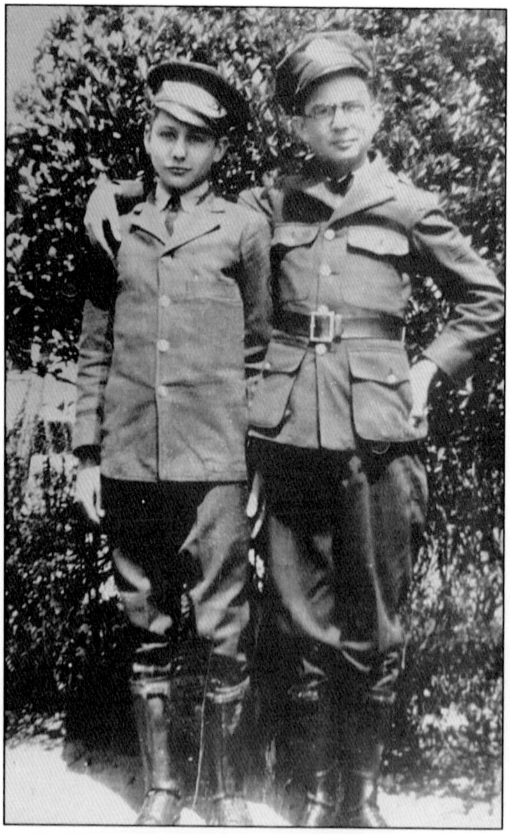

Western Union Messenger Boys. This 1929 photograph shows G.T. Daniel Jr. (left) and Randolph Knight (right), who delivered telegrams in Dublin on their bicycles.

The Macon, Dublin, and Savannah Railroad. The MD&S Railroad was the second railroad to come to Laurens County. Trains began running to Dublin in 1891, and in 1901, the line was extended through East Dublin, Catlin, Minter, and Rockledge on to Vidalia. This photograph taken in the early 1900s shows the No. 107 Engine bound for Dublin from Vidalia.

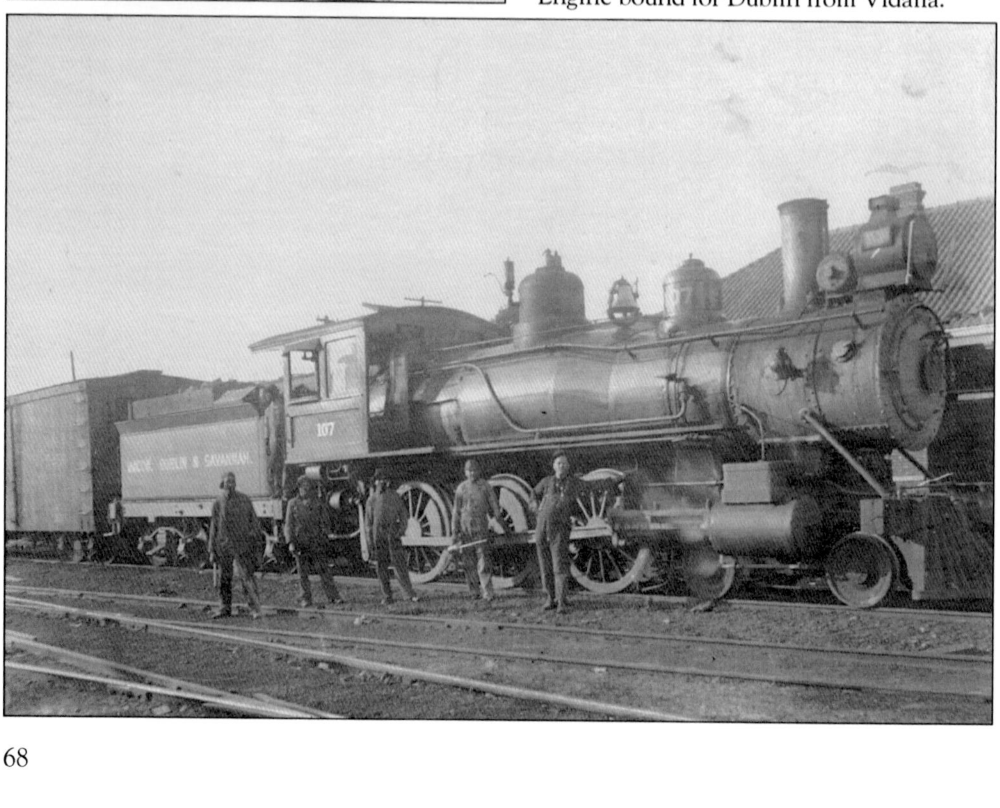

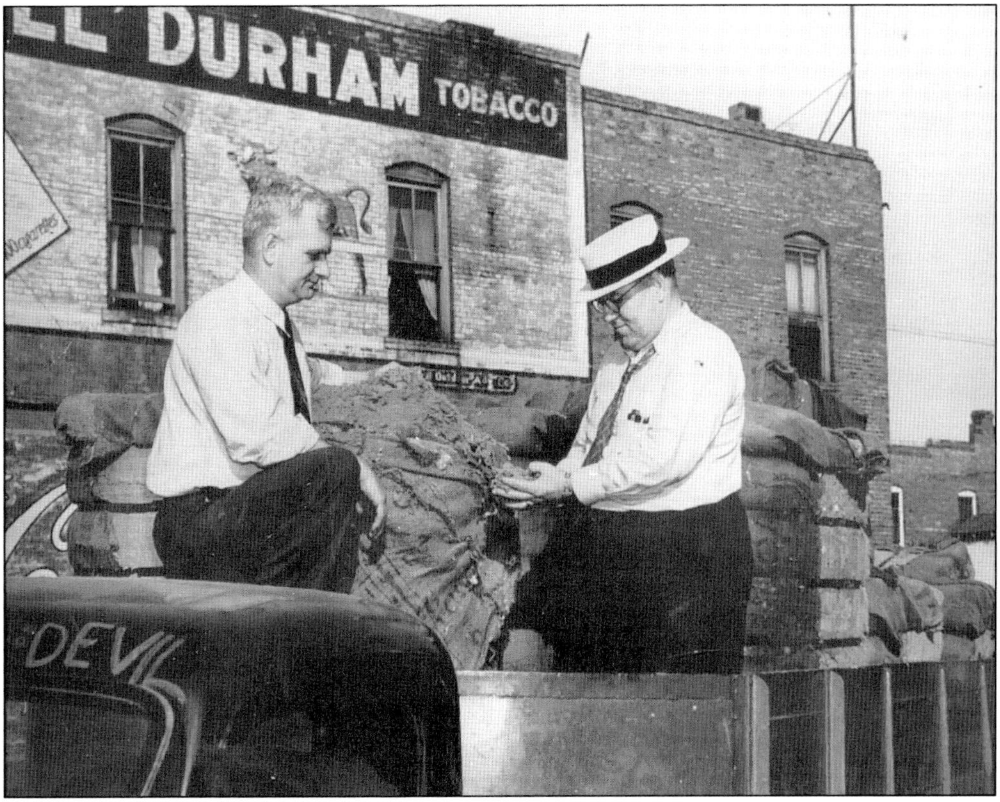

Making the Grade. O.L. Chivers and a cotton buyer are shown looking over a load of cotton that had just arrived at the Chiver's Warehouse at Five Points at the intersection of West Madison, South Lawrence, and Telfair Streets. The building in the background is the Cummings Building, which was built by D.D. Cummings and was the center of the African-American business community of Laurens County for the first half of the 20th century.

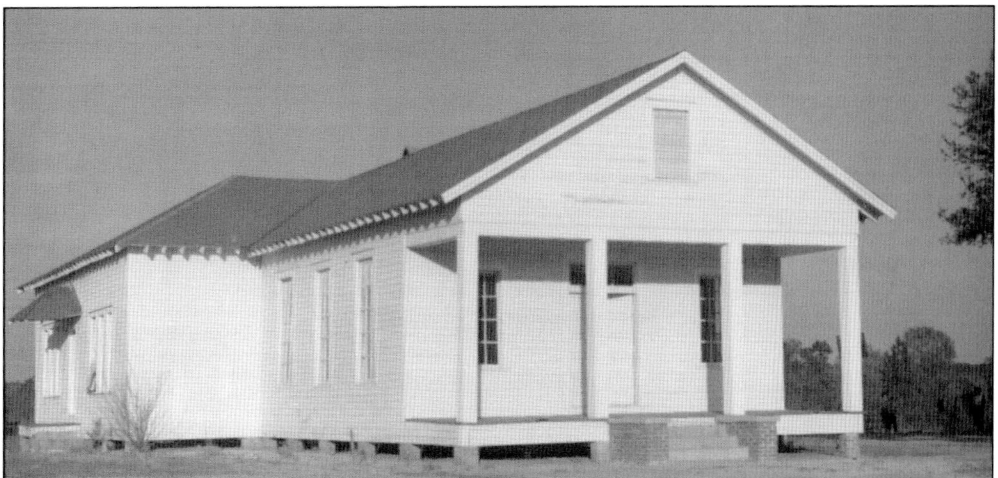

Rockledge Methodist Church. The Methodist Church at Rockledge was founded in 1908 under the leadership of Rev. C.L. Glenn and William H. Smith. The church building remains on its original site and is still an active congregation.

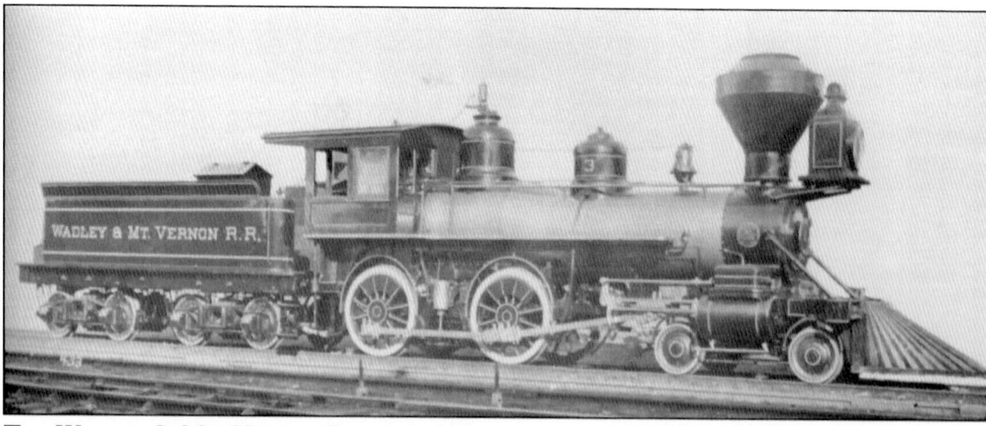

THE WADLEY & MT. VERNON RAILROAD. This engine of the Wadley & Mt. Vernon Railroad pulled carloads of timber, dry goods, and passengers between Rockledge and Wadley from the 1890s until the 1910s.

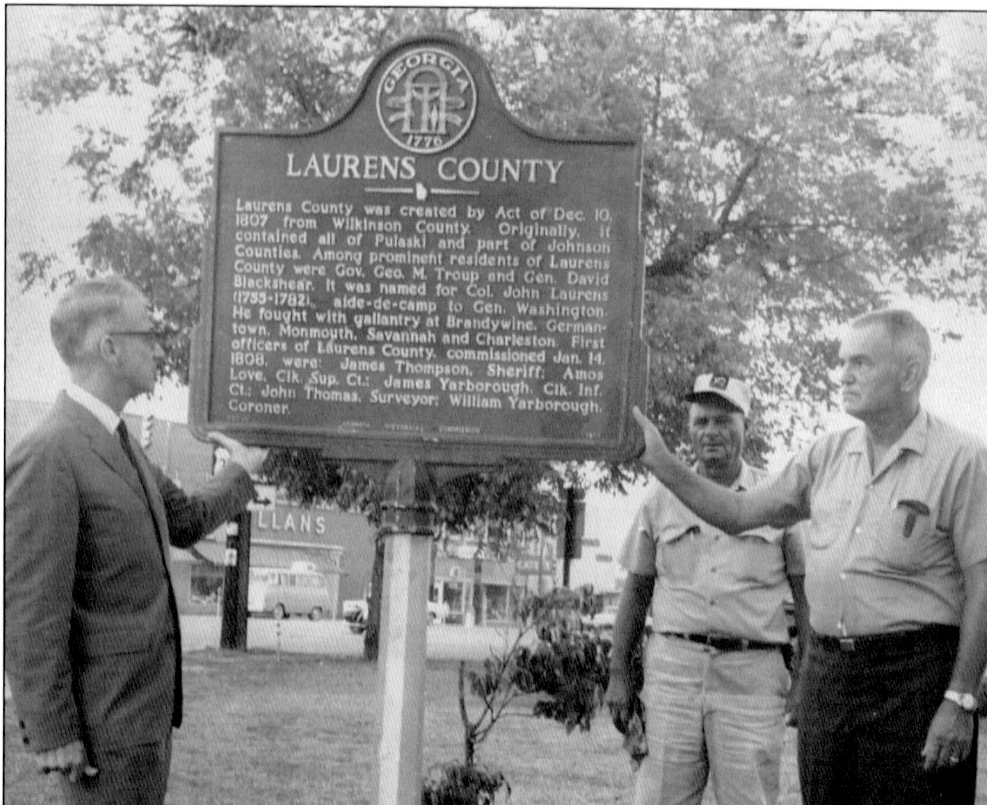

KEEPER OF OUR HISTORY. John Ross (left), the founder of the Laurens County Historical Society and the director of the Dublin-Laurens Museum for over 20 years, is shown in this photograph with workmen replacing the historical marker in front of the courthouse. Ross and his wife, Dorothy, led the formation of the historical society. Because of their efforts, the Dublin-Laurens Museum is one of the best small city museums in Georgia.

Three

LIFE IN LAURENS COUNTY

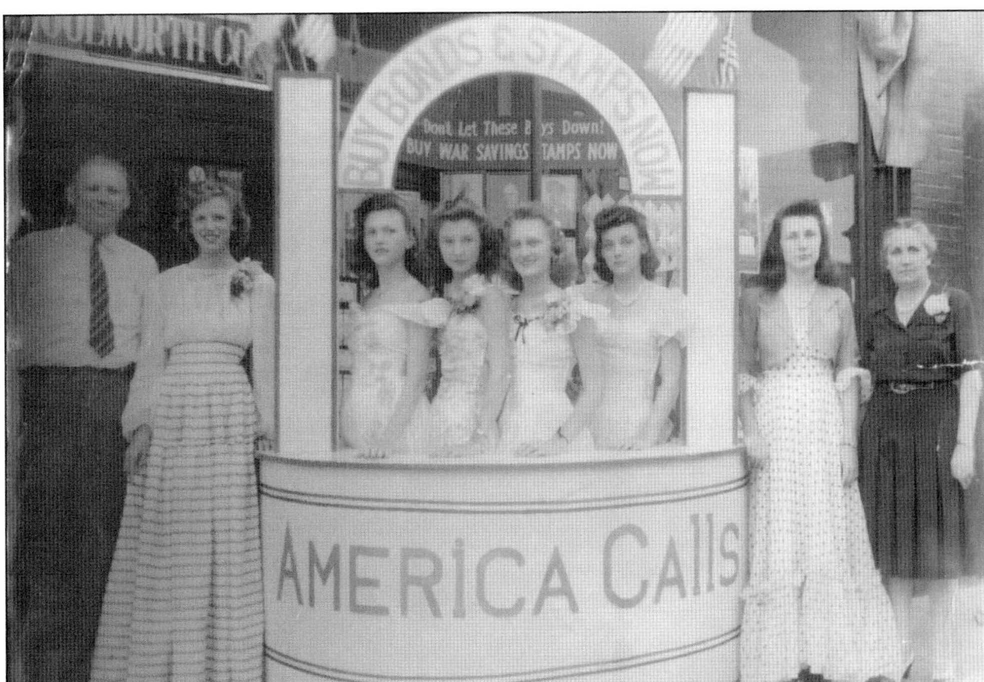

AMERICA CALLS. The people of Laurens County answered their country's call during World War II with unparalleled patriotism and service. This c. 1942 photograph shows a War Bond Booth in front of Woolworth's in Dublin. Seen, from left to right, are Harry Johnson, Helen Adams, Clyde Chivers, Betty Anne Smith, Caroline Brigham, Barbara Fay Bedingfield, Betty Page, and Mrs. B.B. Page.

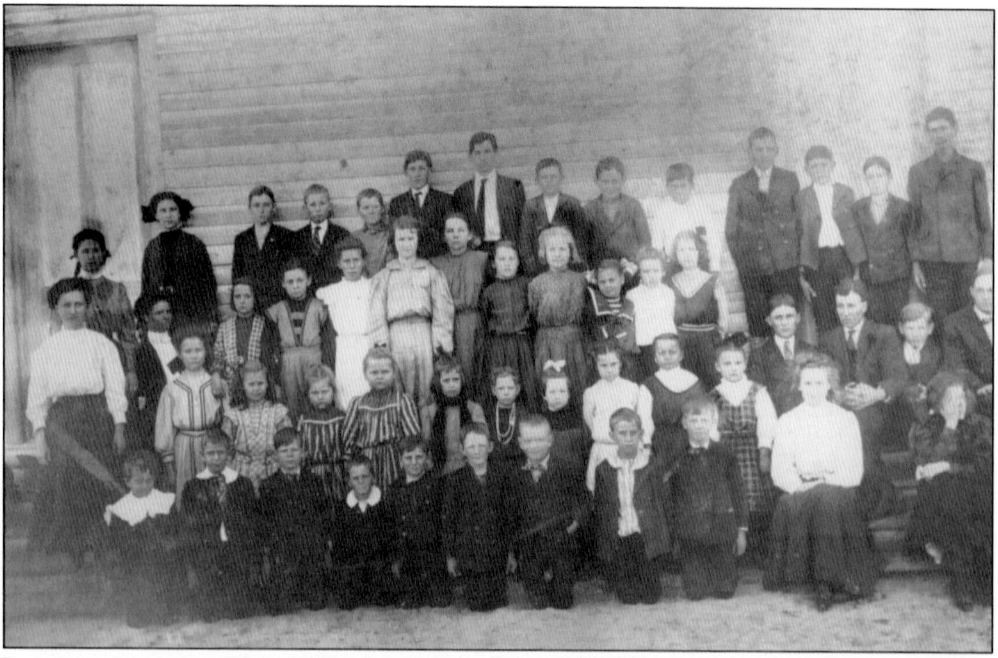

Leaches Academy. This 1895 photograph shows Miss Johanna Carter's class at Leaches Academy, which was located north of Pleasant Springs Baptist Church in Carter's District. The building was later used as St. Paul Nazarene Church, before it was moved to the Nazarene Campground near Adrian.

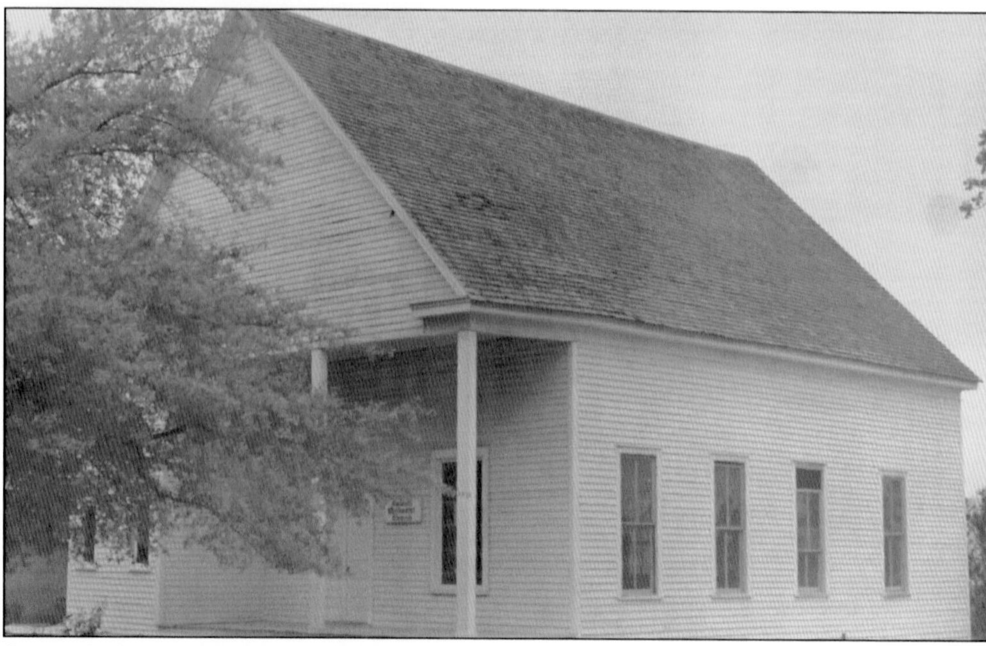

Carter's Chapel Methodist Church. This 1940s photograph shows the second and current building of Carter's Chapel Methodist Church. It was built in 1885 and was named for Edith Calhoun Carter, one of the founding members. The church is located on U.S. Highway 80 East in eastern Laurens County.

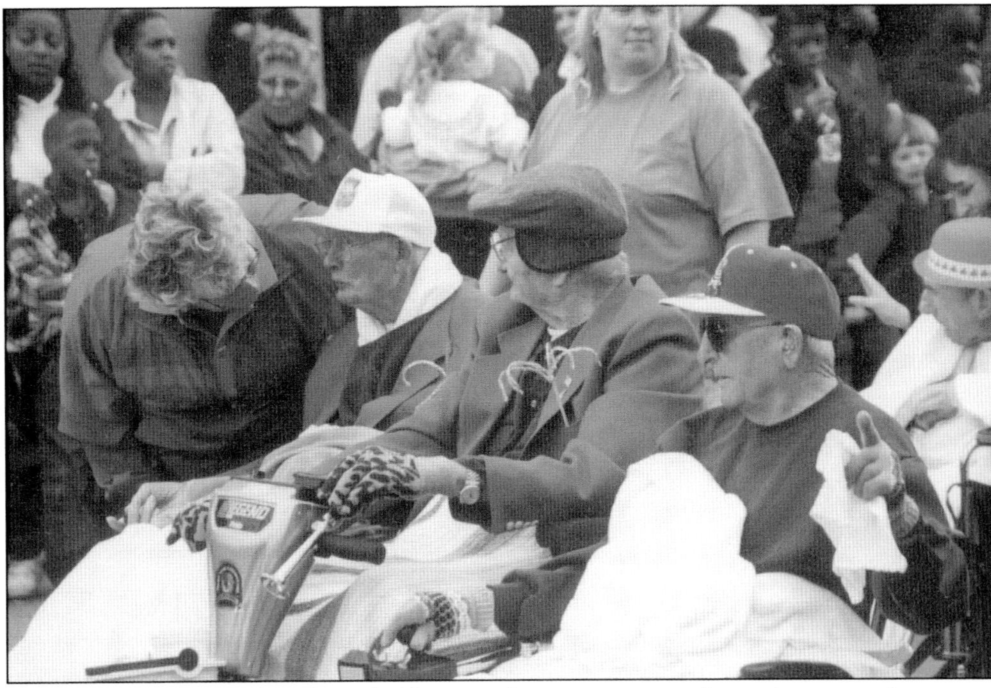

America Remembers. More than a half-century later, we must not forget the men and women of "The Greatest Generation." This photograph taken at the annual St. Patrick's Parade in March of 2000 shows some of our heroes who did no less than save the world from imperialism.

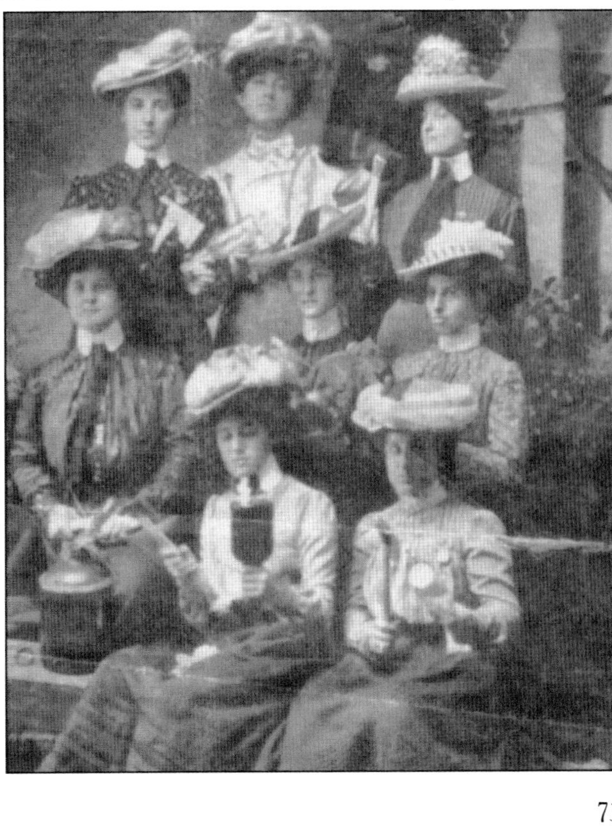

The Carrie Nation Band. This group of young women based in Dublin united to form a band to promote the prohibition of alcohol. Included in the photograph are Connie Berliner, Hortense Morris, Dena Baum, Pearl Wachtel, Annie Josephson, Gertie Wachtel, and Adeline Baum.

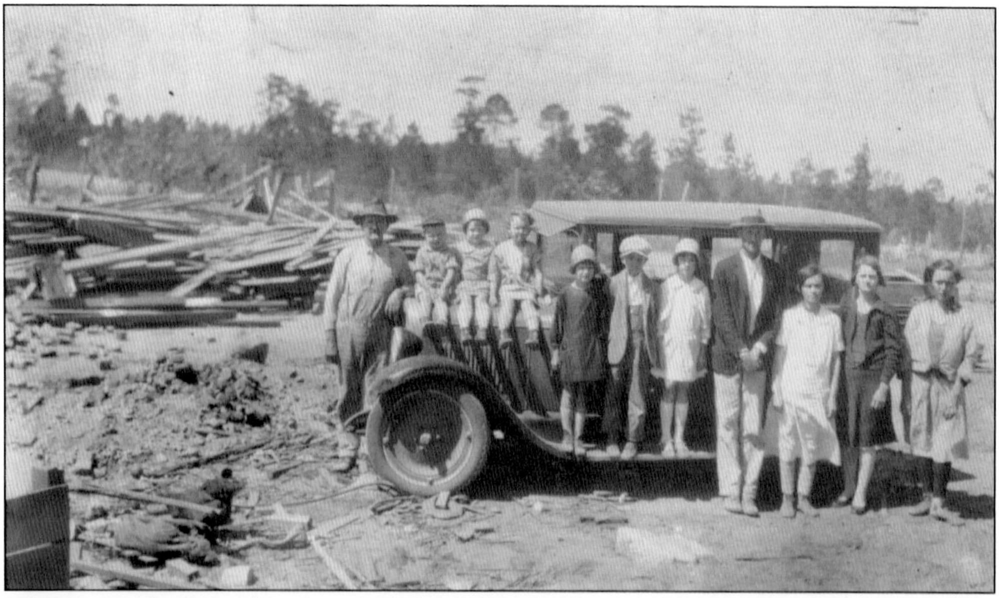

SURVIVORS. Shown in this unusual photograph is the family of M.J. Crumpton, who raced his Chevrolet car through fields and woods to escape the deadly tornado that struck the Dexter community in April of 1929. The family returned to their home, only to find that it had been completely destroyed.

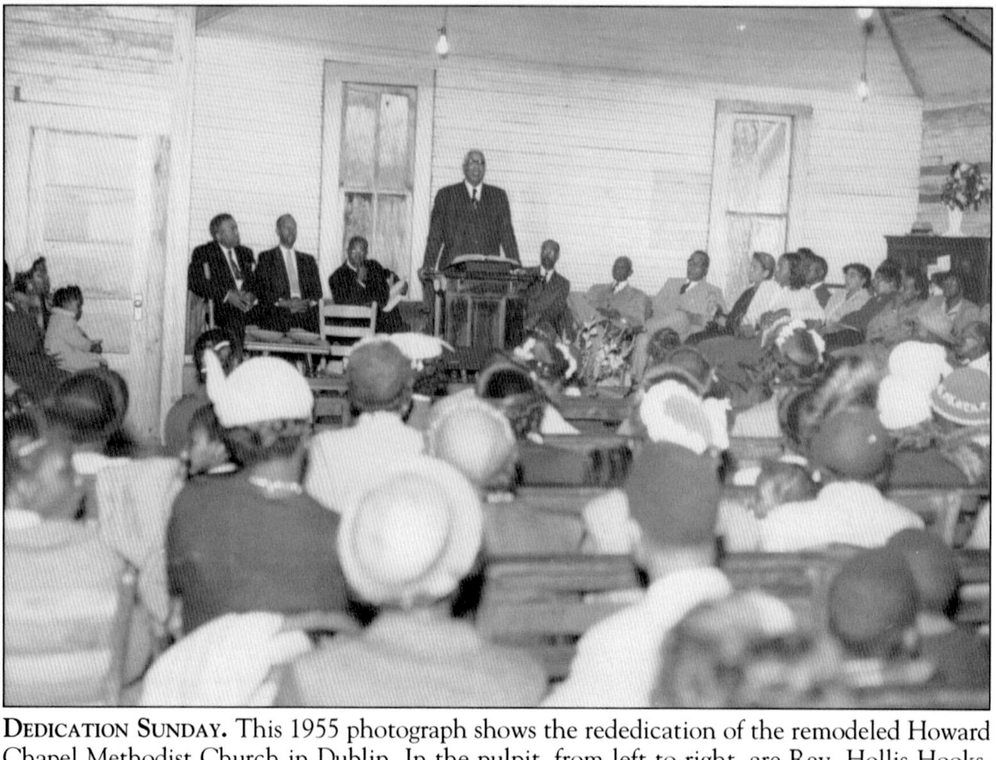

DEDICATION SUNDAY. This 1955 photograph shows the rededication of the remodeled Howard Chapel Methodist Church in Dublin. In the pulpit, from left to right, are Rev. Hollis Hooks, Rev. Amos Holmes, Rev. C.W. Prothro, Rev. W.J. Mason, and Dr. U.S. Johnson, the presiding elder of the African Methodist Episcopal Church.

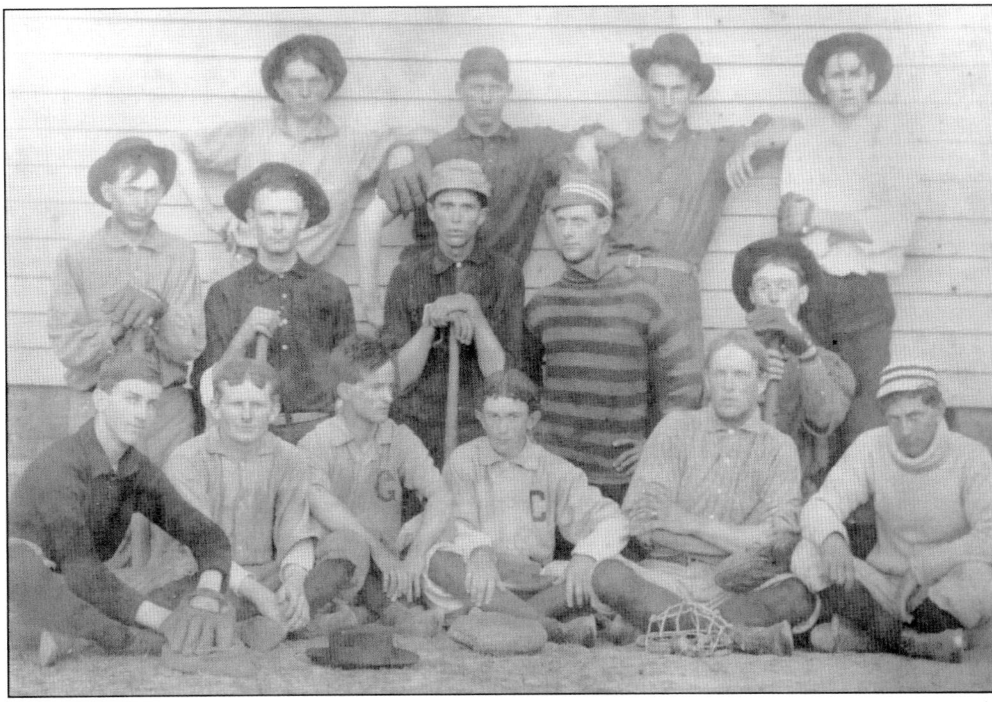

BASEBALL AS IT WAS MEANT TO BE. This group of handsome young men from the Bethsaida community made up one of the county's best school baseball teams around the turn of the 20th century.

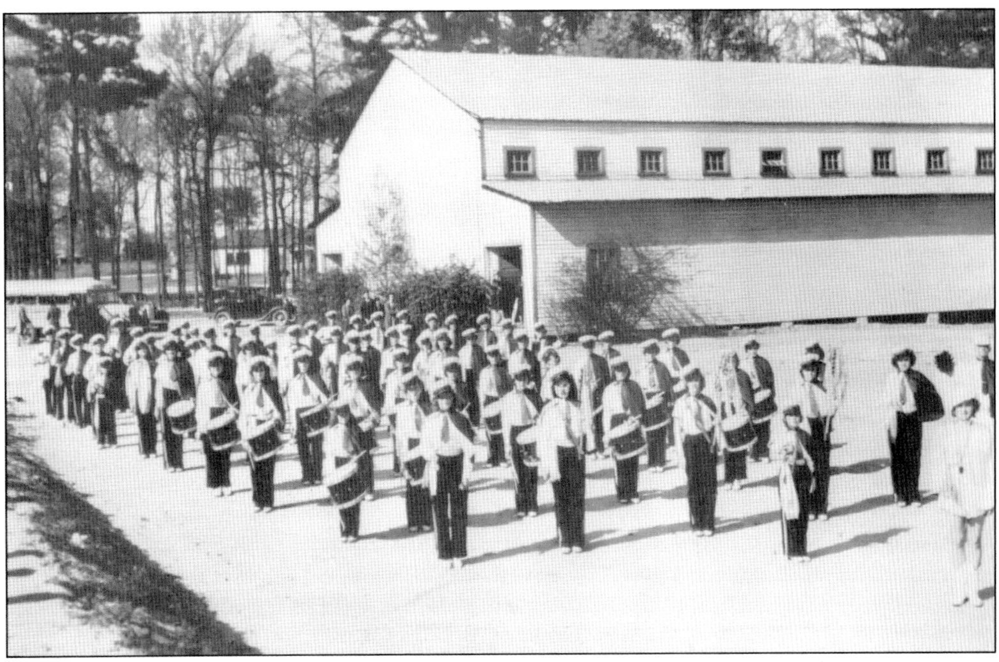

THE LAURENS COUNTY DRUM AND BUGLE CORPS. Musicians from schools of Laurens County are shown in this 1940 photograph outside the Hargrove Gym in Stubbs Park. The band was a popular attraction at parades and festivals and once played for President Franklin D. Roosevelt.

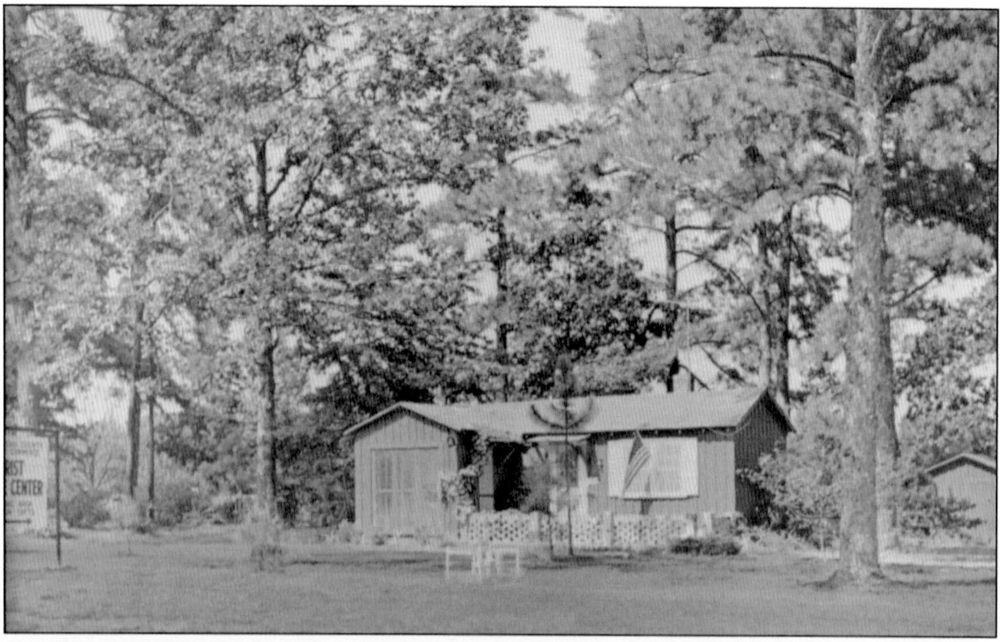

The Welcome Center. In 1963, Laurens County, Dublin, and the Dublin-Laurens Chamber of Commerce established the first municipal welcome center in Georgia, 2 miles north of Dublin on Highway 441. The center welcomed thousands of visitors every year until the completion of the interstate system in Georgia in the 1970s.

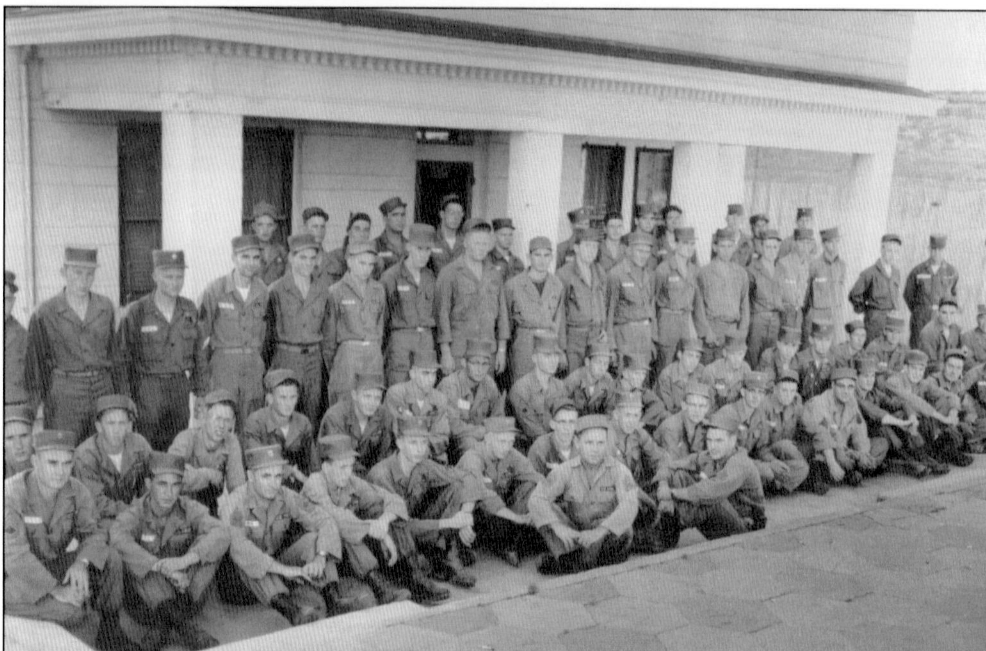

The Georgia National Guard. This 1956 photograph shows Headquarters and Headquarters Company of the 1st Battalion, 121st Infantry, Georgia National Guard. The unit, shown in front of the Laurens County Jail on South Franklin Street, was called out on a 36-hour search for an escaped prisoner in the Dexter area.

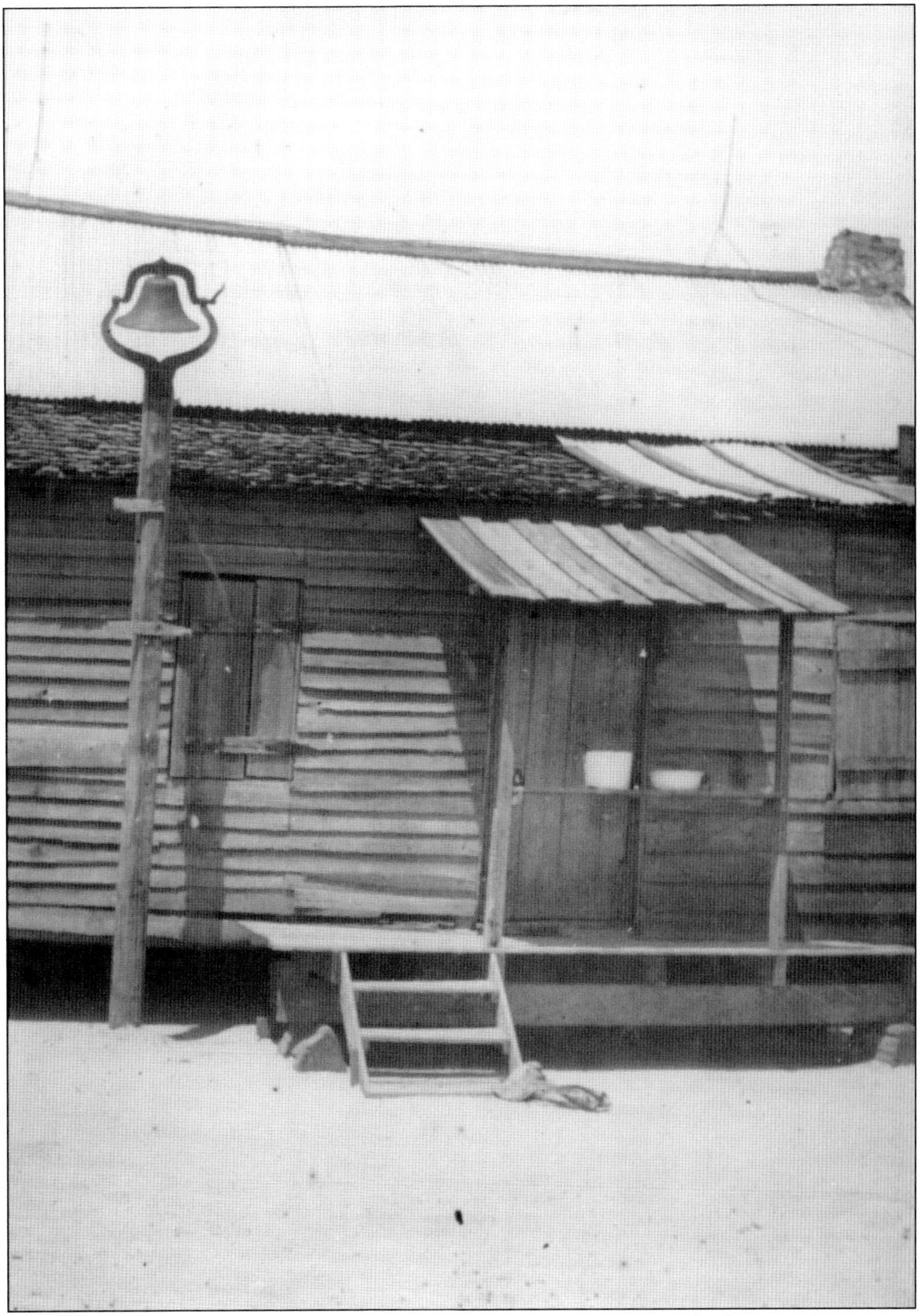

LOG KITCHEN. This 1940 photograph shows the 19th-century log kitchen at the Reason Andrew Bedingfield home in Rentz. Kitchens were built separate from the house to prevent the spread of fire to the main house and to reduce the heat in the main house during the summer months.

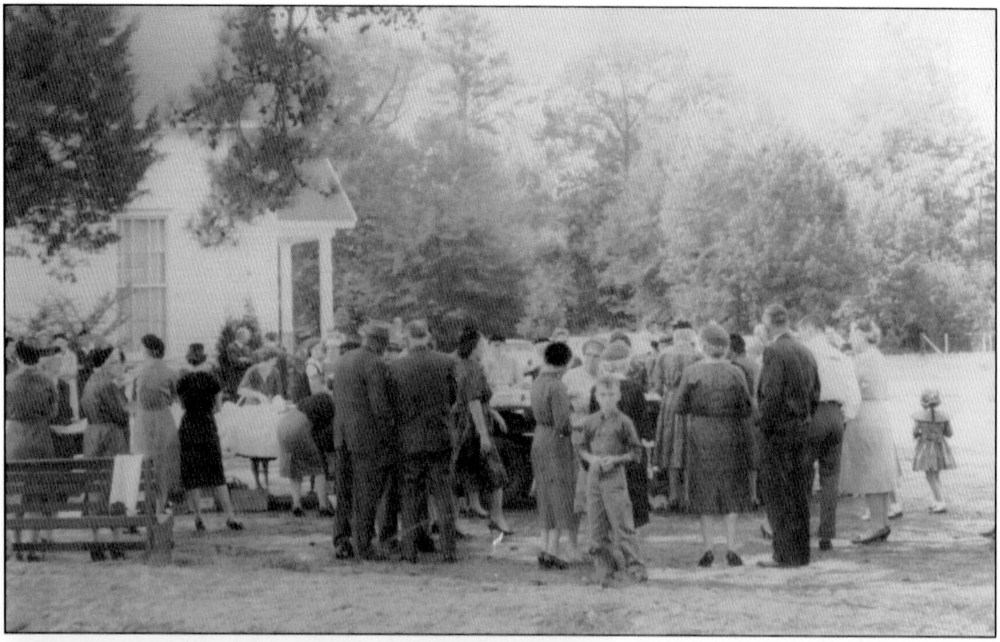

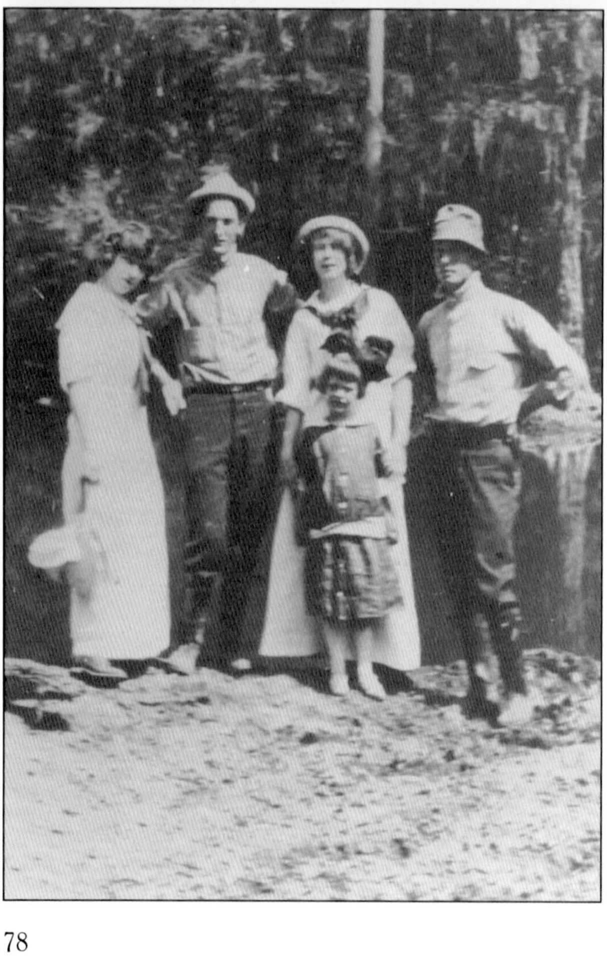

Celebration at Boiling Springs. Members and friends gather to celebrate the anniversary of Boiling Springs Methodist Church in northeastern Laurens County. The church was founded in 1851 and is the oldest wooden Methodist church in the South Georgia Conference and one of the oldest Methodist church buildings in the state.

Camping on Turkey Creek. In the early decades of the 20th century, residents of Laurens County enjoyed the clear cool waters of Turkey Creek near its mouth on the Oconee River. Shown in this photograph, from left to right, are Sarah Orr, Melvin Tarpley, Annie Simons, and Manley Smith. The young girl in the front is Sophie Street.

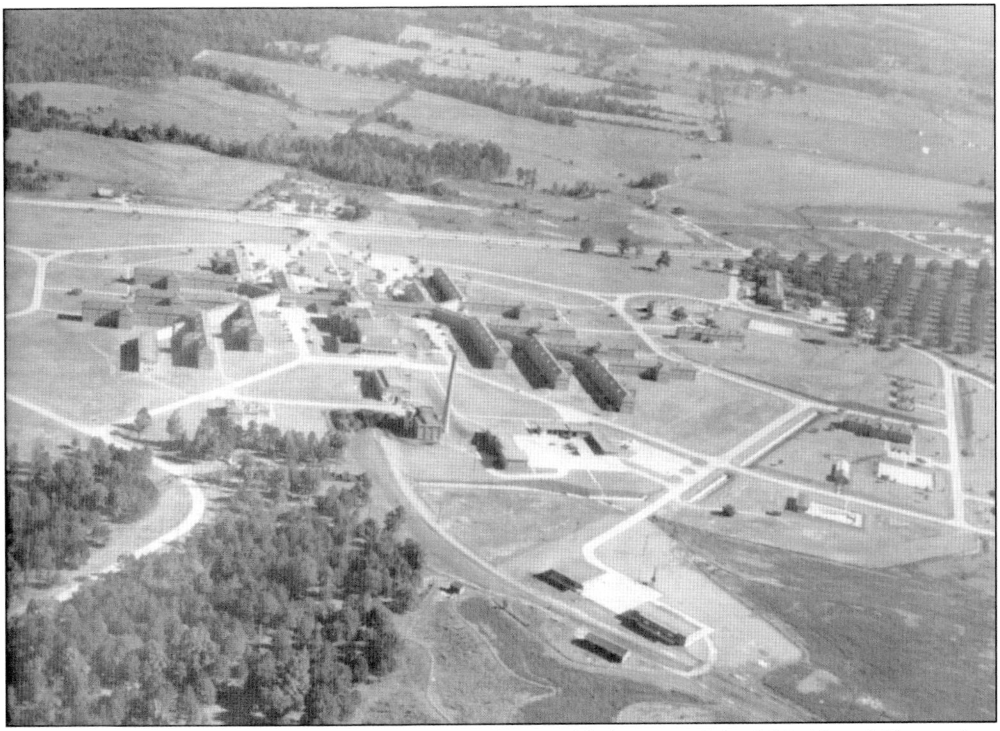

THE VETERANS ADMINISTRATION HOSPITAL. The establishment of the U.S. Naval Hospital in 1945 brought a tremendous and permanent boost to the county's economy. New families from all over the country moved to Dublin and made valuable and long-lasting contributions to the community. The fields at the top of the photograph were soon covered with new homes.

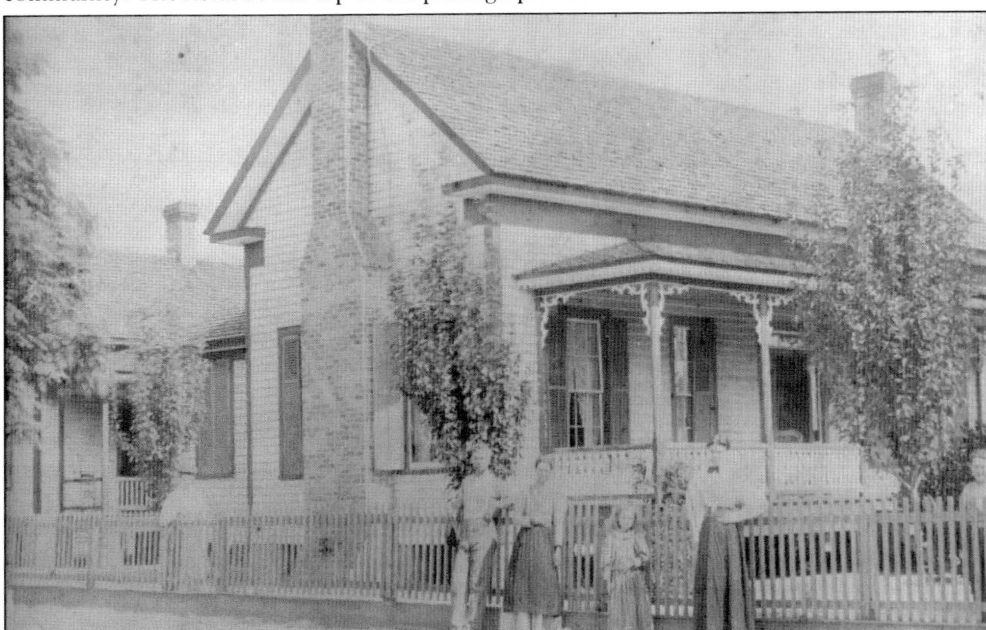

GEORGE W. CARTER HOME. This beautiful home, shown in 1897, belonged to George W. Carter who lived near Scott, Georgia, in the extreme eastern end of Laurens County.

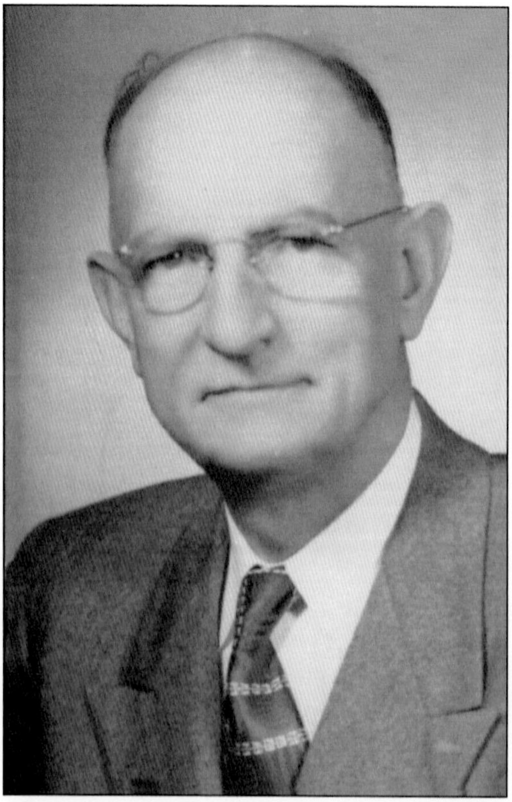

Tom Linder. Tom Linder, a native of Laurens County, served as Georgia's commissioner of agriculture from 1935 to 1937 and from 1941 to 1955, making him Georgia's second longest-serving commissioner of agriculture.

Fields of Cotton. It was called by some "Laurens County snow." In the summers, cotton blooms covered the land like snow. Laurens County was perennially at the top of Georgia counties in cotton production. The field in this late-19th-century photograph was owned by George W. Carter. Notice that deadened pine trees were left in the field.

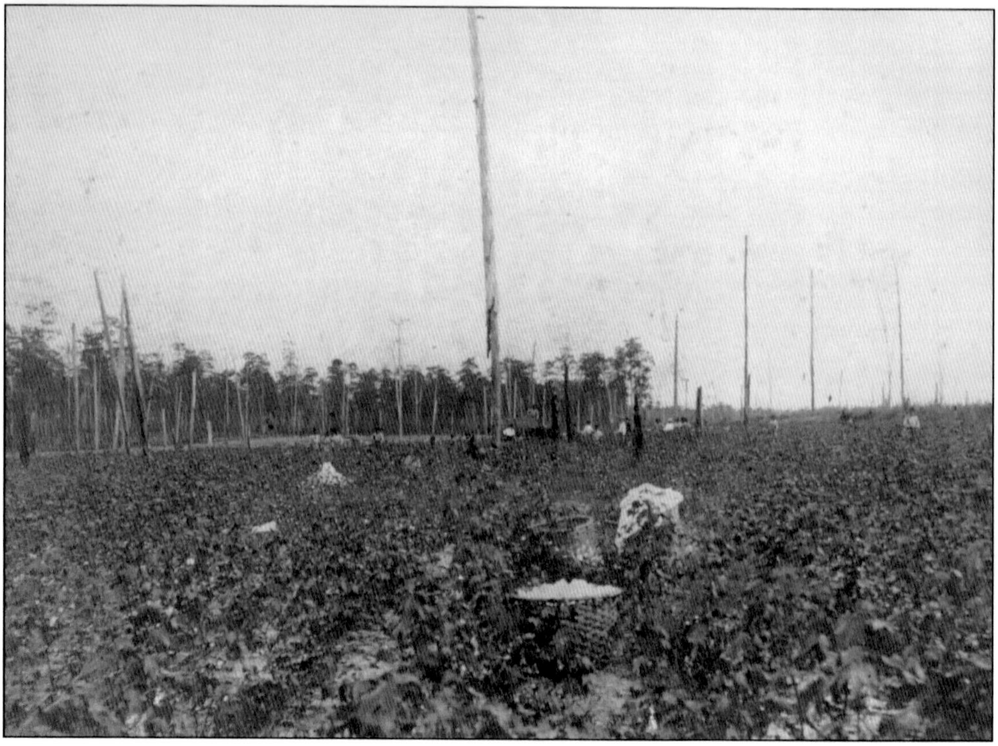

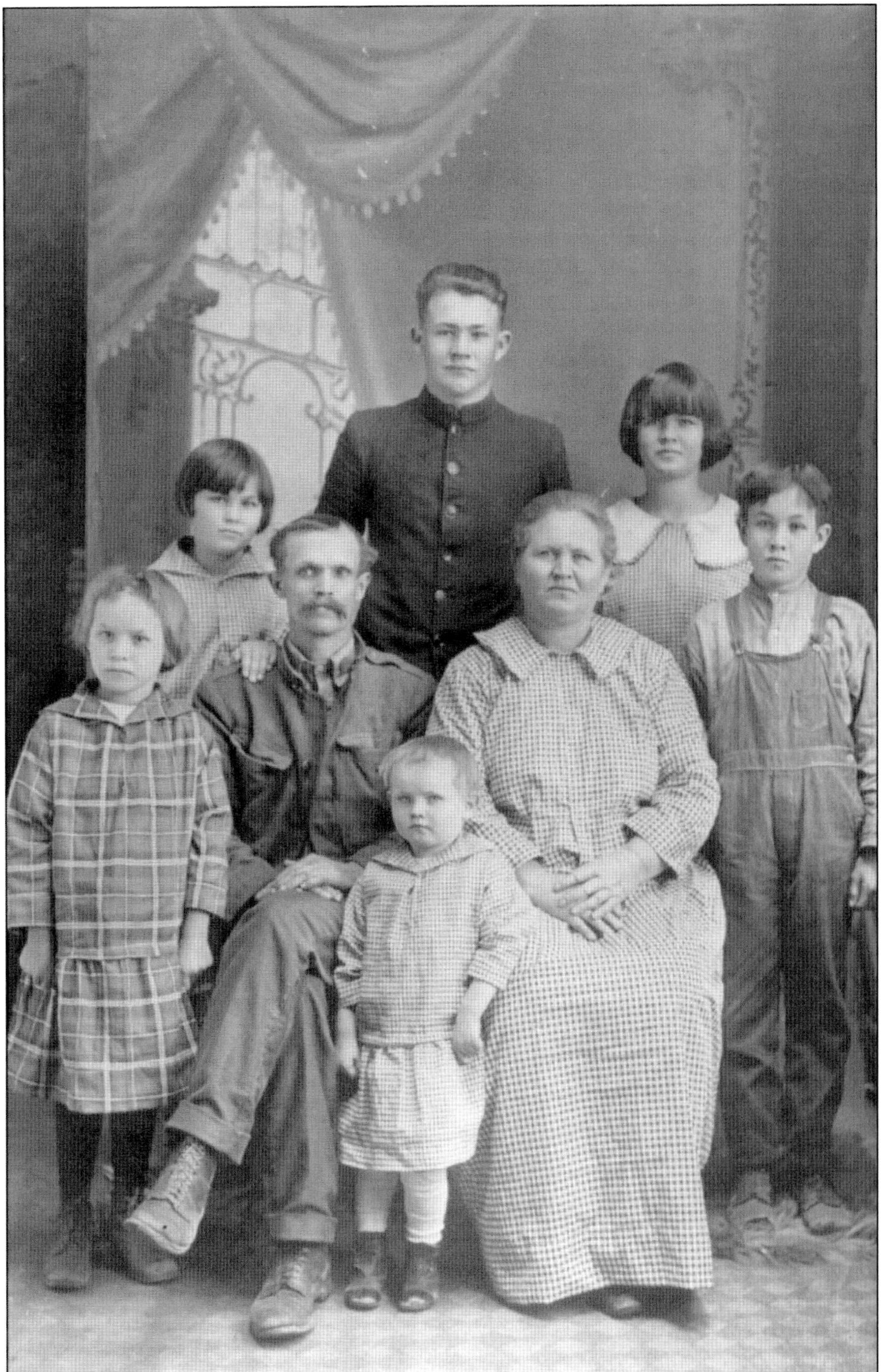

The J.T. Dixon Family. The Dixon family was typical of a Laurens County family in the 1920s. They lived and worked every day on their farm in the Rock Springs community in southern Laurens County.

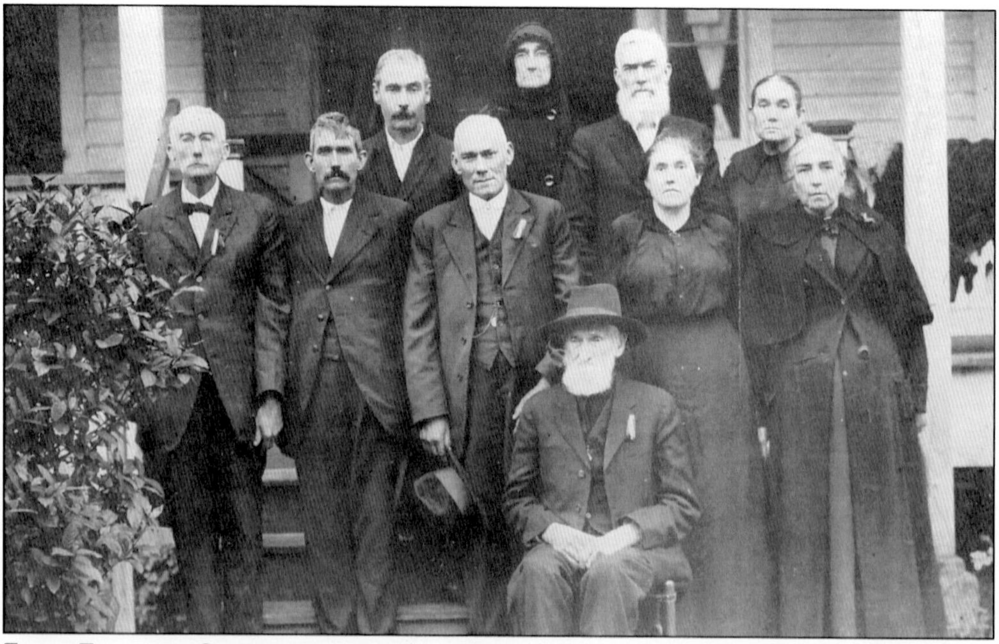

Zenus Fordham, Centenarian. Rarely did people who were born in the early 19th century ever live to be 100 years of age. Zenus Fordham was one of the most popular centenarians of his day. He was the progenitor of a large family. Shown in this 1919 photograph, from left to right, are (front row) Zenus Fordham; (middle row) William J. Fordham, Jeff Perry, Ben Fordham, Fannie Perry, and Onie Miller; (back row) ? Miller, two men (of whom one is Jim Fordham and the other is unidentified), and Mrs. W.J. Fordham.

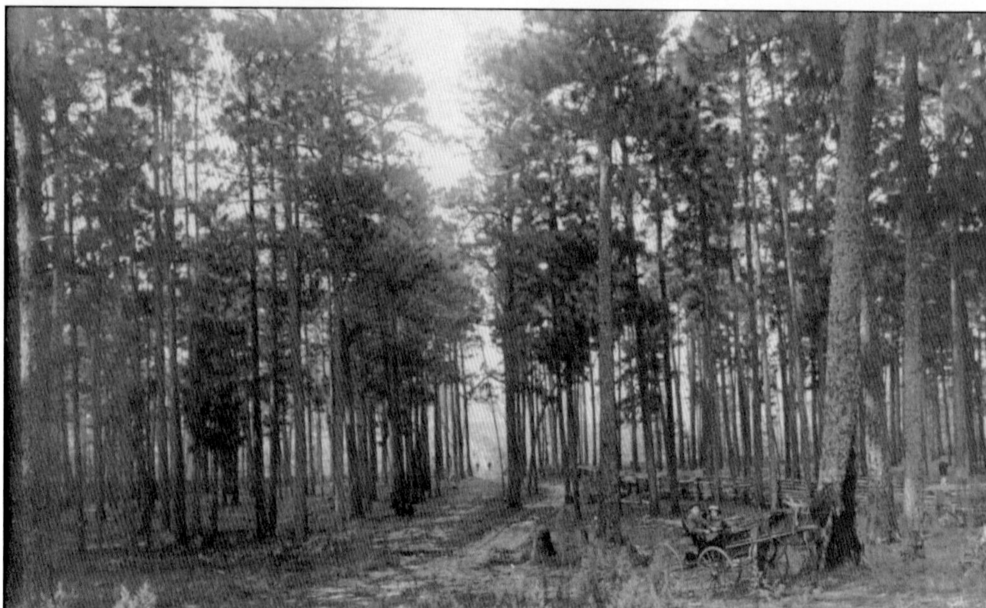

Old County Roads. In the 19th century a good road was one where two wagons could pass each other without going off in the ditch, if the road had a ditch at all. This road ran in front of the T.J. Perry home on Moore's Station Road, west of Dublin.

Fiftieth Wedding Anniversary. Shown in this 1911 photograph, from left to right, are an unknown Methodist minister, Rev. Charles Augustus Moore, and his wife, Nancy Ellen Hicks Moore. The Moores were celebrating their 50th year of marriage. Reverend Moore was one of the most well-known and longest-serving Methodist ministers in Laurens and the surrounding counties.

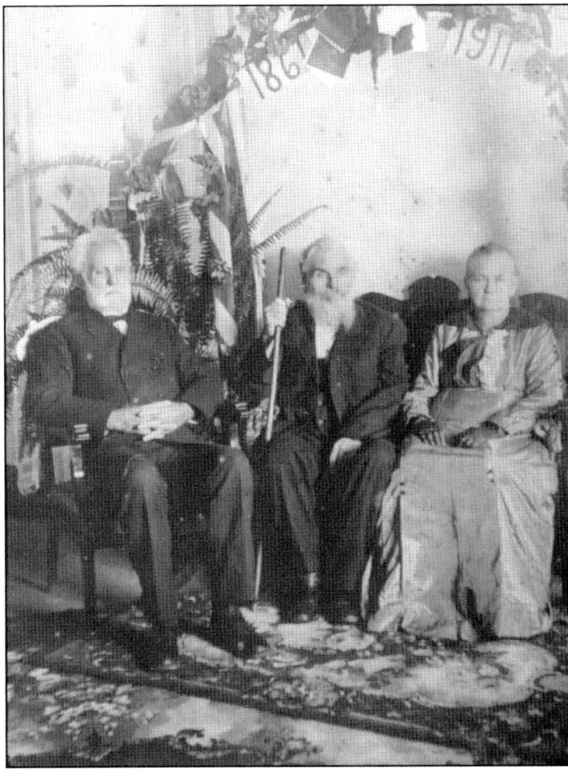

Washington Street Presbyterian Church. This modern brick church was established on South Washington Street in Dublin in 1953 by the members of Henry Memorial Presbyterian Church to promote the beliefs of the Presbyterian church in the African-American community.

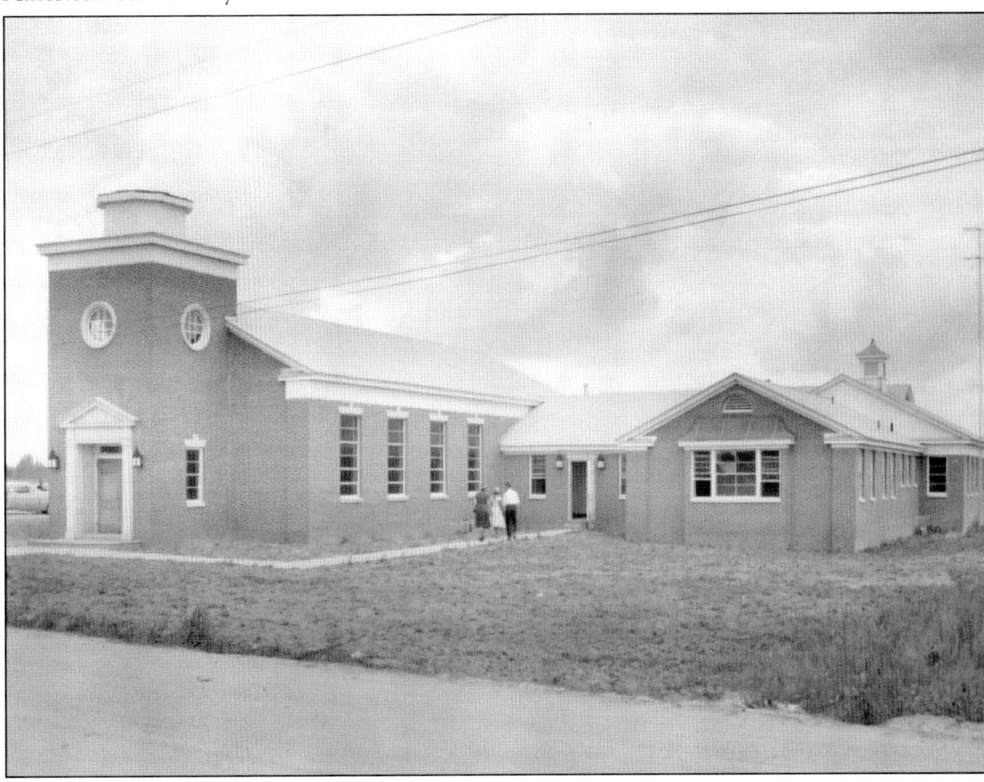

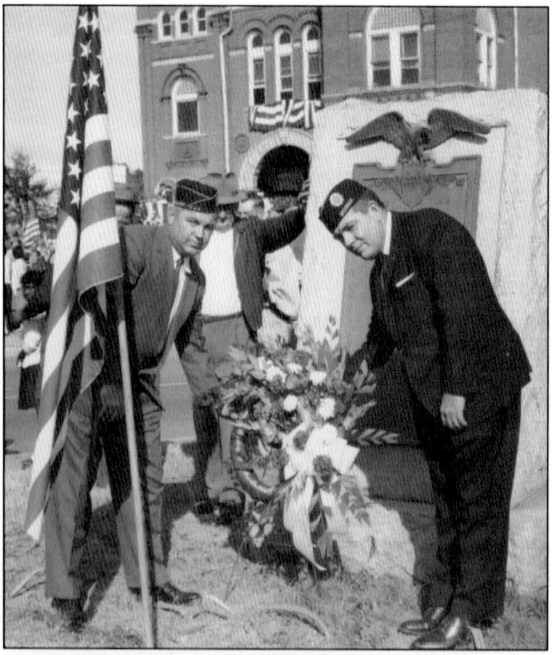

GONE BUT NOT FORGOTTEN. Members of the American Legion place a wreath on the monument to the men of Laurens County who gave their lives for their country in World War I.

THE MARTIN THEATER. Remember when you could go to the movie with a dollar, get something to eat and drink and come home with change? This 1950s photograph shows the concession stand in the lobby of the Martin Theater in Dublin. For four decades the theater was a favorite place for thousands of Laurens County residents, especially on Saturdays.

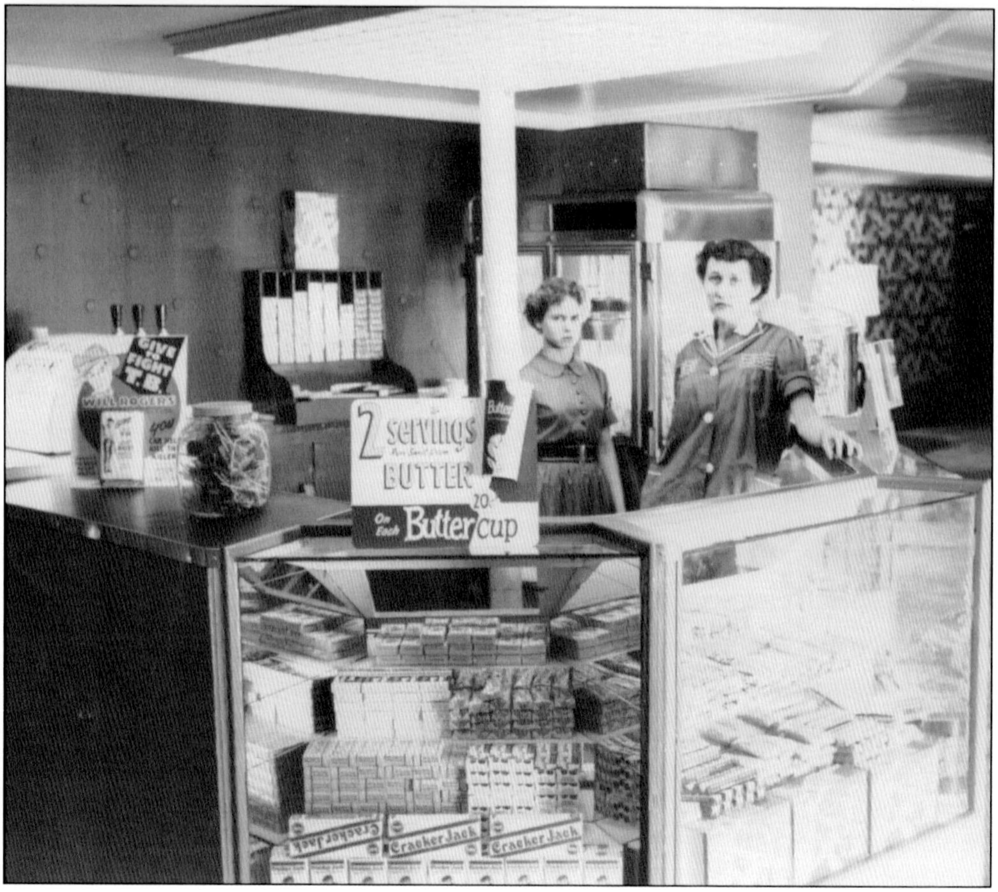

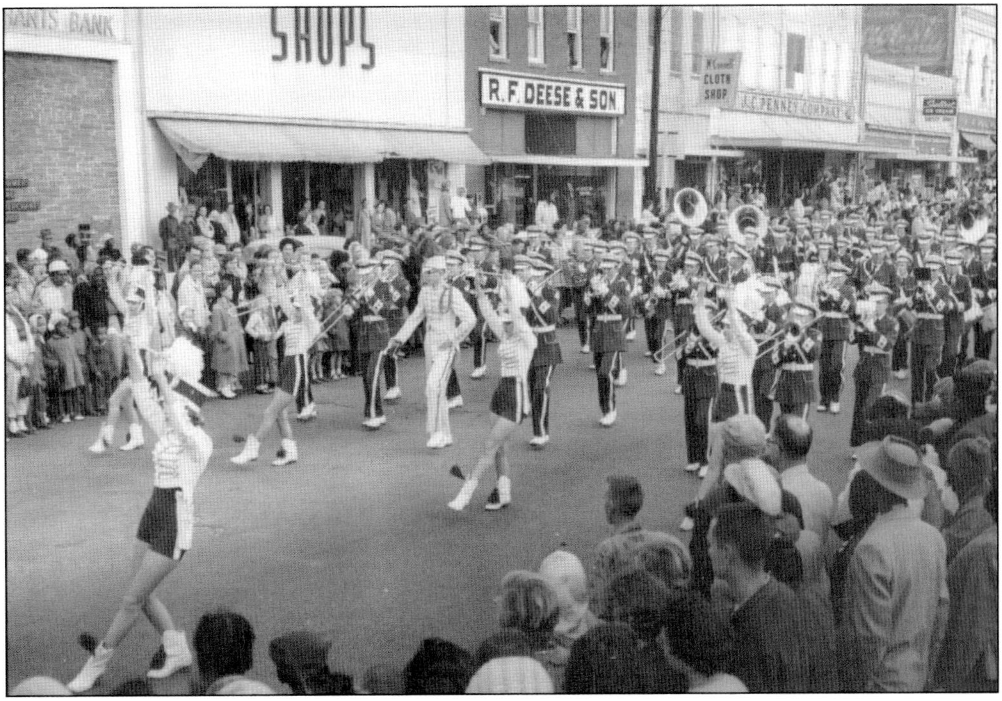

We All Love A Parade. Parades in Dublin were always fun. Many high schools held parades on Homecoming Days. In this early 1960s photograph, the Dublin Dixie Irish Band marches down the first block of West Jackson Street.

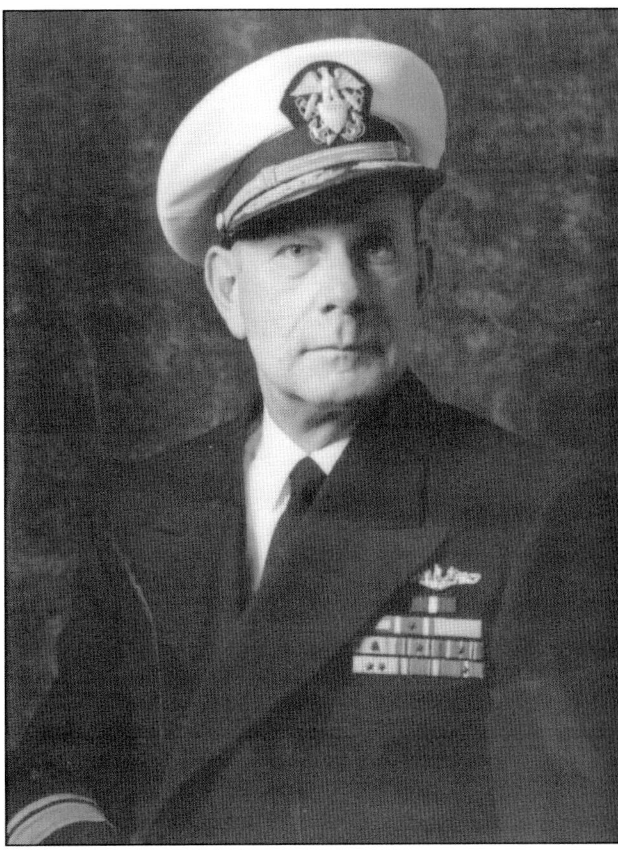

Adm. Robert E. Braddy. Admiral Braddy was a native of Dublin who attended the Naval Academy in the 1920s. While in command of the U.S.S. *Bernadou* in the Mediterranean Sea in World War II, Braddy was awarded the Navy Cross, the nation's second highest award for heroism.

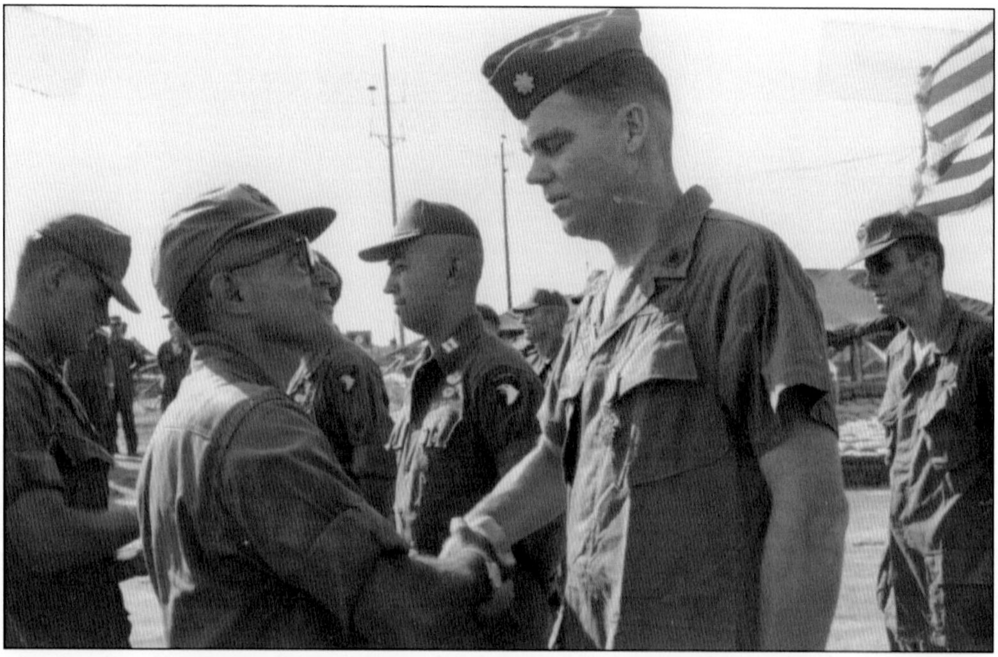

MAJ. JAMES WILKES. Shown receiving one of his numerous medals is Maj. James Wilkes, who was a representative of the brave men and women of Laurens County who served their country during the Vietnam War. In 306 missions in Vietnam, Major Wilkes was awarded two Distinguished Flying Crosses, a Silver Star, and fifteen Air Medals. Wilkes served as a Forward Air Controller, or FAC, and flew a light modified civilian aircraft at extremely low altitudes to aid ground troops and fighter pilots in spotting enemy ground troops.

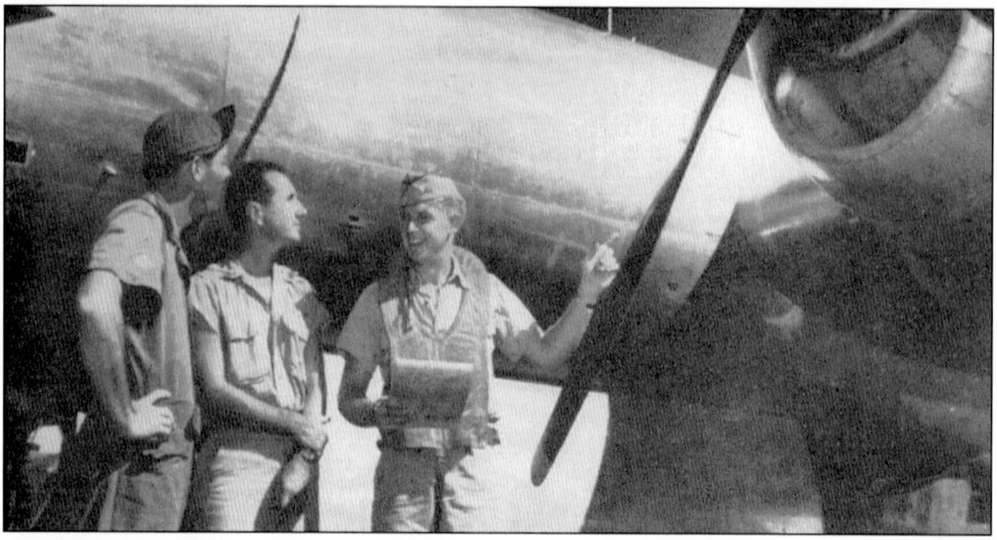

THE PILOT OF THE LUCKY IRISH. In the center of this photograph is Capt. William Arlington Kelley. Captain Kelley taught and coached at Dublin High School before entering the Army Air Corps in World War II. He named his plane "The Lucky Irish" and was the leader of the first crew in the 20th Air Force to complete 30 missions. While ferrying home another plane to headline the 7th War Bond Drive, Kelley and nine of his crew were killed when their plane crashed into the ocean.

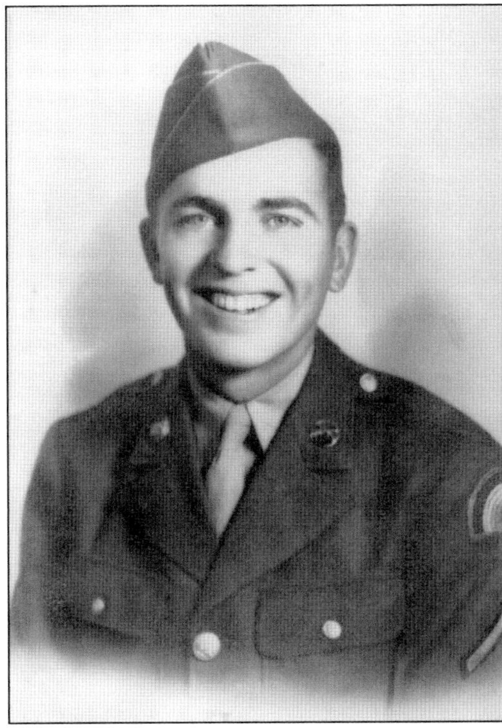

A True American Hero. Frank Zetterower Jr. was loved and respected by all who knew him. On January 6, 1945, while leading his squad in an attack on German positions near Gambsheim, France, Sergeant Zetterower was killed in action while trying to save the life of a buddy. For his heroism, Zetterower was awarded the Silver Star, the nation's third highest award for heroism.

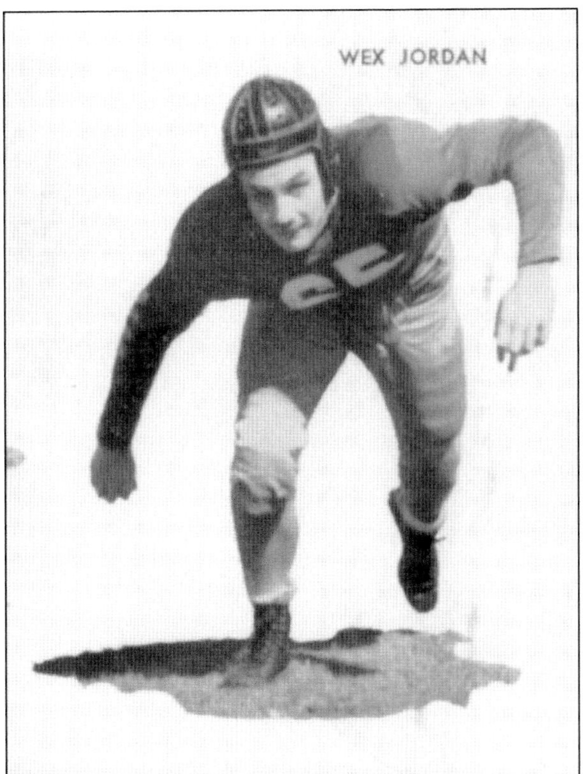

The Fiddling Fullback. Wex Jordan was a popular young man on the campus of Dublin High School for his fiddle playing, good looks, and athletic ability. As a guard for Georgia Tech, he was cited as being one of the best in the Southeast. On November 11, 1943, while training in a navy fighter plane, he was killed when his plane crashed.

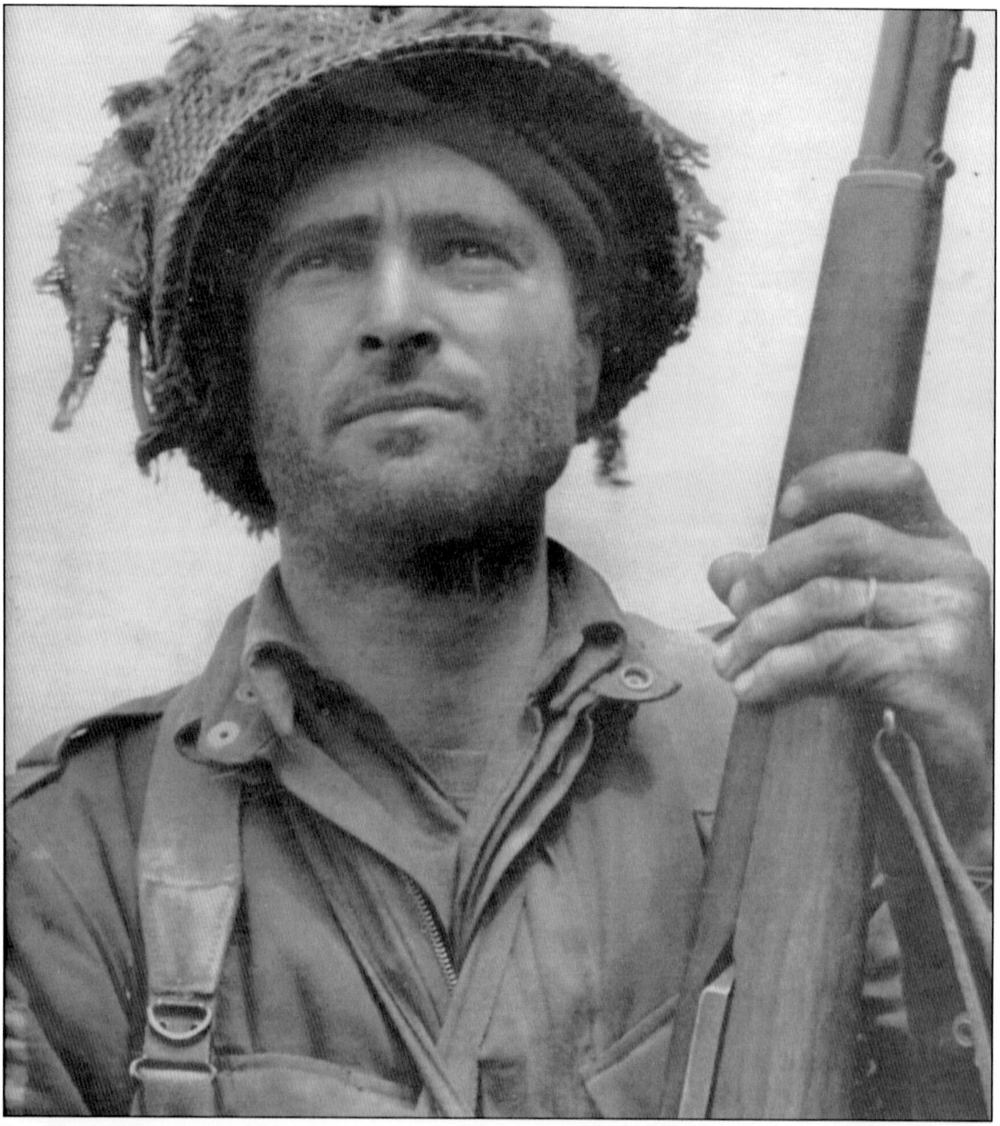

Lt. Kelso Horne. Lt. Kelso Horne, a member of the 82nd Airborne Division, parachuted on to Normandy soil early on the morning of June 6, 1944, hours before the D-Day invasion was launched on the shores of Normandy. A *Life* magazine photographer captured this image of Lieutenant Horne, and it made the cover of the magazine in August of 1944. Horne's face has become a symbol of the hundreds of thousands of soldiers who took part in the invasion, which brought about an earlier end to the war.

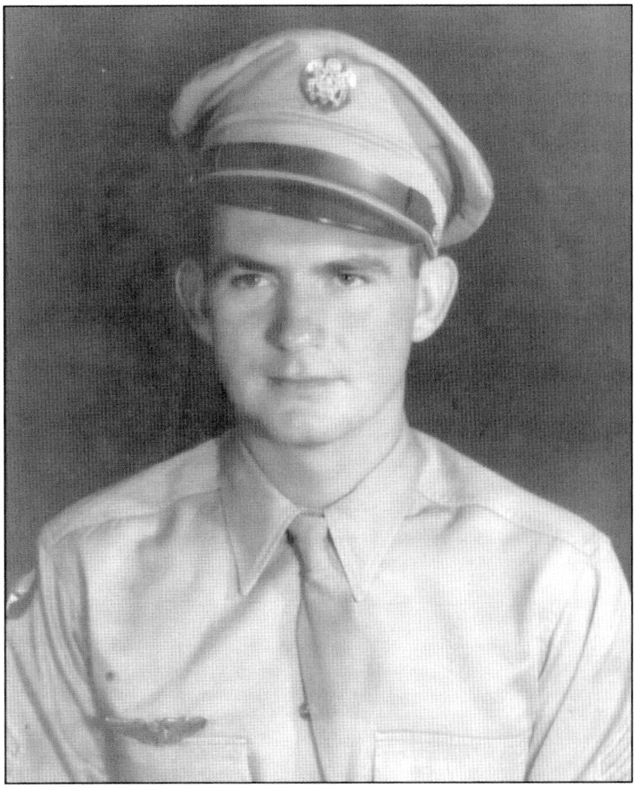

SGT. W.J. GAY. This native of Dublin completed his 25 missions over Europe as a gunner before the age of 21. Nearly one of out every sixteen Americans who died in World War II were members of the 8th Air Force, who flew mission after mission to bomb Germany into submission.

BUSY DAY AT THE BANK. This late 1940s photograph shows the lobby of the Citizens and Southern Bank of Dublin, which was then located in the old First National Bank Building on South Jefferson Street in Dublin.

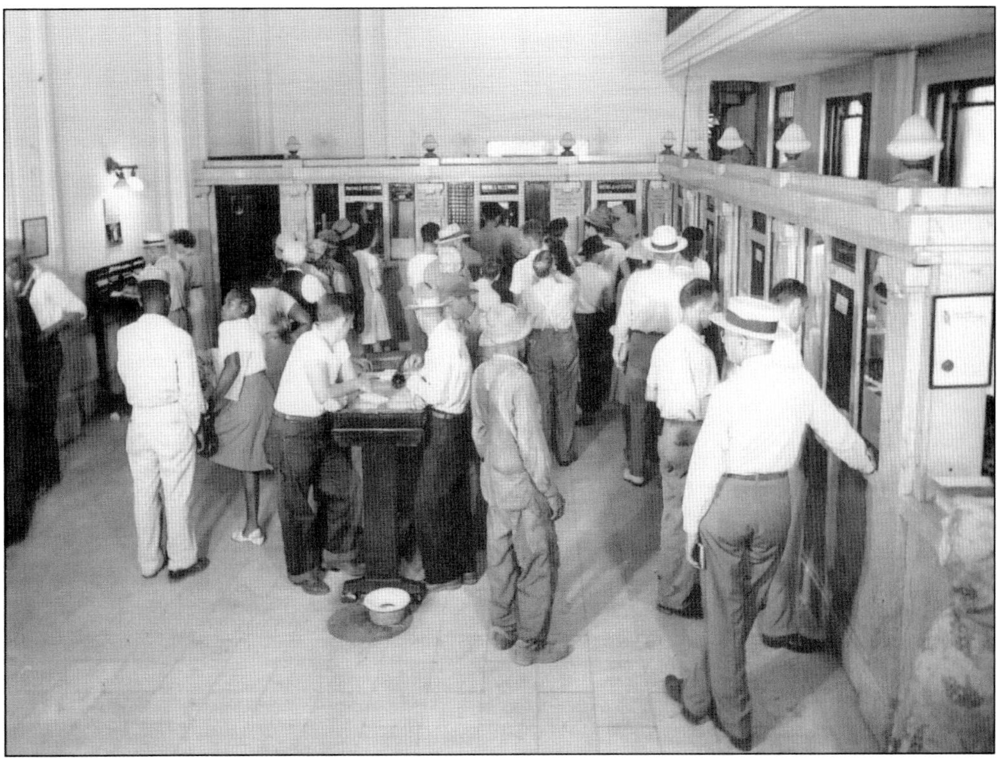

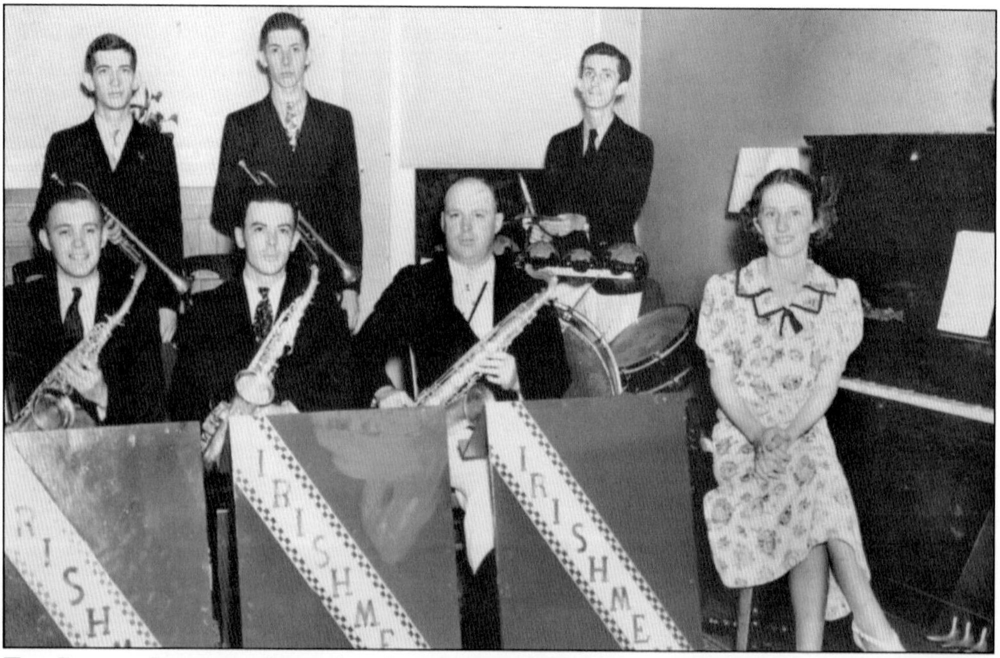

The Dublin Irishmen. Dance bands were popular in Laurens County for most of the 20th century. Shown in this 1930s photograph are the Dublin Irishmen; from left to right are (seated) Louis Smith, Ed Powel (the band leader), Ira S. Chappell Jr., and Arlena Everson Snider; (standing) Talmadge Veal, Luther B. Word Jr., and Billy Keith.

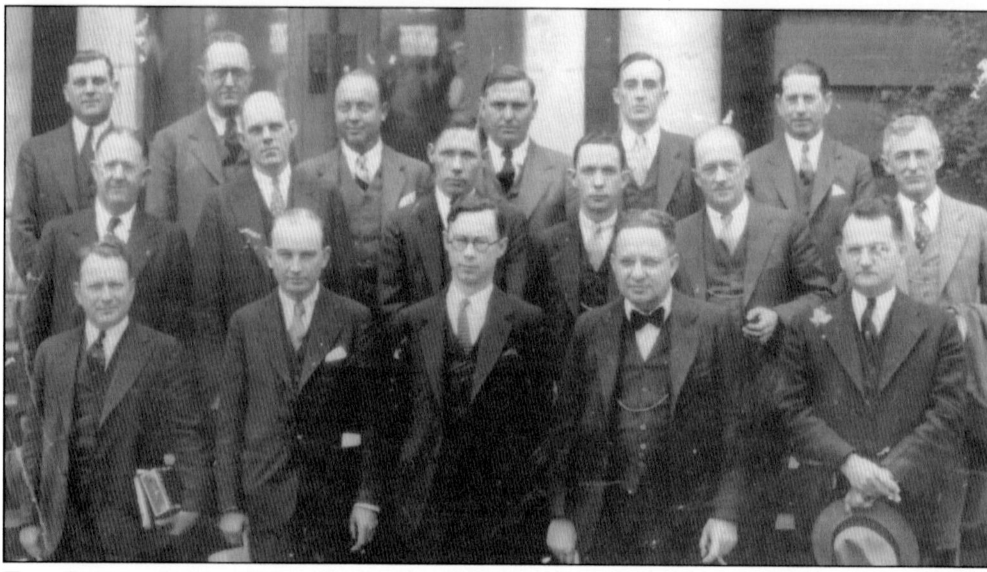

The Dublin Lions Club. Fraternal organizations have been the driving force in the development of Laurens County for over a century and a half. Shown in this 1930s photograph is the Lions Club, which was founded in 1924 and is one the oldest Lions Clubs in Georgia and Laurens County's oldest civic organization. From left to right are (front row) Roy Flynt, Carl Nelson, C.U. Smith, L.C. Gray, and A.J. Hargrove; (middle row) T.A. Curry Sr., Pasto Phelps, Hardeman Blackshear, unidentified, Bob Hightower, and Carl Hilbun; (back row) Ben Belue, P.M. Watson Sr., L.A. Whitlock, Nelson Carswell Sr., Sam Swinson, and Jim Allen.

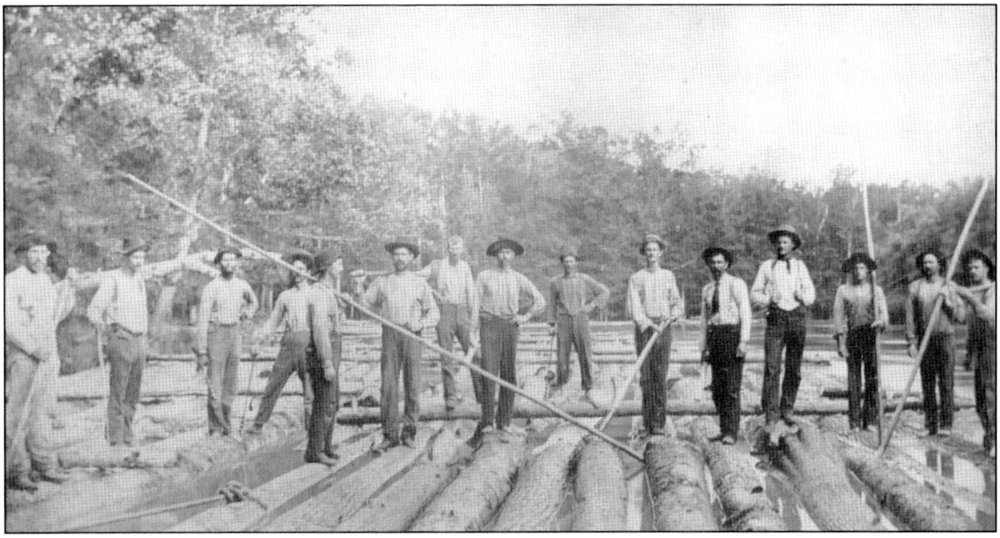

LOG RAFTING ON THE OCONEE. While Laurens County was served by many railroads, there were none close to the Oconee River. For decades in the late 19th and early 20th centuries, men banded logs together into rafts and floated them to the large sawmills at the mouth of the Altamaha River in Darien.

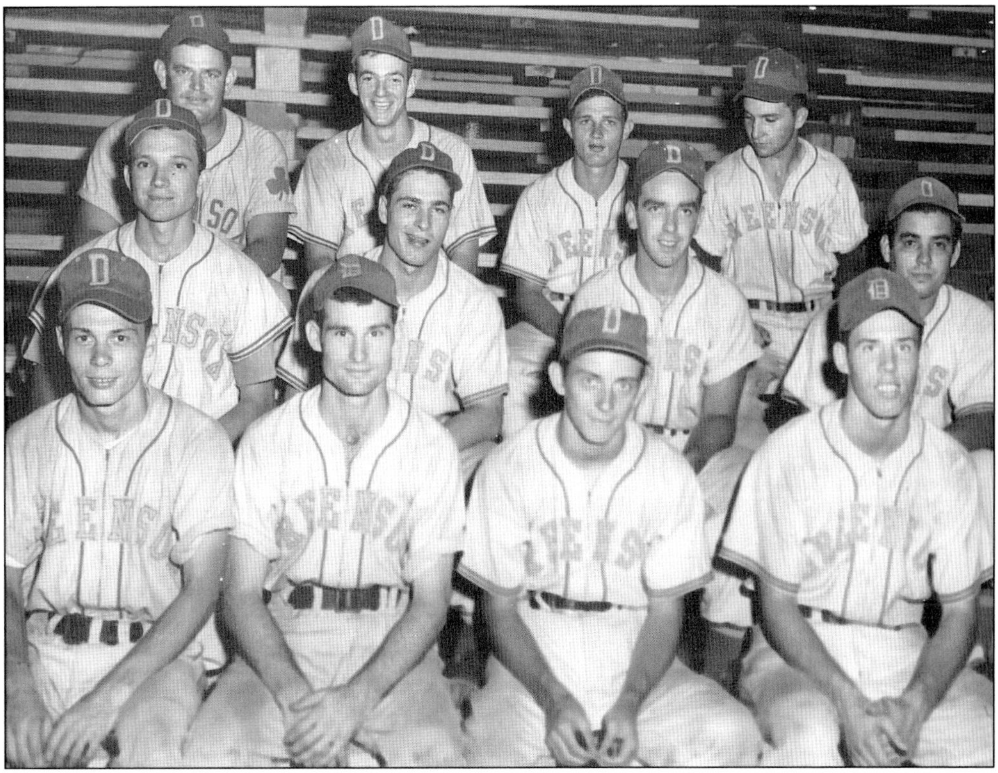

THE DUBLIN GREEN SOX. The Green Sox were Dublin's entry in the Georgia State League from 1949 to 1955. Shown in this picture is the 1952 team, which played in Lovett Park on Kellam Road in Dublin. Don Vaughn, shown in the second row and second from the left, pitched for the Green Sox and returned to Dublin after marrying local girl Barbara Lee.

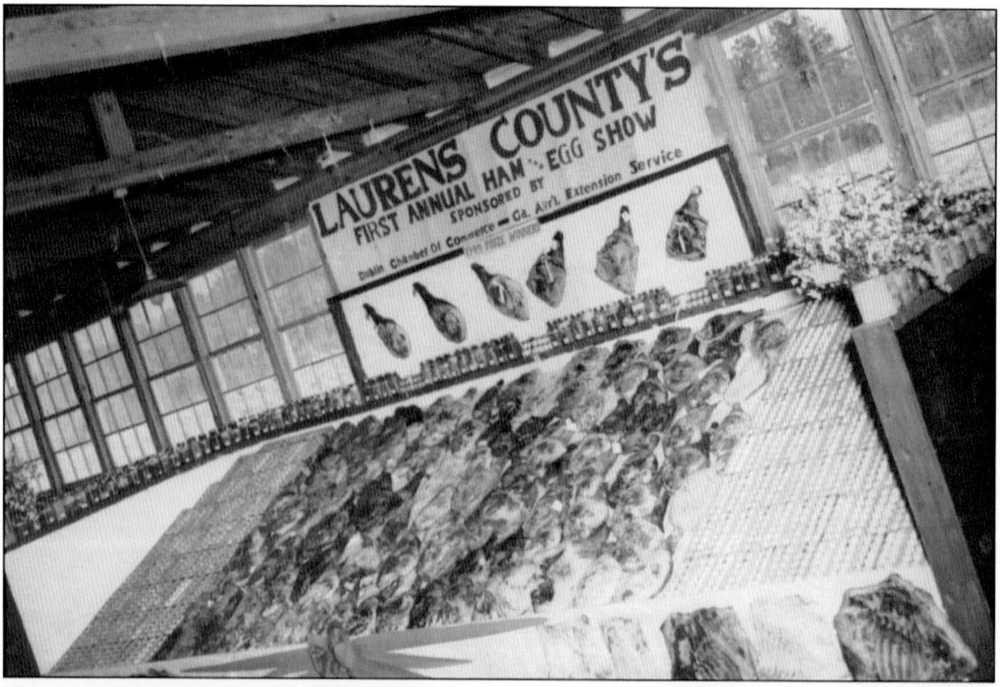

Ham and Eggs. Local farmers showed their prize-winning hams and eggs in the First Annual Ham and Egg Show held in 1949.

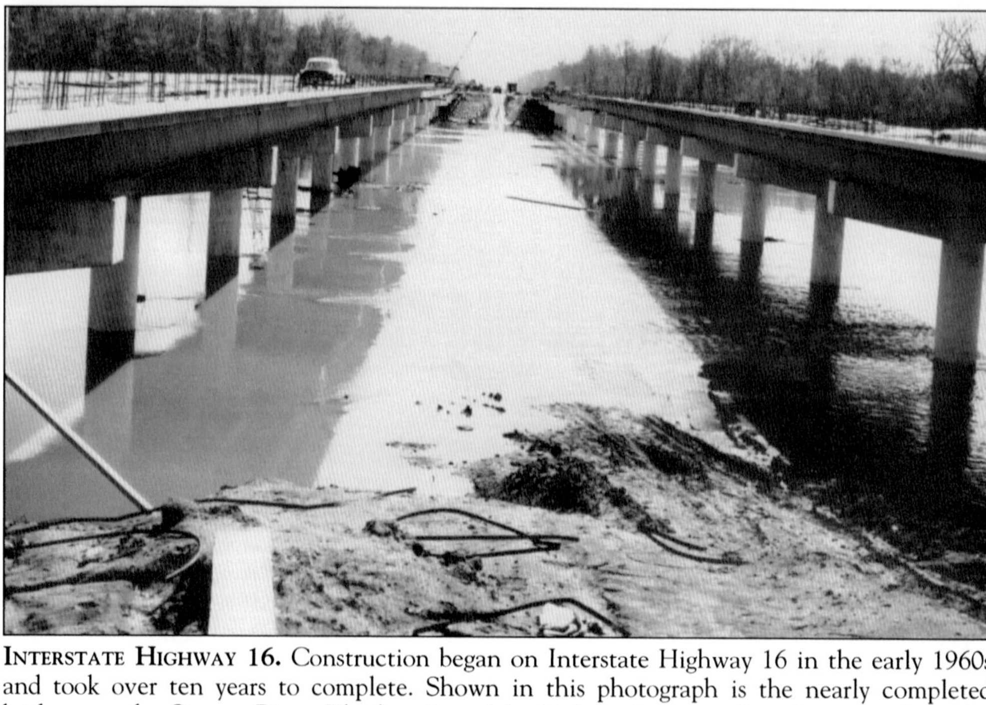

Interstate Highway 16. Construction began on Interstate Highway 16 in the early 1960s and took over ten years to complete. Shown in this photograph is the nearly completed bridge over the Oconee River. The location of the highway has contributed immensely to the growth of the county in the last half of the 20th century and will continue to do so for the centuries to come.

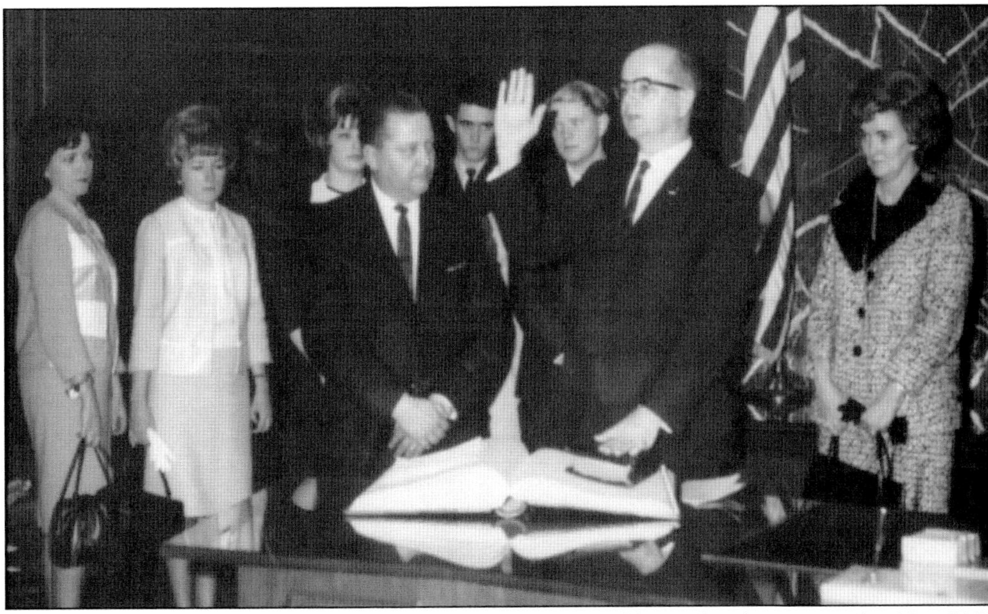

Dublin Judge Gives Oath of Office to Governor. Dublin judicial circuit judge Harold E. Ward swore in controversial governor Lester Maddox (with right hand raised) just moments after his election by the Georgia Legislature in 1967.

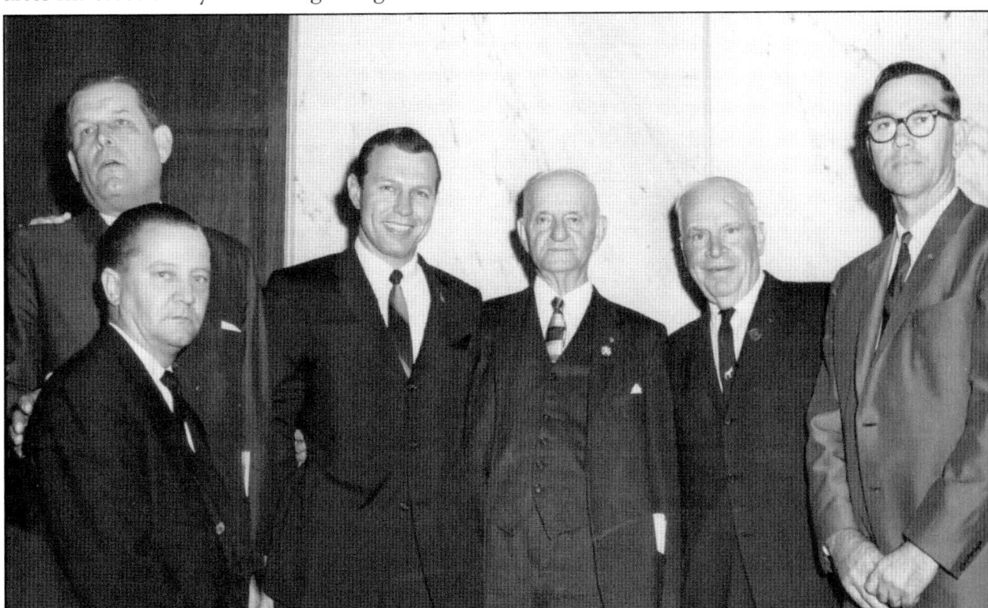

Laurens County Courthouse Dedication. The present Laurens County Courthouse was dedicated in 1964. Shown in this photograph are, from left to right, Congressman Elliott Hagan, Judge Harold E. Ward, Governor Carl Sanders, Congressman Carl Vinson, U.S. Secretary of Commerce Luther Hodges, and Don Lamb of the Dublin-Laurens Chamber of Commerce. After several bond issues were defeated by Laurens County voters, Congressman Vinson was able to secure the first federal funds ever appropriated for the construction of a county courthouse in the United States.

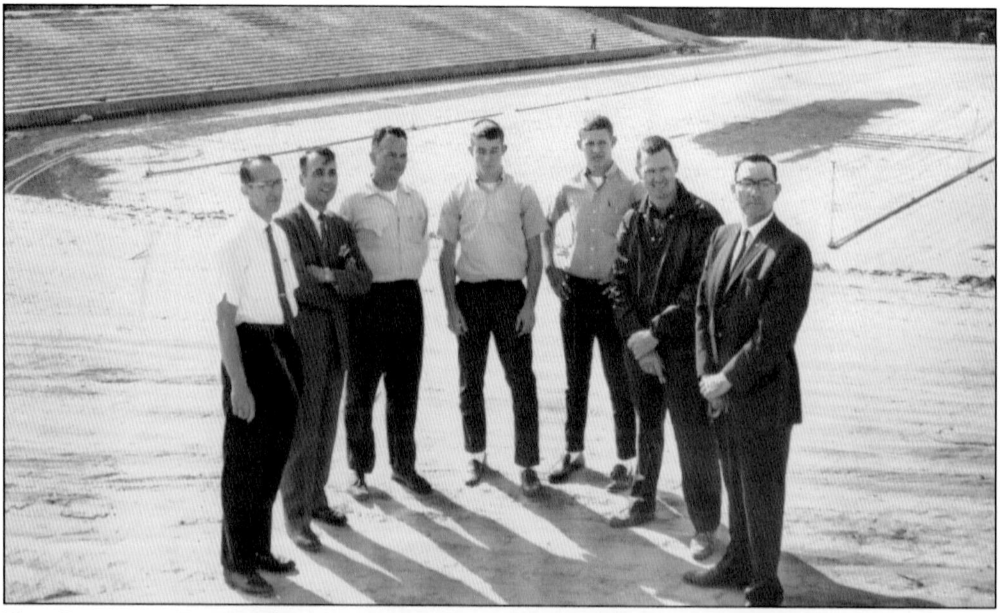

The Shamrock Bowl. The civic-minded citizens of Dublin joined together in 1962 to build an 8,000-seat stadium for the Dublin Irish football team, who were state champions in 1959, 1960, and 1963. Shown in the photograph, from left to right, are Leonard Swida, unidentified, Fred Middlebrooks, Jim Nelson, Carl Stone, Coach Minton Williams, and Don Lamb, who spearheaded the project.

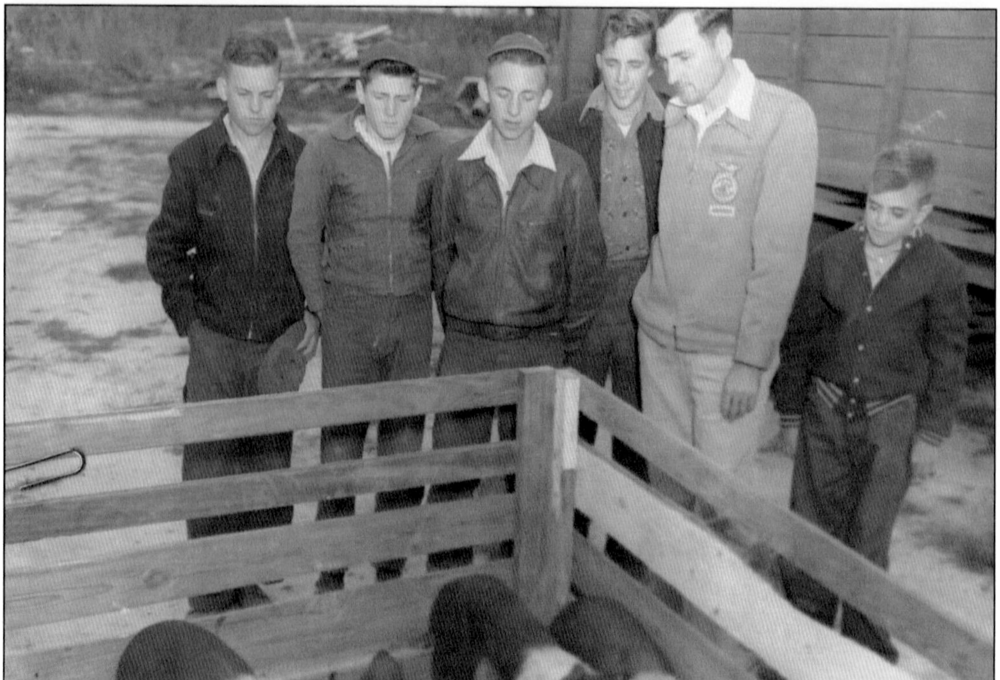

Future Farmers of America. The Future Farmers of America (FFA) have been active in Laurens County for decades. Here a young group of future farmers admire a fine group of young hogs at an FFA County Show in 1950.

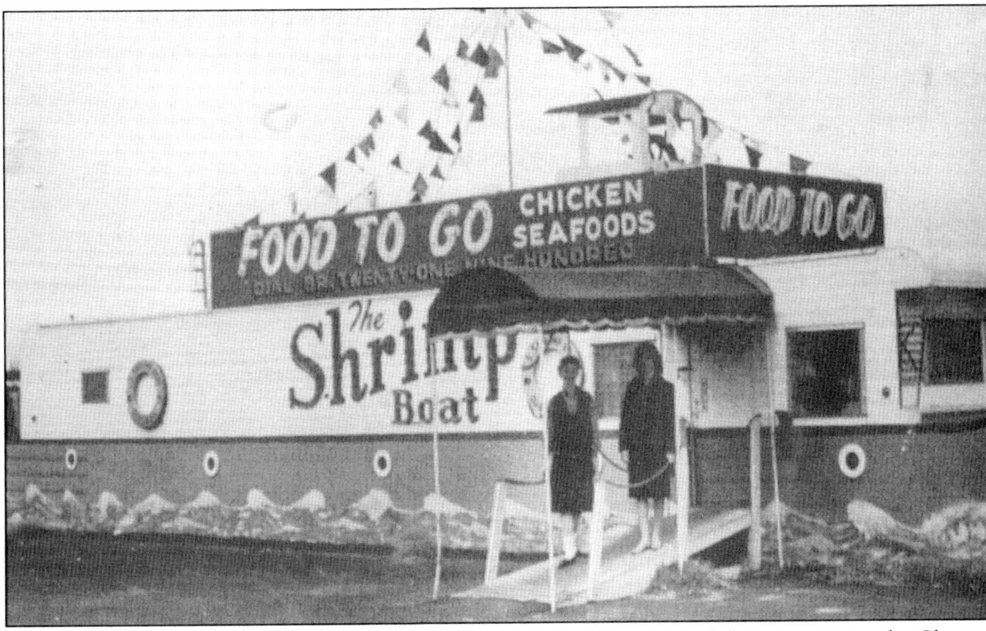

THE SHRIMP BOAT. One of most unique restaurants in the history of the county was the Shrimp Boat Restaurant at 1513 Rice Avenue in Dublin. It is shown here *c.* 1960.

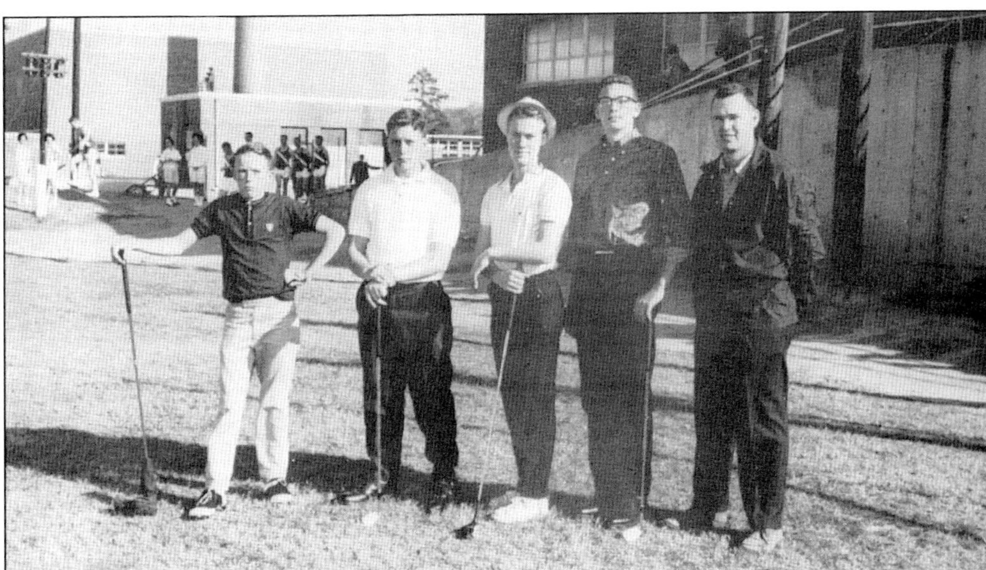

GOLF CHAMPIONS. The 1962 Georgia State AA Golf Champions are, from left to right, Spec Hall, Robert Swinson, Richie Cummings (state medalist), Tom Perry, and Coach Minton Williams. The team won the championship in only their second year of play. Swinson was the state medalist in 1965, when the Irish linksters won their second consecutive championship.

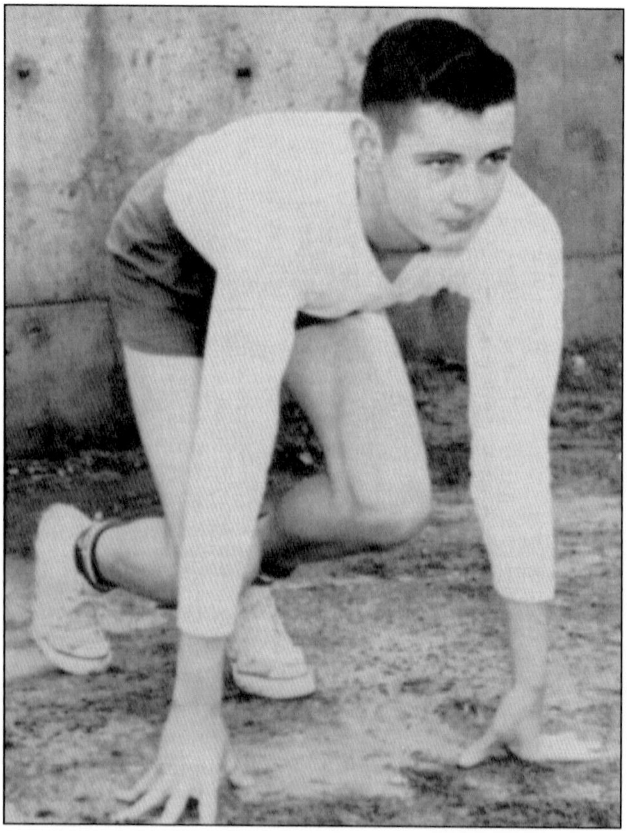

American Champion. In 1959, Ira Welborn, a Dublin High track star, finished in a second place tie in the region track meet. Welborn didn't give up on pole vaulting. In 1976, he shattered the American record for pole vaulting by a man over 30 with a vault of 14 feet 9 inches at the Master's Track and Field.

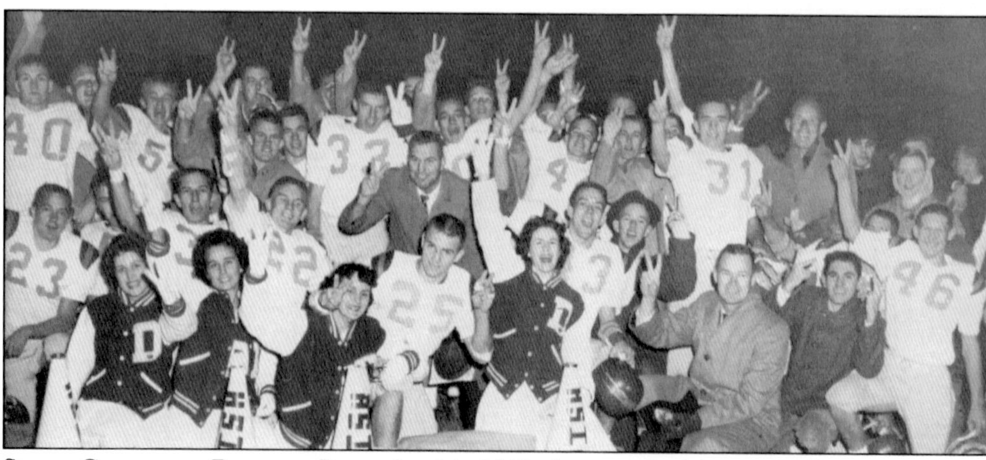

State Champions Back to Back. In this 1960 photograph, Minton Williams, shown on the first row giving the victory sign, led his team to their second straight Class A football championship. The Dublin Irish came back in 1963 to win their third championship in five years.

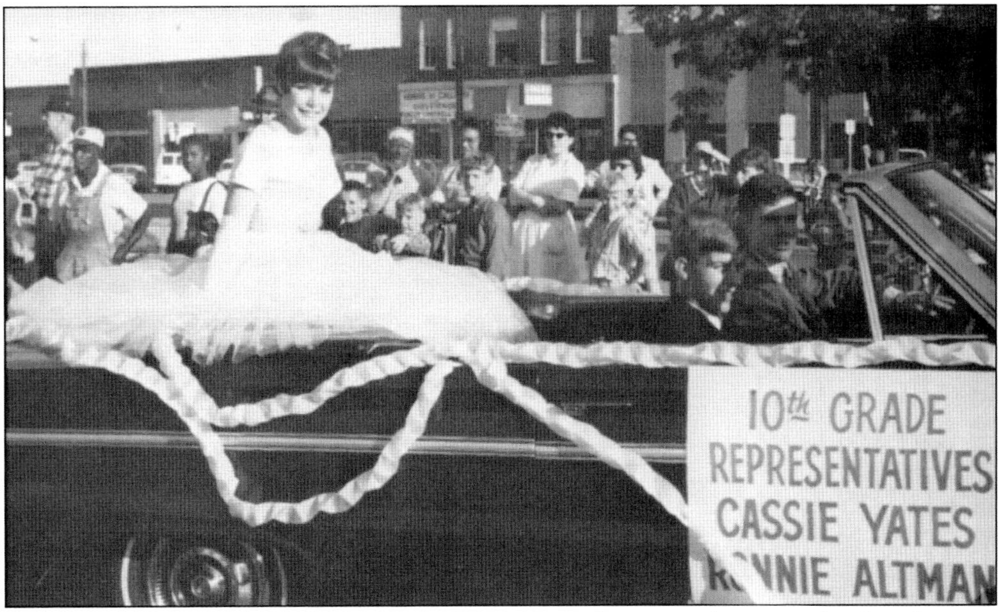

Homecoming Parades. Homecoming parades were popular events for many schools and county citizens in the 1960s. Shown in this 1966 photograph is tenth grade representative Cassie Yates. Cassie left Dublin before her graduation from high school and landed in Hollywood where she starred in movies and television, including *Rich Man, Poor Man II* and *Barnaby Jones*, as well as the 1978 film *Convoy*.

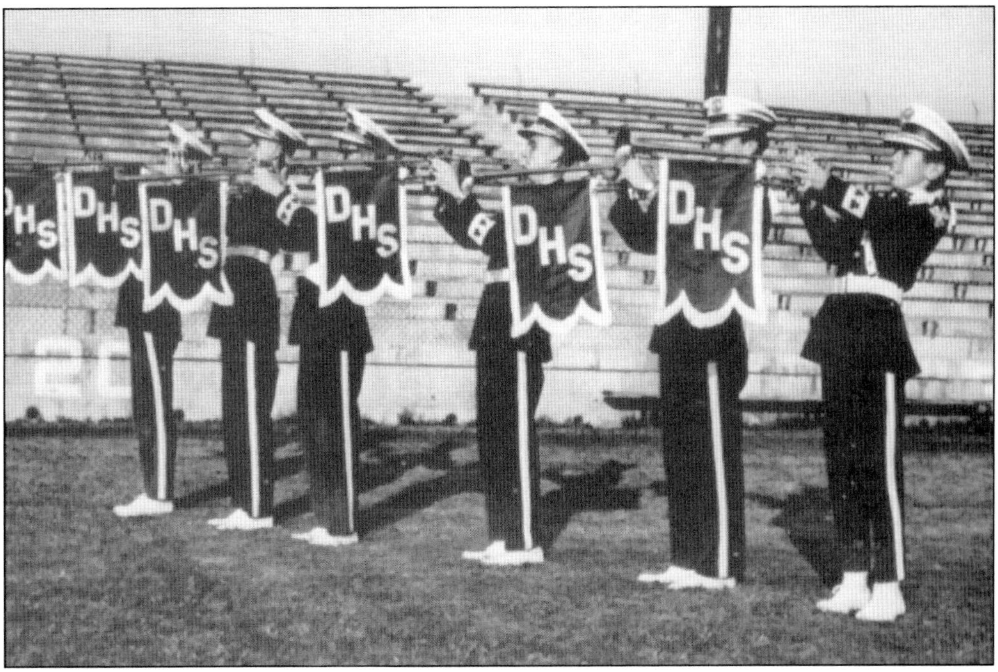

The Dixie Irish Marching Band. Under the direction of John Hambrick and Jim Willoughby, the Dixie Irish Marching Band of Dublin High School was one of the most outstanding bands in the state of Georgia. Shown in this 1966 photograph is the herald trumpet section, one of the band's trademarks.

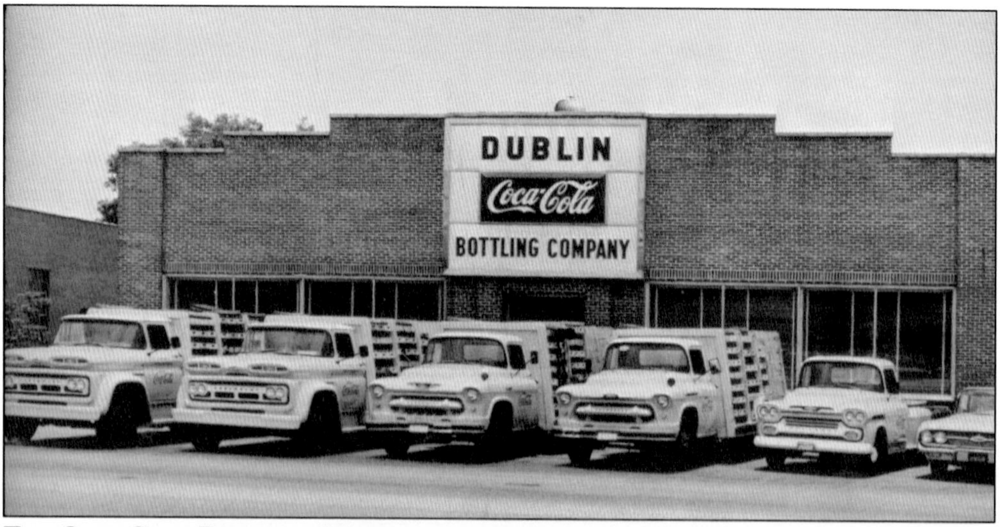

The Coca-Cola Bottling Company. Coca-Cola has been a part of Laurens County for over a century. The Holmes family of the Condor community began the bottling of Coca-Cola in the late 1890s in various locations all over the state of Georgia. Shown in this 1960s photograph is the company's plant and fleet of trucks at its offices at 415 East Jackson Street in Dublin.

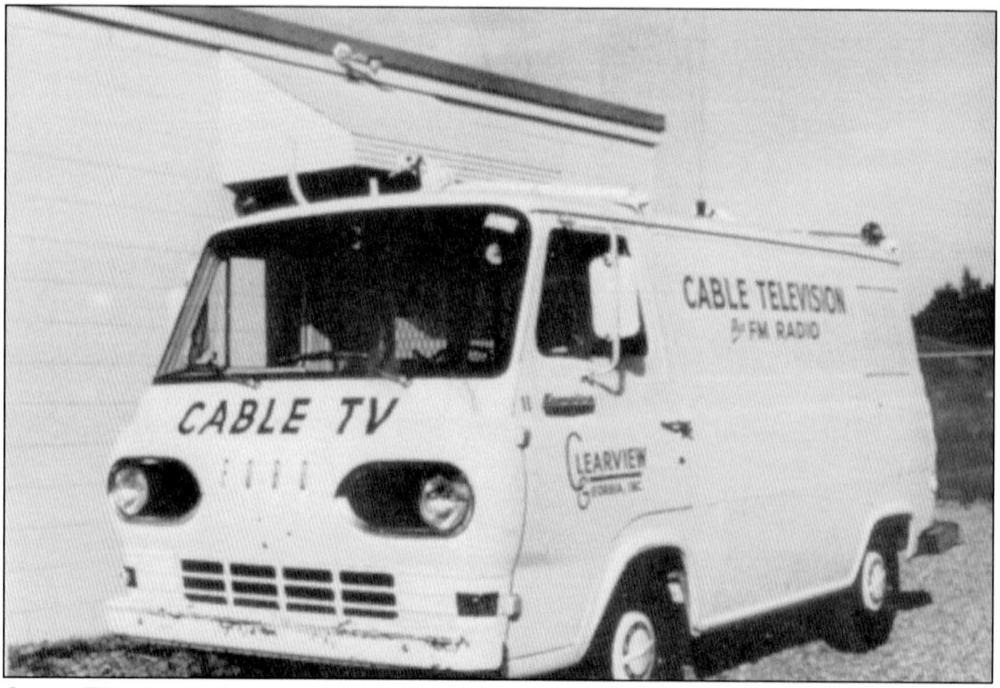

Cable TV. A new luxury was introduced into Dublin homes in 1965, with the advent of cable television. Clearview Cable Company gave its viewers a choice of seven channels. At the dawn of the 21st century, cable is available in many parts of the county with hundreds of channels available.

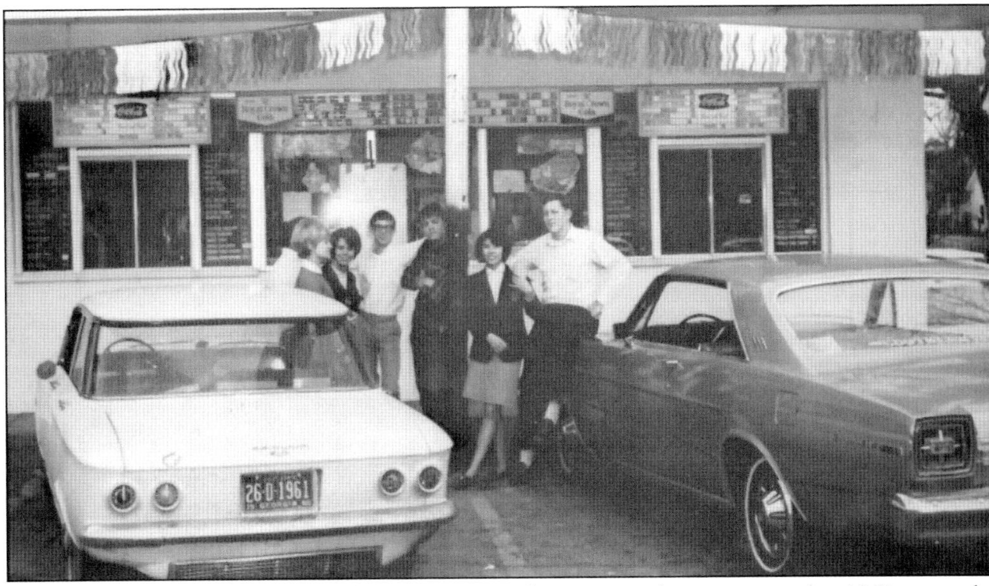

The Castle Drive-In. One of the more popular teenage hangouts in the 1960s was the Castle Drive-In on North Jefferson Street in Dublin. Here, one could order the typical fare of hamburgers, hot dogs, and milkshakes.

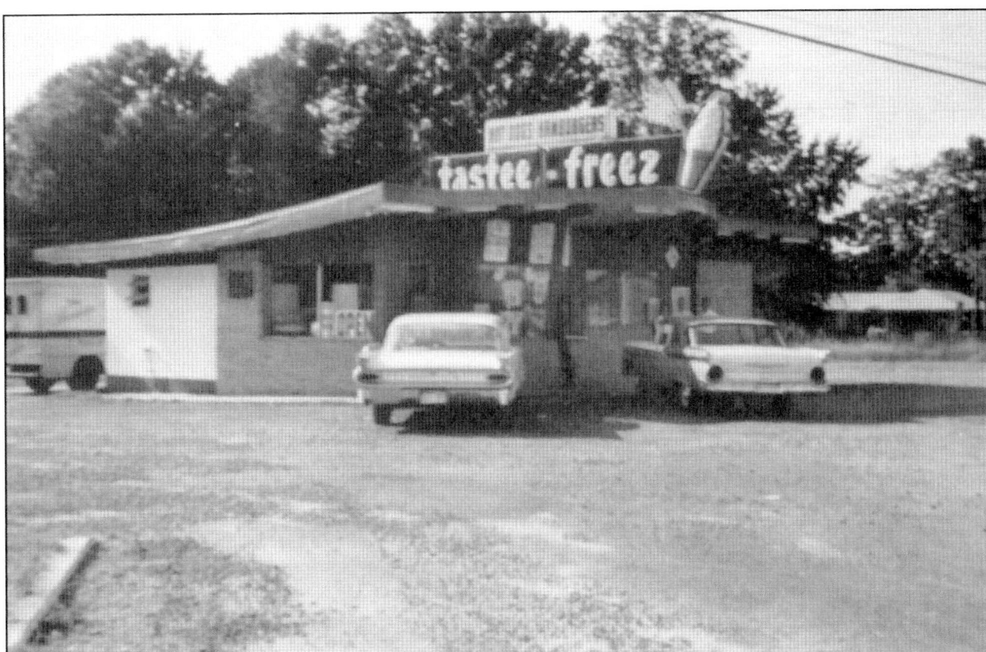

The Tastee Freeze. Another popular teenage hangout was the Tastee Freeze on North Jefferson Street. Teenagers cruised the strip and circled around the drive in a maneuver that came to be known as "Breezing the Freeze."

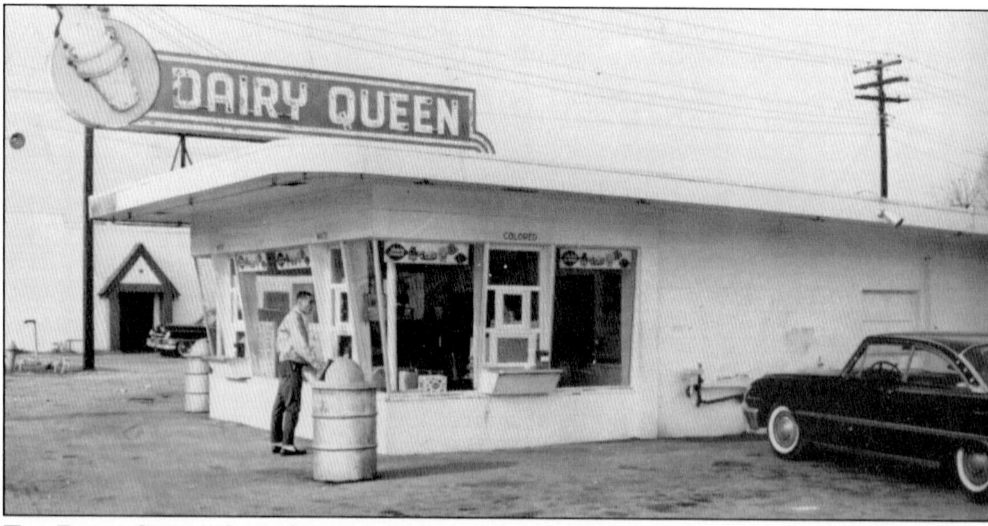

The Dairy Queen. One of Laurens County's first franchise restaurants was the Dairy Queen on East Jackson Street in Dublin. In its early days the Dairy Queen sold only its delicious ice cream treats.

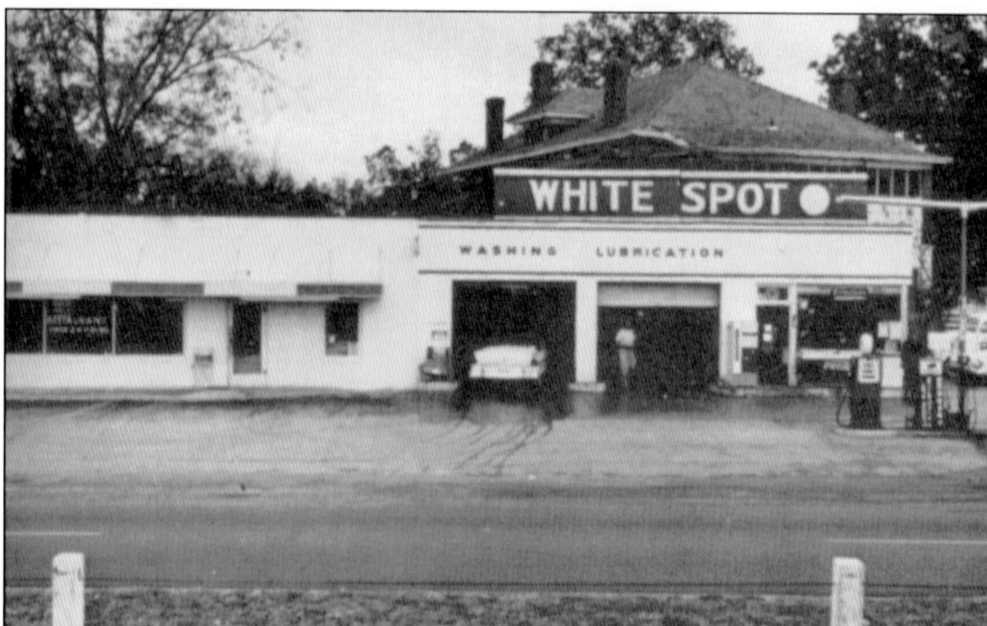

The White Spot. The White Spot Restaurant and Service Station was a landmark in Laurens County for several decades. It was located on Veteran's Boulevard where the Farmers State Bank now stands.

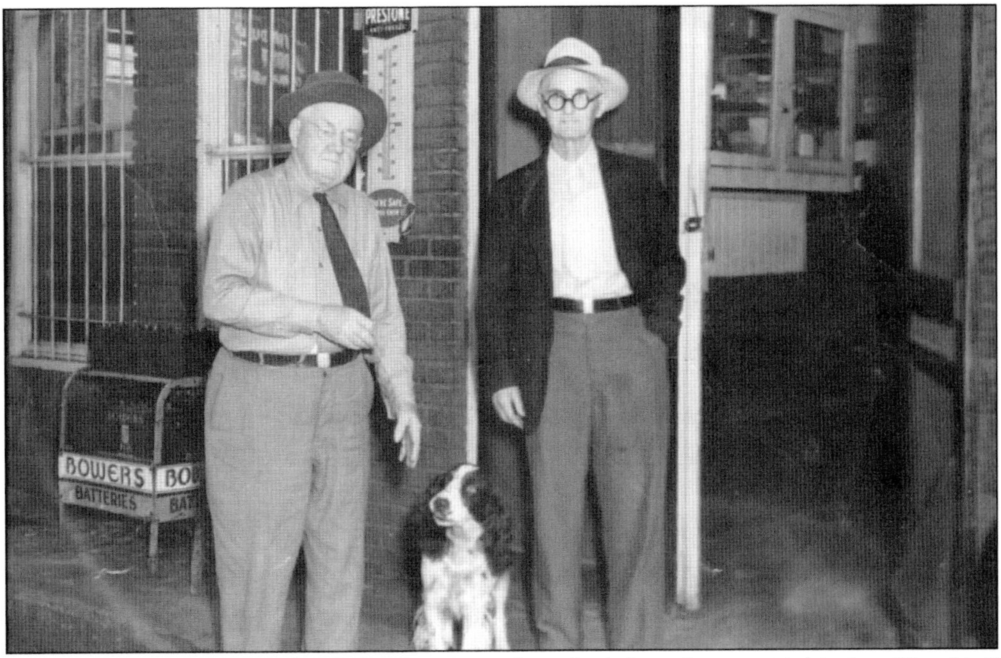

A Man and His Dog. Arthur J. Toole, pictured on the left, is shown with his dog, "Smokie." Toole was a longtime agent at the railroad depot in Dublin. Smokie loved ice cream so much that a local drug store established a charge account for the dog.

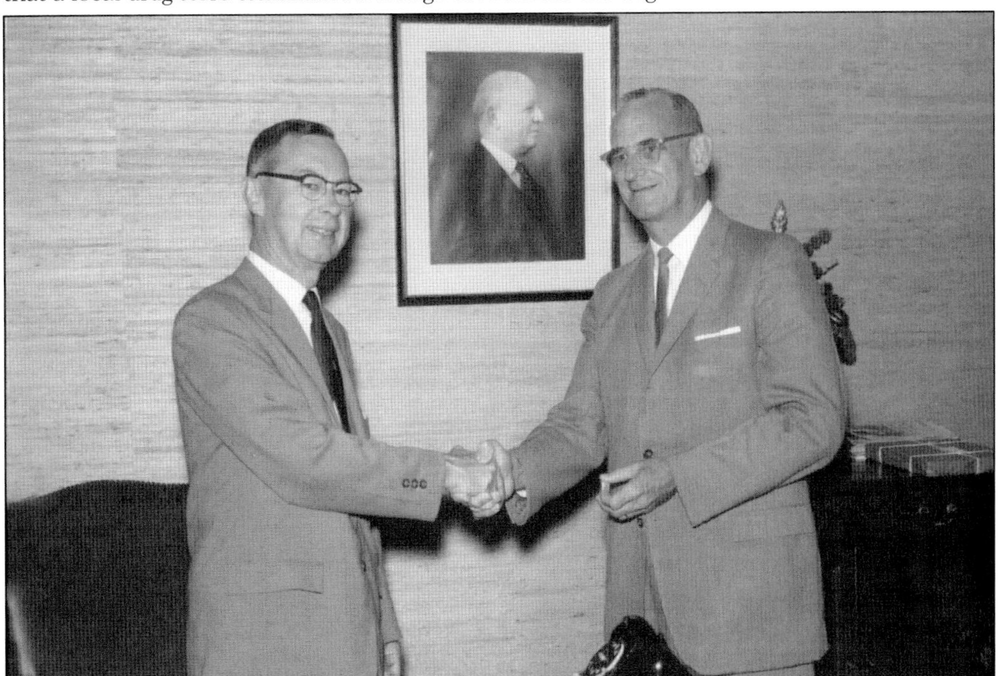

Changing of the Guard. The Citizens and Southern Bank rescued the finances of Laurens County after the First National Bank closed in 1928. On the left, bank president Charles U. Smith, who worked in the bank for four decades, congratulates Winfield "Wink" Simmons, who succeeded Smith as president.

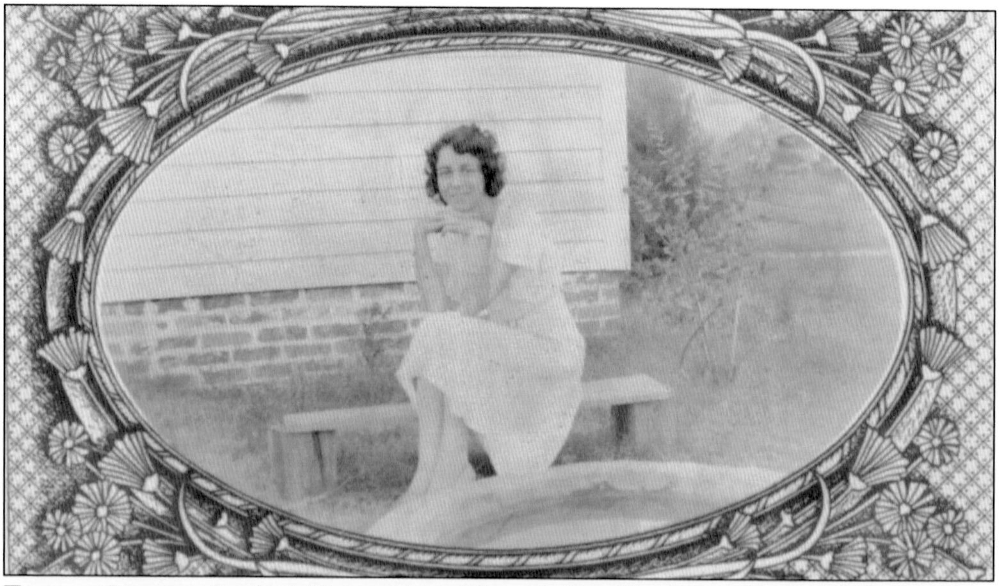

TEENAGE LAWYER. Aretha Miller graduated from Dublin High School and, at the age of 18, became Laurens County's first female attorney and one Georgia's first female lawyers. She worked as a legal secretary following high school but never attended law school. Prior to 1941, lawyers were required to pass an oral exam but did not have to have a law degree to practice. Miss Miller passed the exam and worked as a lawyer for 35 years. Miss Miller was one of the youngest female attorneys in the history of Georgia.

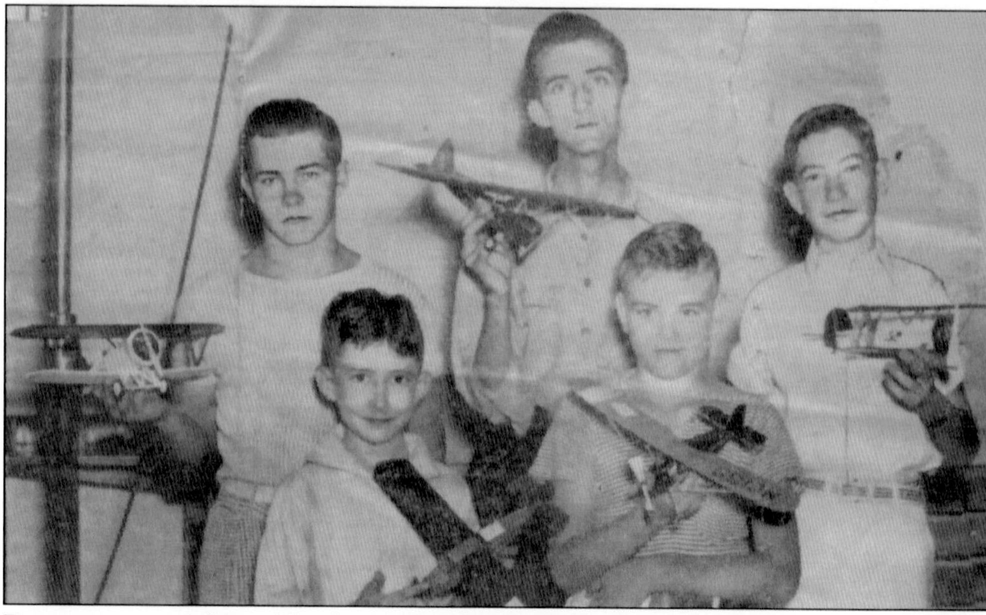

DREAMING OF THE SKIES. This late 1930s photograph shows the winners of a model airplane contest. From row left to right are (front row) Bluford Page and Clifford Prince Jr.; (back row) Herbert Moffett Jr., Billy Keith, and McGrath Keen. Page and Keen grew up to fly in the Armed Services. Keen, who commanded the B-29 "The Lucky Lady," took great pride in the fact that many of his missions didn't drop bombs but food to starving prisoners of war who had been liberated from Japanese P.O.W. camps.

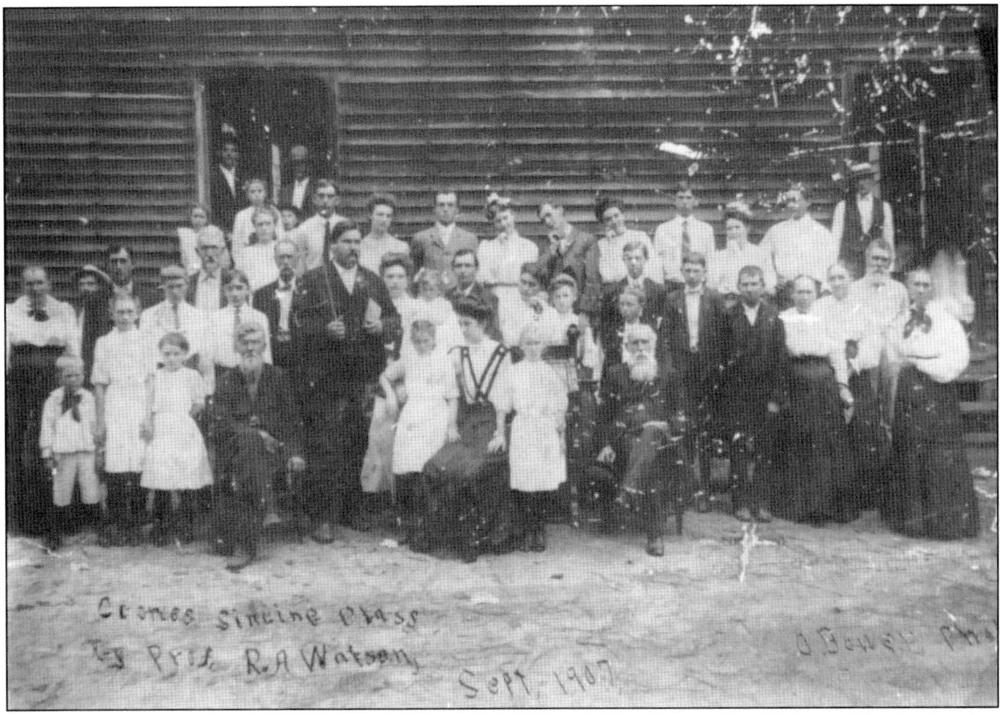

Singing Convention. All-day "sings" were popular events in Laurens County. Shown in this 1907 photograph is a convention led by R.A. Watson, who is the first man standing on the front row.

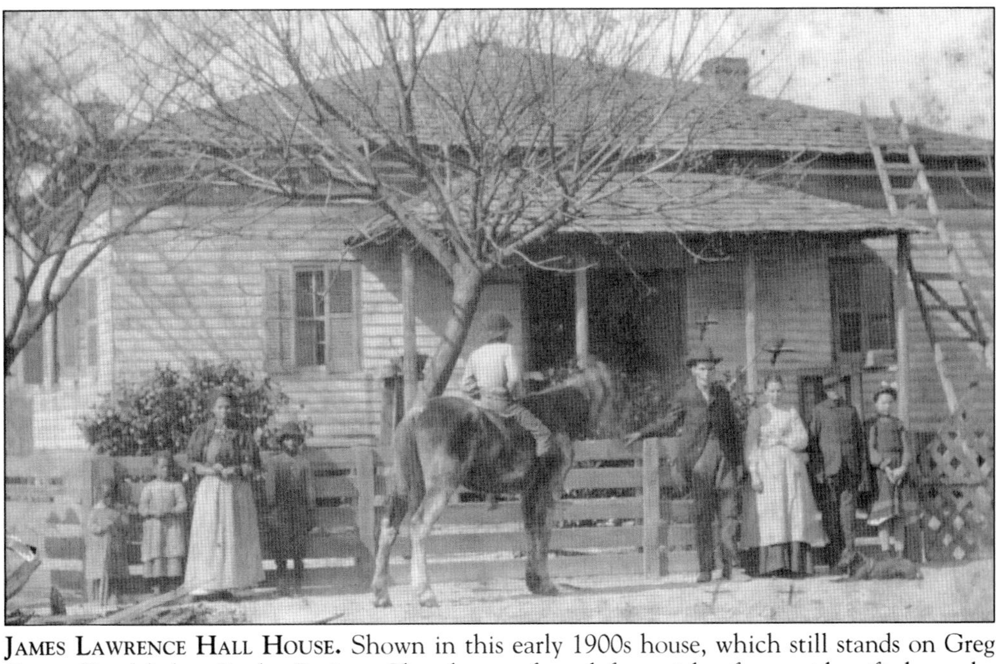

James Lawrence Hall House. Shown in this early 1900s house, which still stands on Greg Couey Road below Poplar Springs Church, are, from left to right, four unidentified people, an unidentifed person on horse, James Lawrence Hall, Benita Gibson Hall, Gordon Hall, and Roxie Hall.

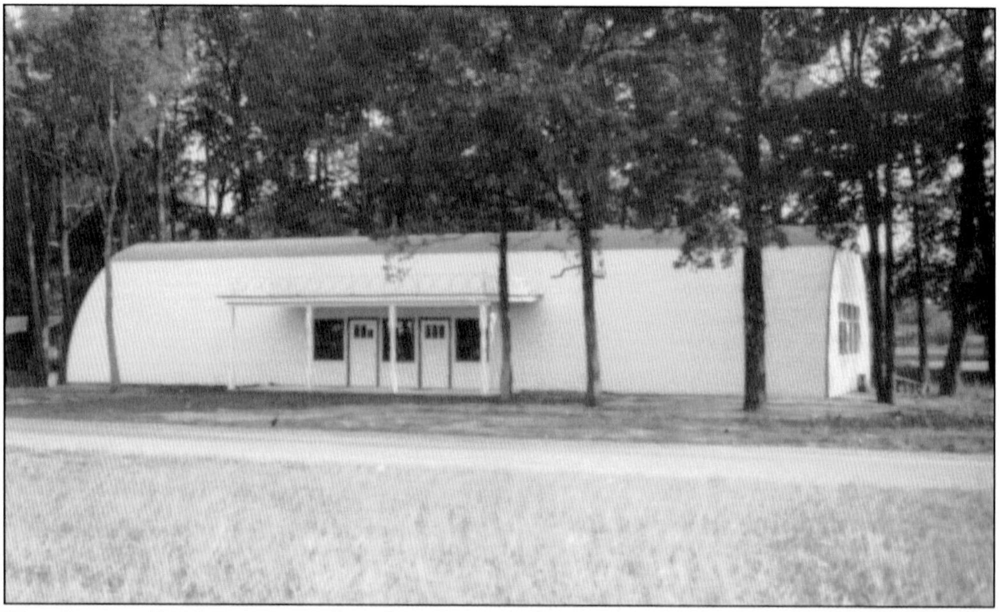

The Shanty. Dublin teenagers found a permanent home in Stubbs Park in the early 1950s with the erection of a Quonset hut which became affectionately known as "The Shanty."

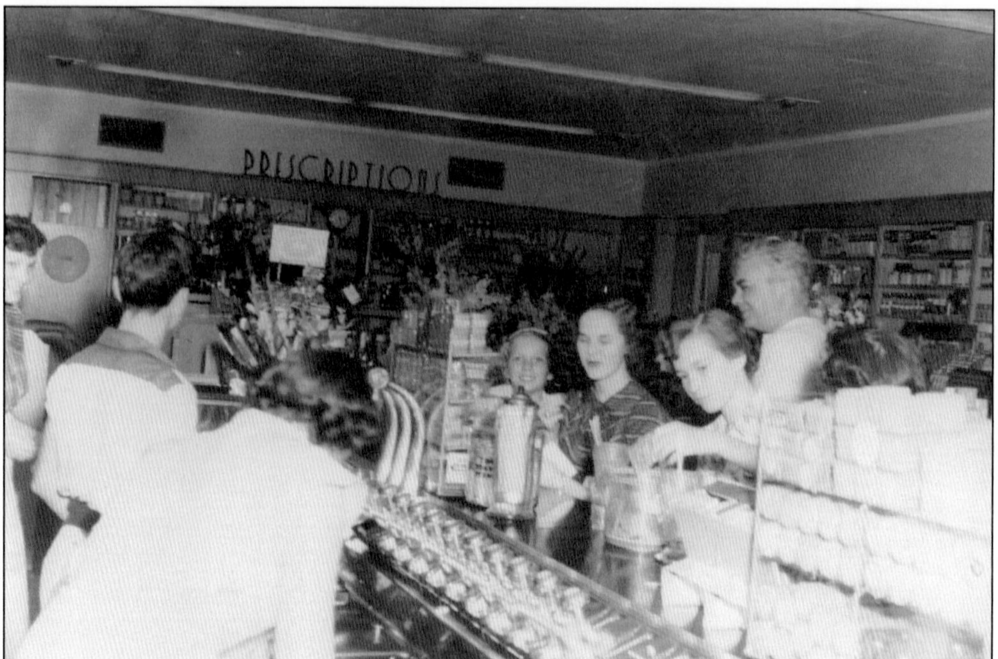

Soda Fountains. Soda fountains were popular with kids of all ages through the middle decades of the 1900s. Shown in this 1950s photograph is the grand opening of the soda fountain at Oatts Drug Store in Dublin.

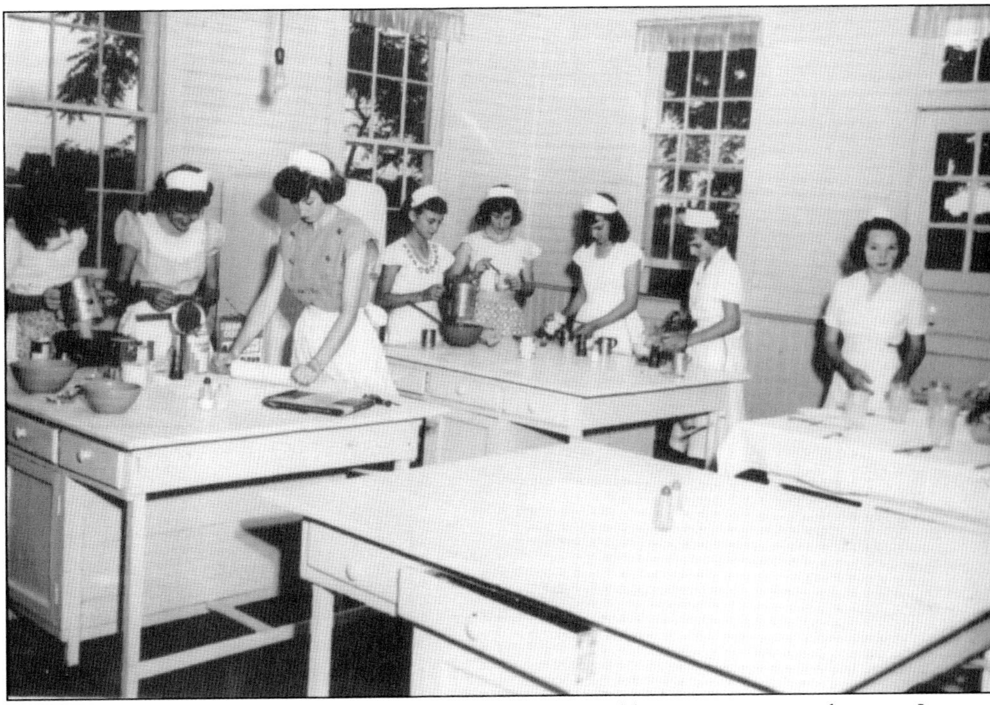

HOME ECONOMICS CLASS. This photograph shows a typical home economics class in a Laurens County high school in 1950.

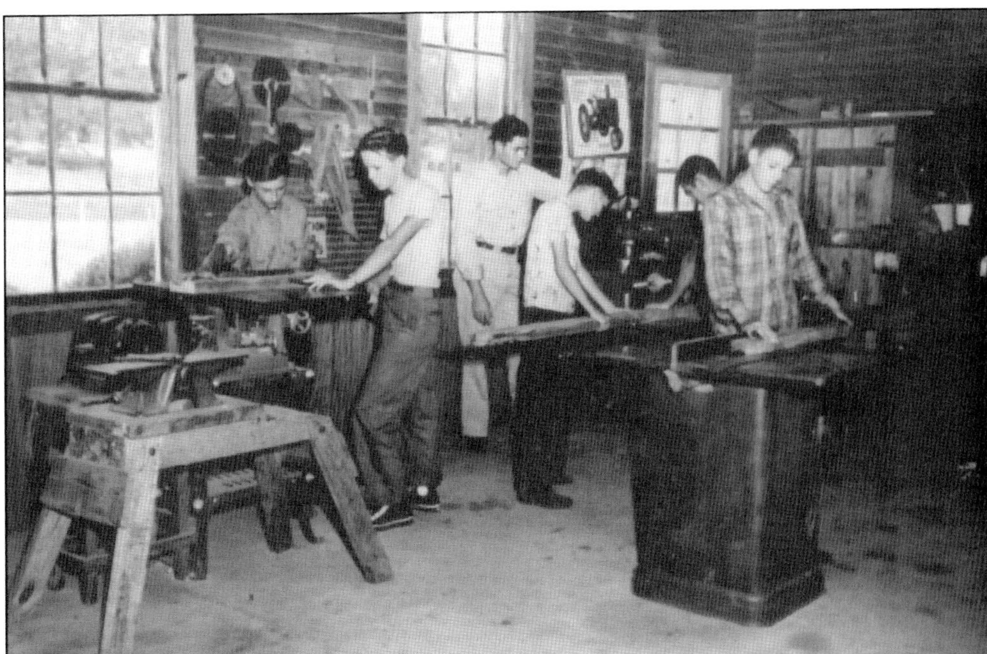

SHOP CLASS. This photograph shows a typical industrial arts class in a Laurens County high school in 1950.

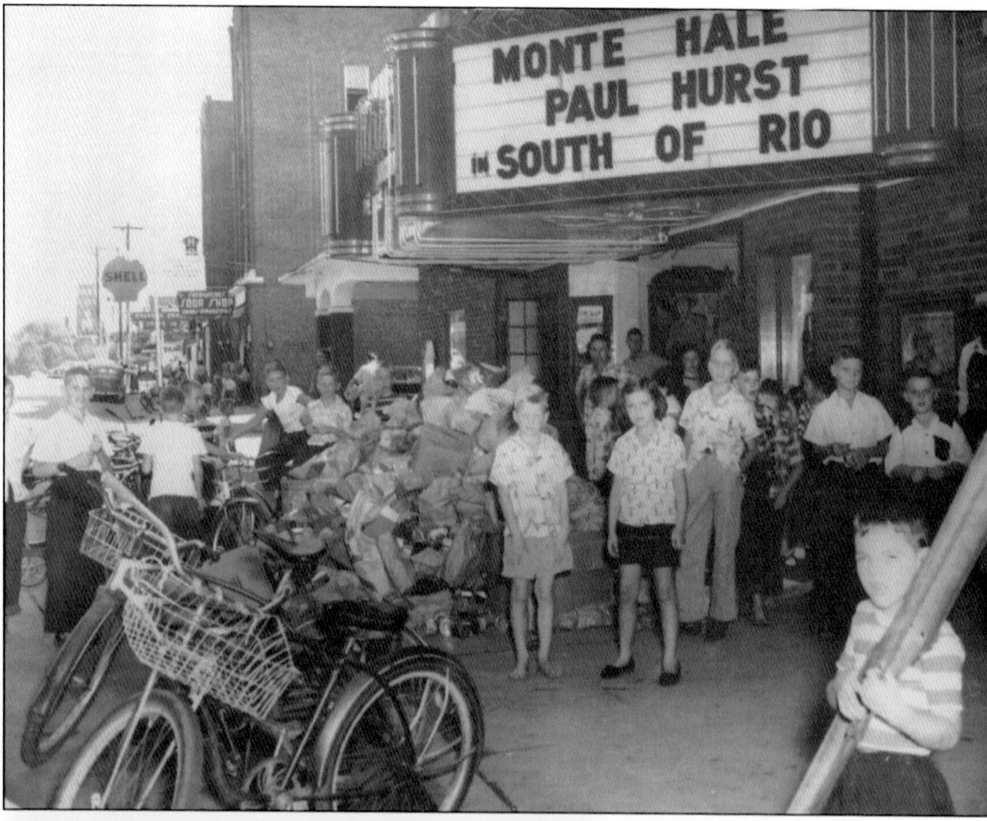

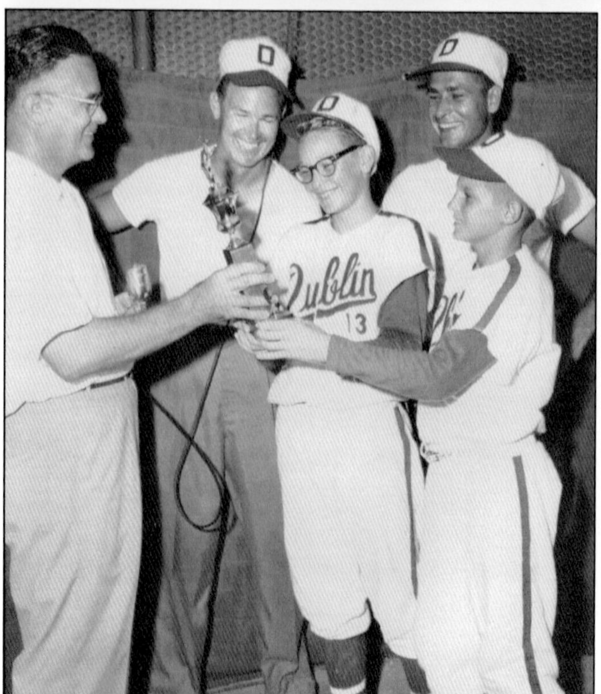

Clean Up Drive. A group of children gathered in front of the Martin Theater in the early 1950s to bring in scrap materials they gathered as a part of the "Clean Up and Fix Up Campaign" in the Better Home Town Program.

1959 District 5 Champions. A District 5 representative presents the championship Little League trophy to the Dublin All Stars. Shown, from left to right, in the photograph are manager Minton Williams, pitcher Tom Perry, coach Don Vaughn, and pitcher Reggie Belote. More than 1,500 people turned out at Little Hilburn Park to see Dublin capture the championship over a team from Macon.

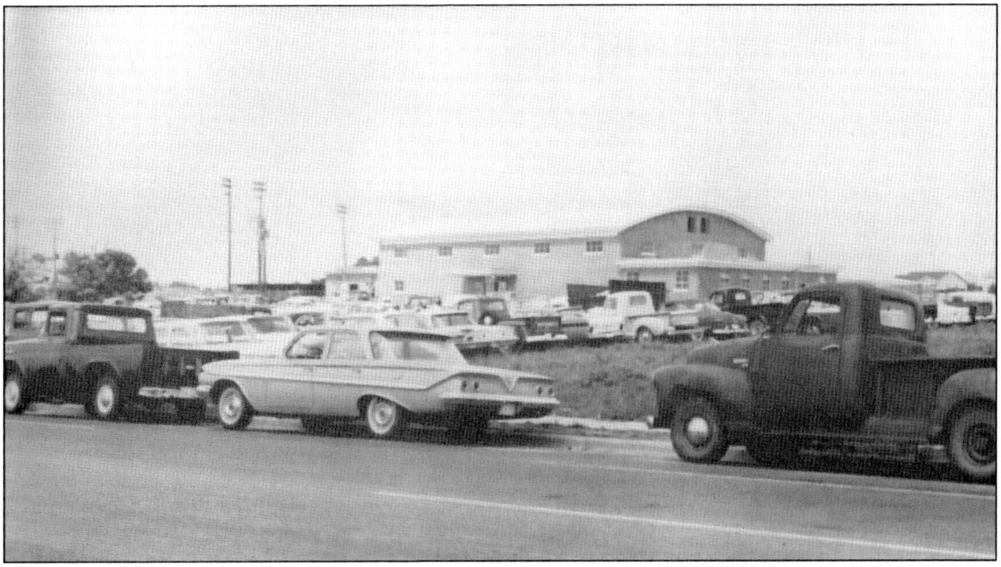

THE LAURENS COUNTY AGRICULTURE CENTER. The commissioners of Laurens County erected a modern building on Telfair Street in Dublin in 1961 to promote the vast and important agricultural industry of Laurens County.

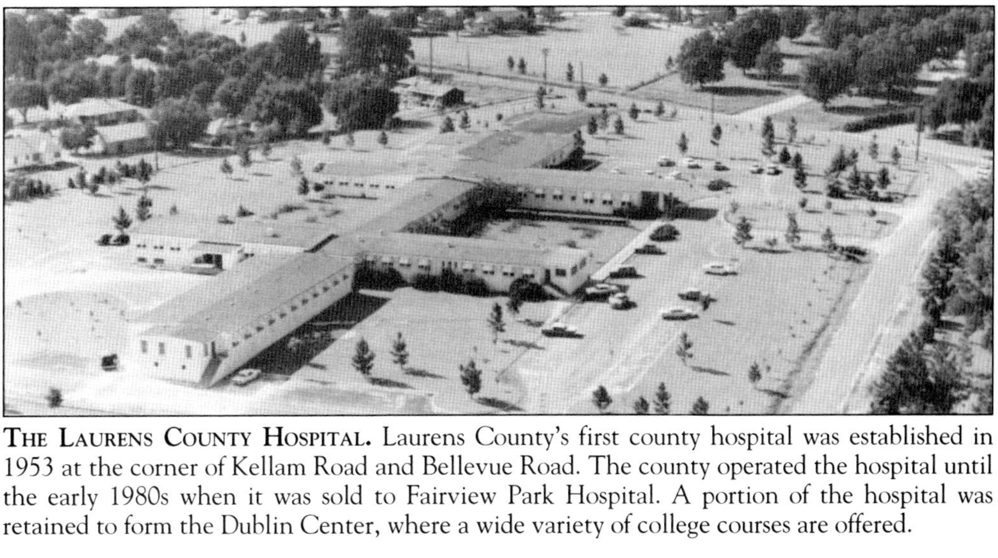

THE LAURENS COUNTY HOSPITAL. Laurens County's first county hospital was established in 1953 at the corner of Kellam Road and Bellevue Road. The county operated the hospital until the early 1980s when it was sold to Fairview Park Hospital. A portion of the hospital was retained to form the Dublin Center, where a wide variety of college courses are offered.

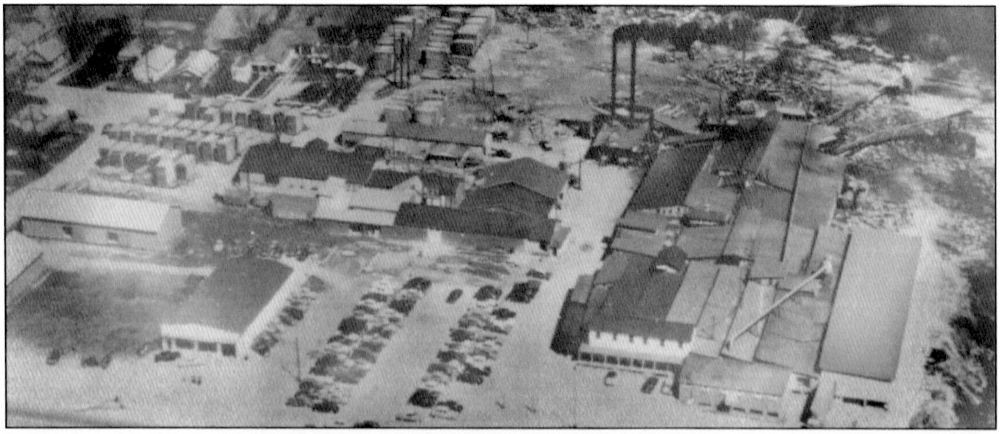

Georgia Plywood Corporation. One of Laurens County's most successful businesses was Georgia Plywood Corporation. The plant, which operated under several names over seven decades, was last owned by W.F. Belote, a Laurens Countian who was one of the largest timber and naval stores dealers in Georgia.

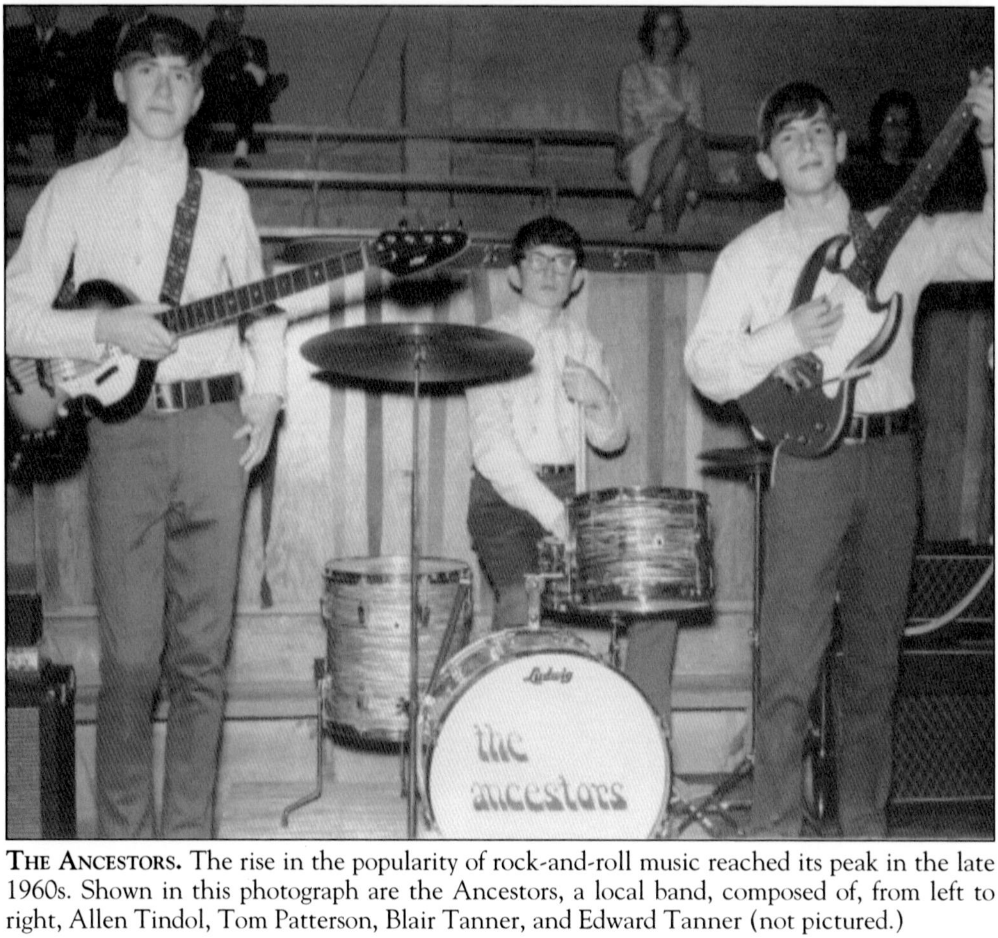

The Ancestors. The rise in the popularity of rock-and-roll music reached its peak in the late 1960s. Shown in this photograph are the Ancestors, a local band, composed of, from left to right, Allen Tindol, Tom Patterson, Blair Tanner, and Edward Tanner (not pictured.)

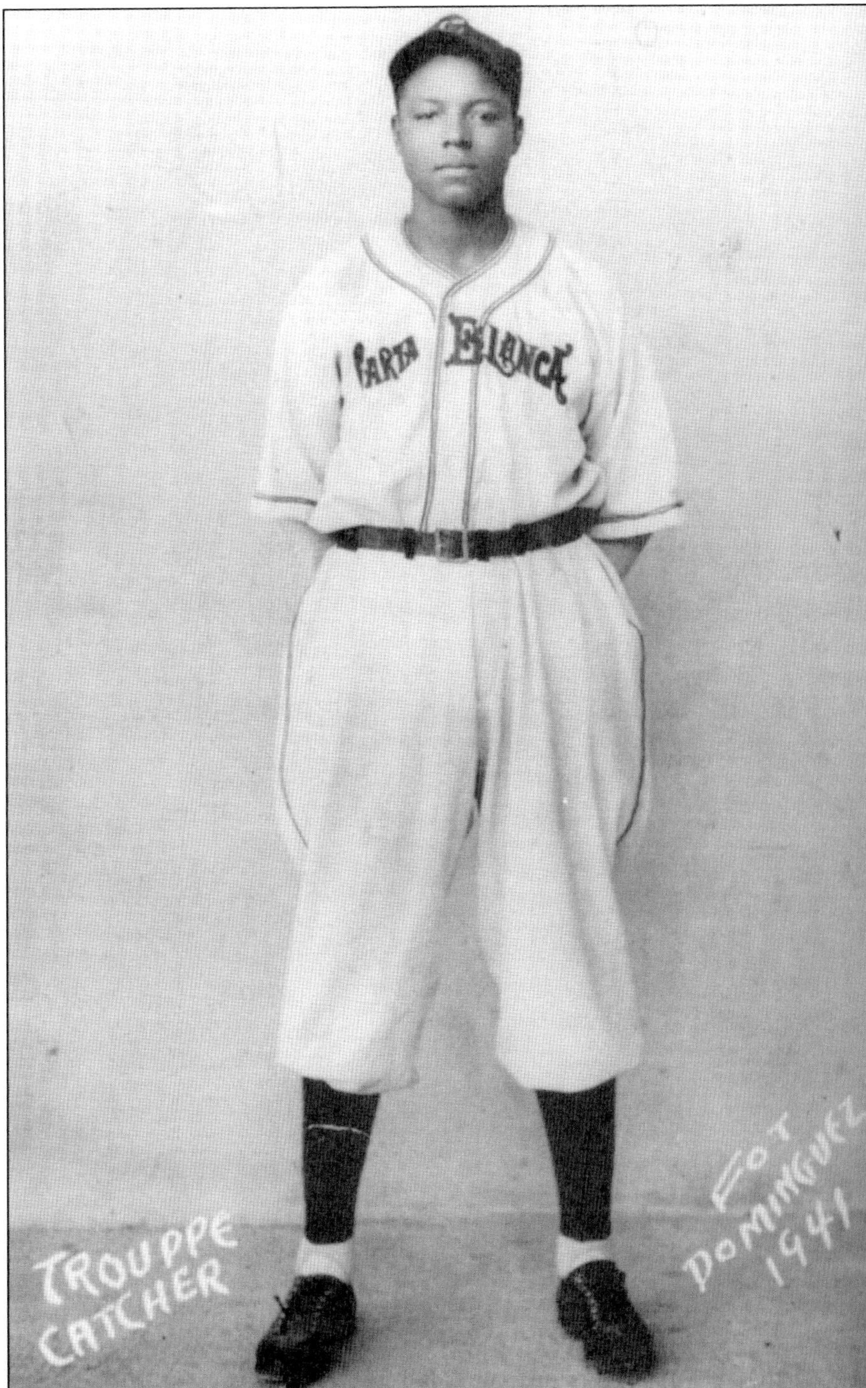

QUINCY TROUPPE. Quincy Trouppe was born in Laurens County on Christmas Day, 1912. After moving to St. Louis, Quincy became an amateur boxer. Quincy also excelled in baseball and played in the Negro Leagues for nearly 20 years and for the Cleveland Indians in 1952. Quincy, who was regarded as one of the best catchers in Negro League history, donated his lifelong collection of baseball memorabilia to the Negro League Hall of Fame.

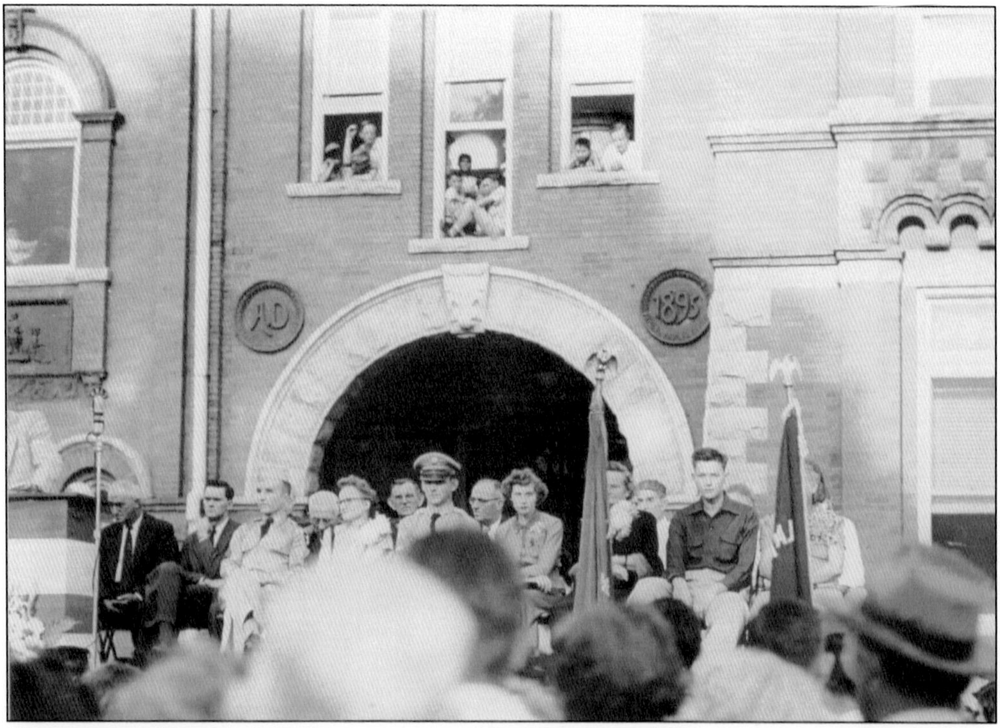

HOMECOMING HEROES. This homecoming celebration was held on October 2, 1953, for three Laurens Countians who had survived the horrors of Korean P.O.W. camps during the Korean War. Seated on the front row in uniform, from left to right, are Emerson Burns, Wesley Hodges, and Tyrois Odom, who is seated between the flags and was not in uniform.

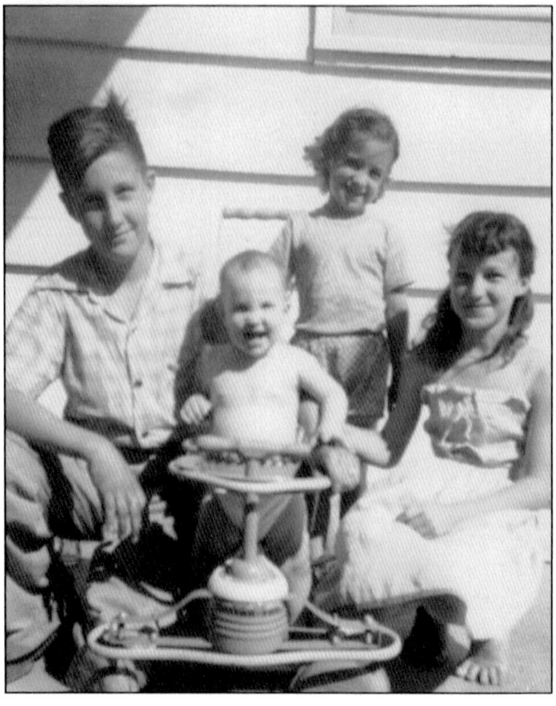

A FINE CADWELL FAMILY. The Colter family of Cadwell is seen in 1951. From left to right are William Jesse, Nancy, Jackie, and Sue. Sue Colter is the new president of the local historical society.

Miss Mattie Tucker. Miss Mattie, who is shown carefully tending to her garden in Cadwell in the 1990s, was a friend to many during her day.

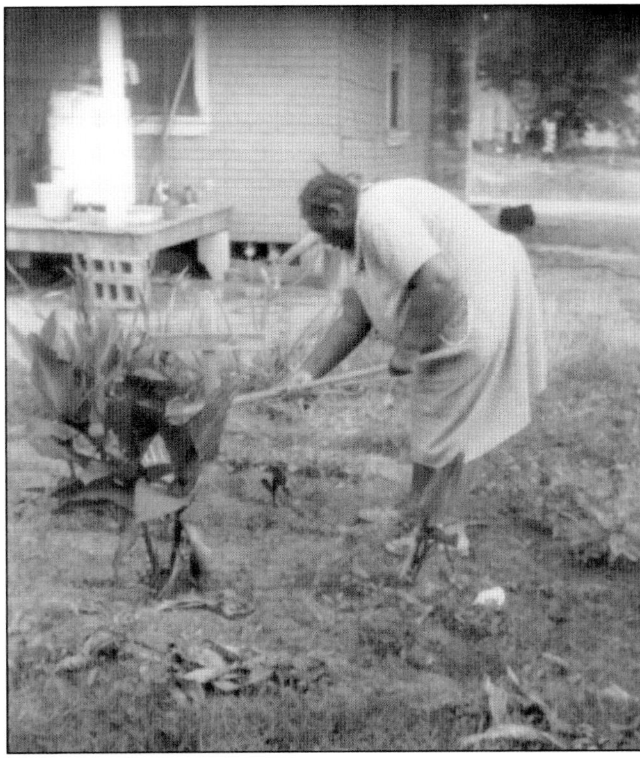

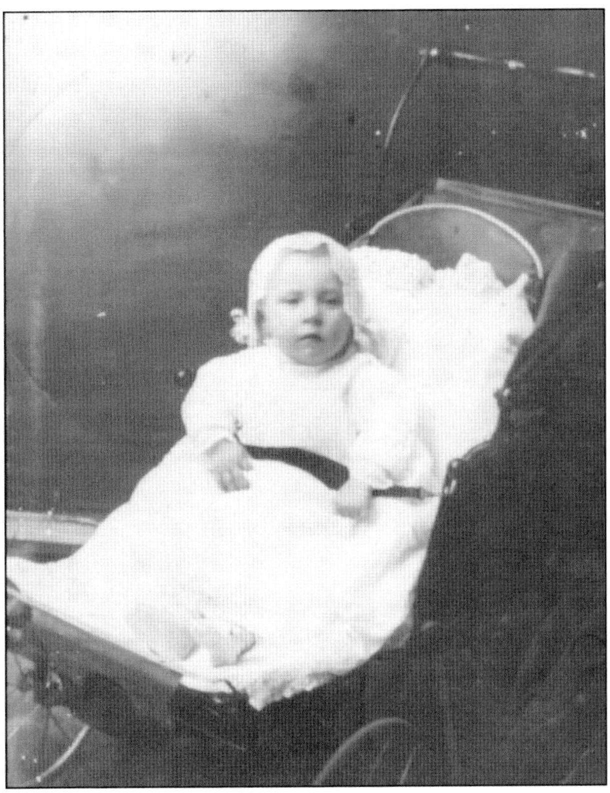

Baby in a Stroller. Babies in strollers were a favorite of photographers in the early 1900s. Shown in this 1912 photograph is Allix Colter of Cadwell.

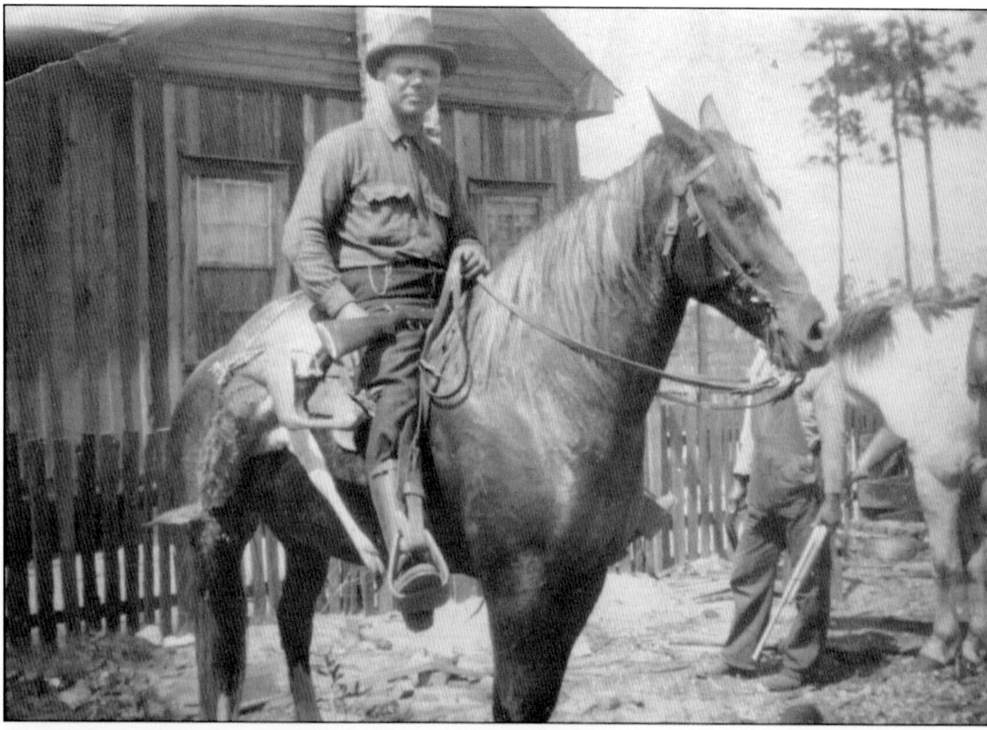

Proud Deer Hunter. John Carter poses in this *c.* 1920 photograph with a deer across the back of his horse. Deer were virtually extinct in Laurens County until restocking efforts began in the early 1940s.

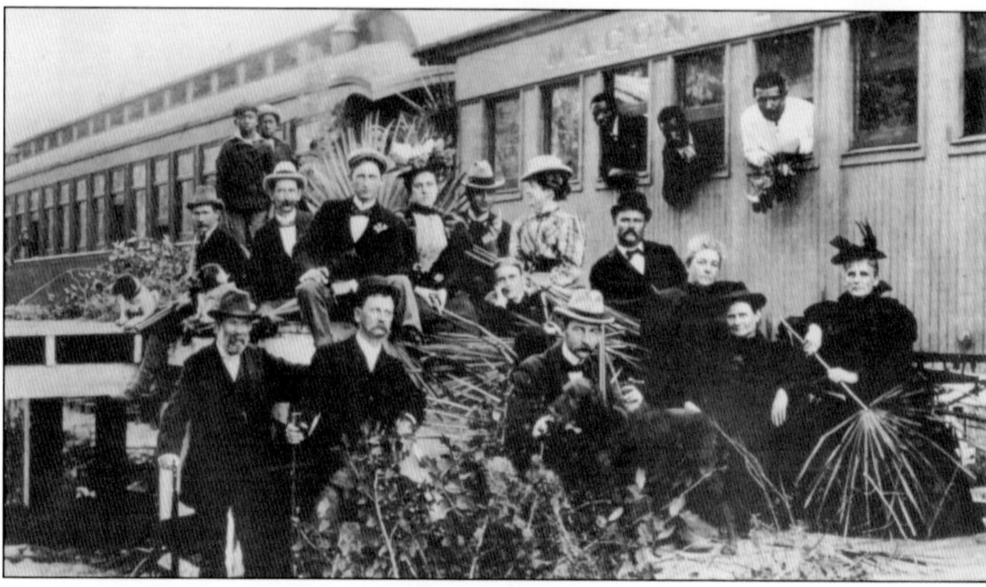

The Macon, Dublin, and Savannah Railroad. Shown in this July 1891 photograph is the VIP party on the inaugural train ride of the railroad. It ran from Macon to Dublin and later to Vidalia, where it picked up a connection to Savannah. Seated in the middle of the front row is James Wright, president of the railroad. To his right is Dudley M. Hughes of Twiggs County, the vice-president of the railroad and a Laurens County farm owner.

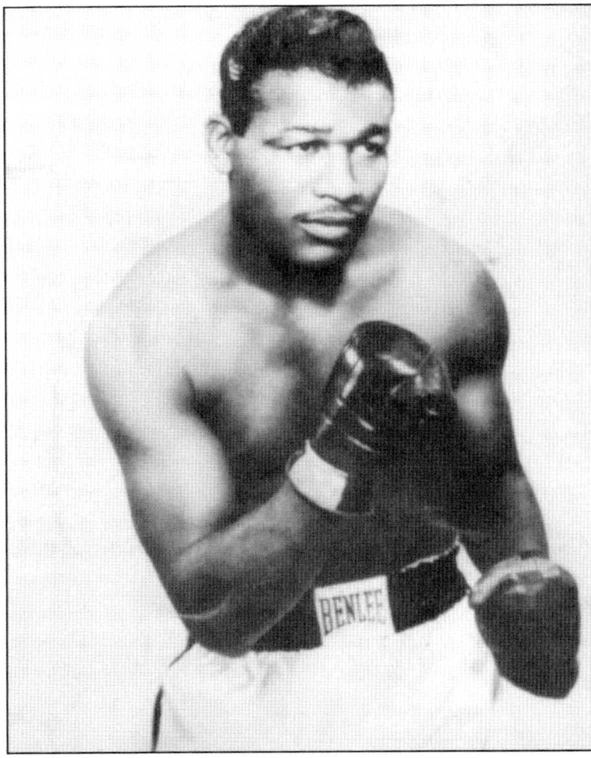

SUGAR RAY ROBINSON. Born Walker Smith Jr., this son of Walker Smith Sr. and Lula Hurst Smith of Laurens County spent many of his childhood days with his grandmother Anna Hurst in Dublin. Smith changed his name to Sugar Ray Robinson and was a six-time world boxing champion. He is known as the greatest pound-for-pound boxer in the history of the sport.

PIANO RECITAL. Betty Jim Burch's class poses for a picture during their 1950 recital in Cadwell. Shown, from left to right, are Iris Moye, Judy Cameron, Sandra Smith, Betty Jo Burch, William Colter, Connie Bedingfield, Jean Smith, Jackie Colter, Brenda Culpepper, Betty Jim Burch, Sue Colter, Annette McCullough, and Martha Ann Carter.

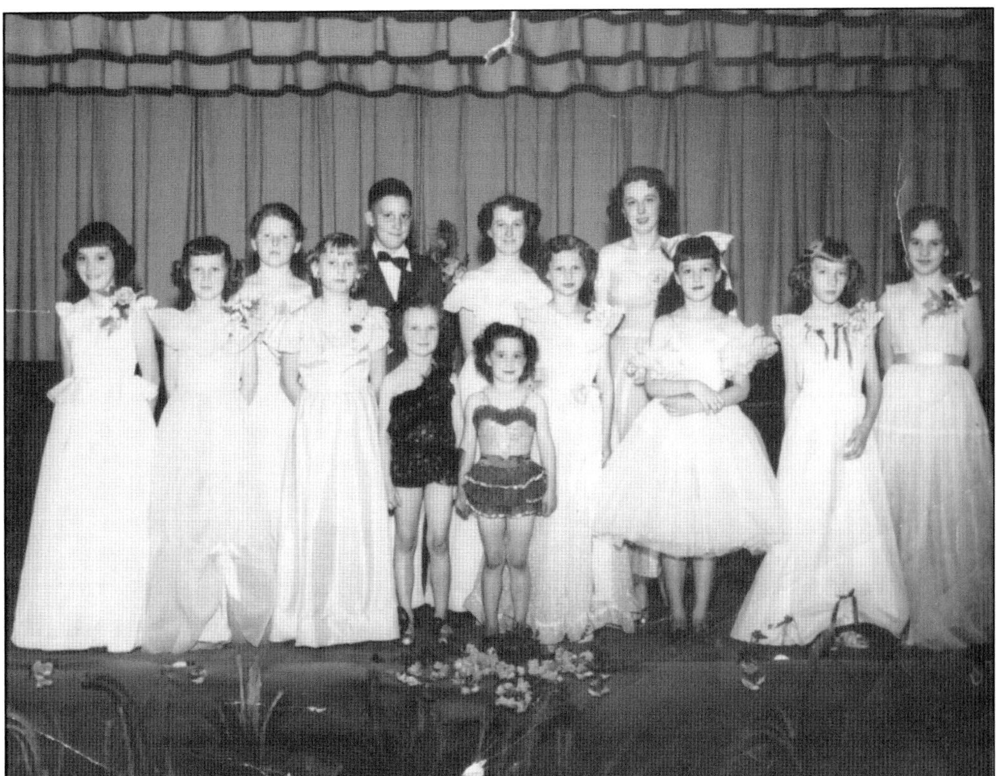

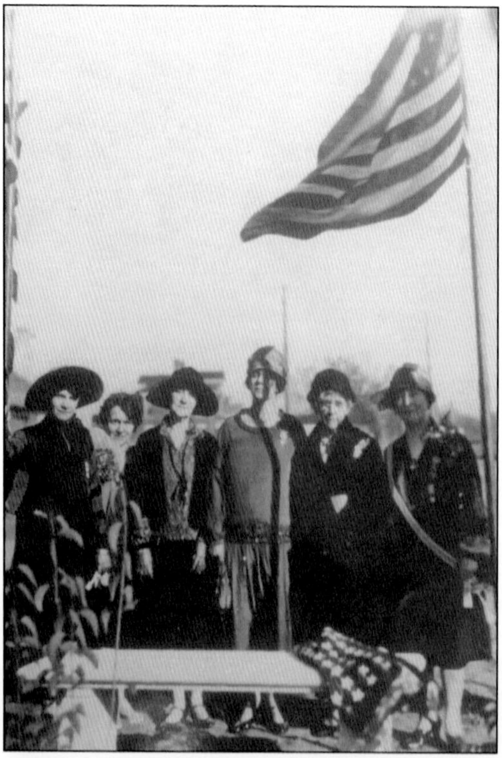

THE SMALLEST PARK. The smallest park in the City of Dublin was established in 1926. Glover Burney donated a small triangular tract of land at the intersection of Bellevue Road and Veteran's Boulevard, which he named in honor of his ancestor James McCall, a captain of the militia in 1774. The John Laurens Chapter of the D.A.R. placed a marble bench in the park in 1926 as a memorial to the men of Laurens County who lost their lives in World War I.

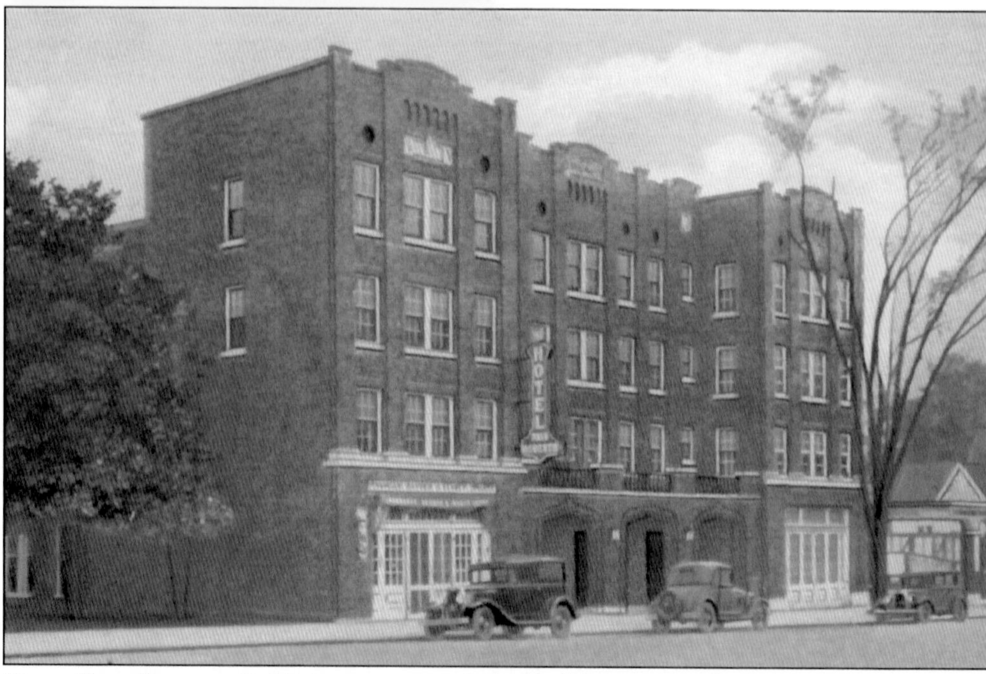

HOTEL FRED ROBERTS. Dublin's premier hotel, the Fred Roberts, was built in 1926. It was named in honor of the president of the chamber of commerce who died during the construction of the building. Visitors in the hotel came from all parts of the country in their travels along Highway 80. The building was restored in the early 1990s as a senior citizens center.

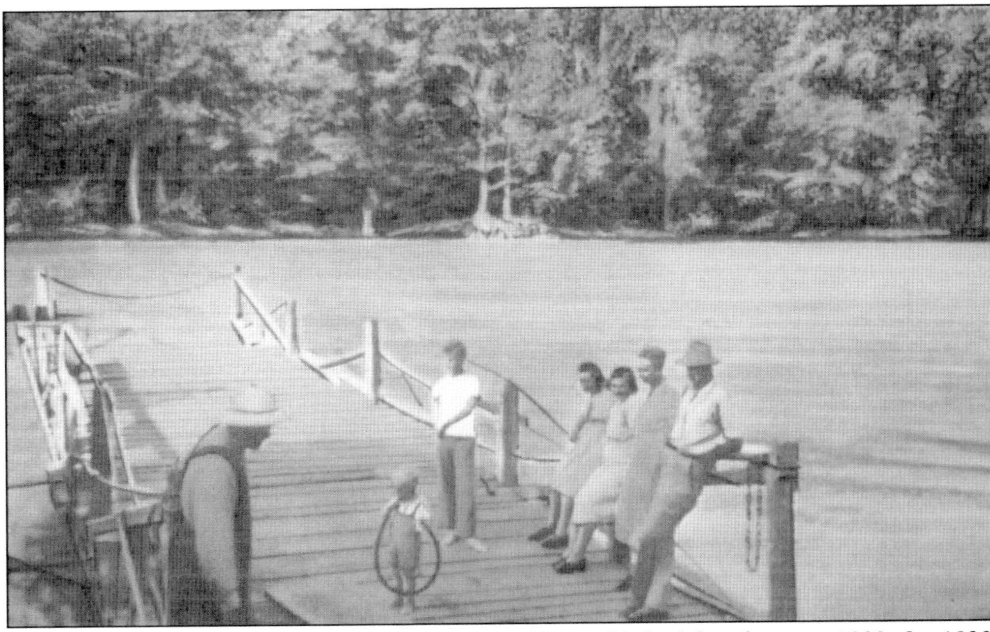

Blackshear's Ferry. Elijah Blackshear originally established his ferry in 1808. In 1820, Blackshear and his brother David bought the old Trammel and Beatty Ferry and established the permanent site of their ferry. The ferry was used for nearly 140 years until it closed in 1947.

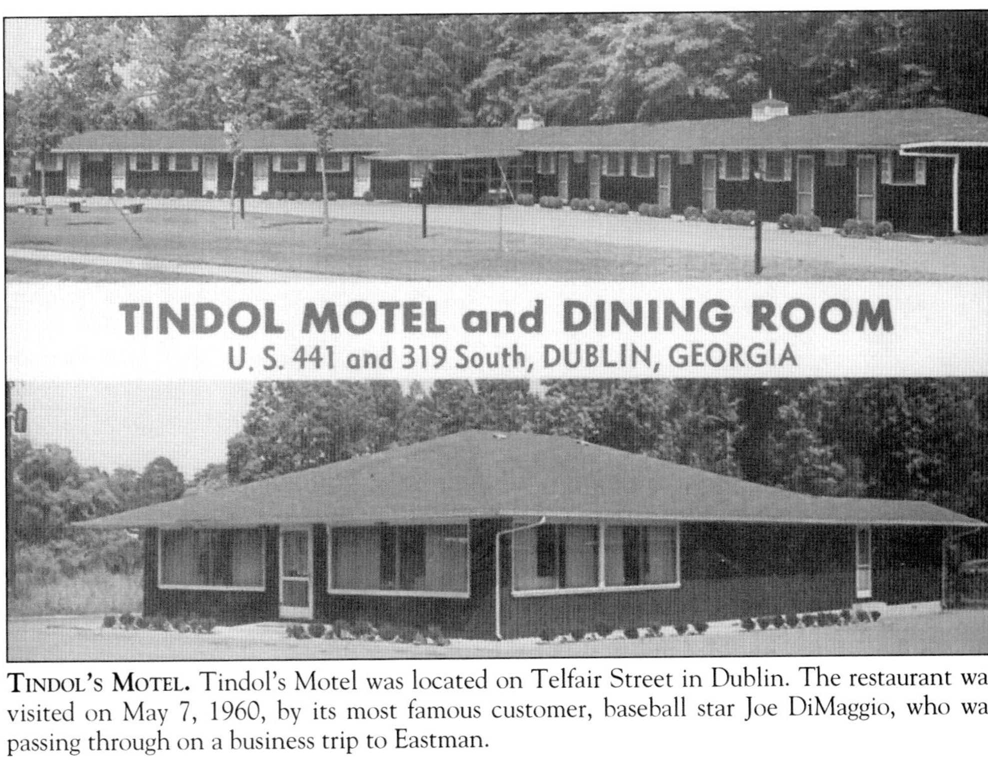

Tindol's Motel. Tindol's Motel was located on Telfair Street in Dublin. The restaurant was visited on May 7, 1960, by its most famous customer, baseball star Joe DiMaggio, who was passing through on a business trip to Eastman.

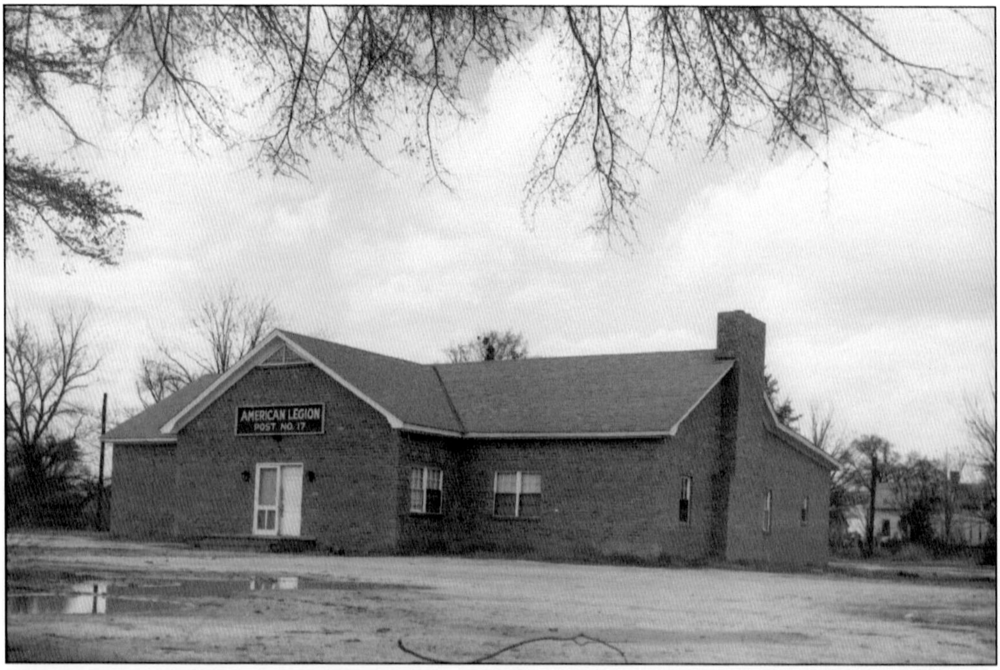

The American Legion. Post No. 17 of the American Legion was established by Roy Flynt in 1919. During the 1950s the members of the American Legion built this commodious modern post building on North Jefferson Street.

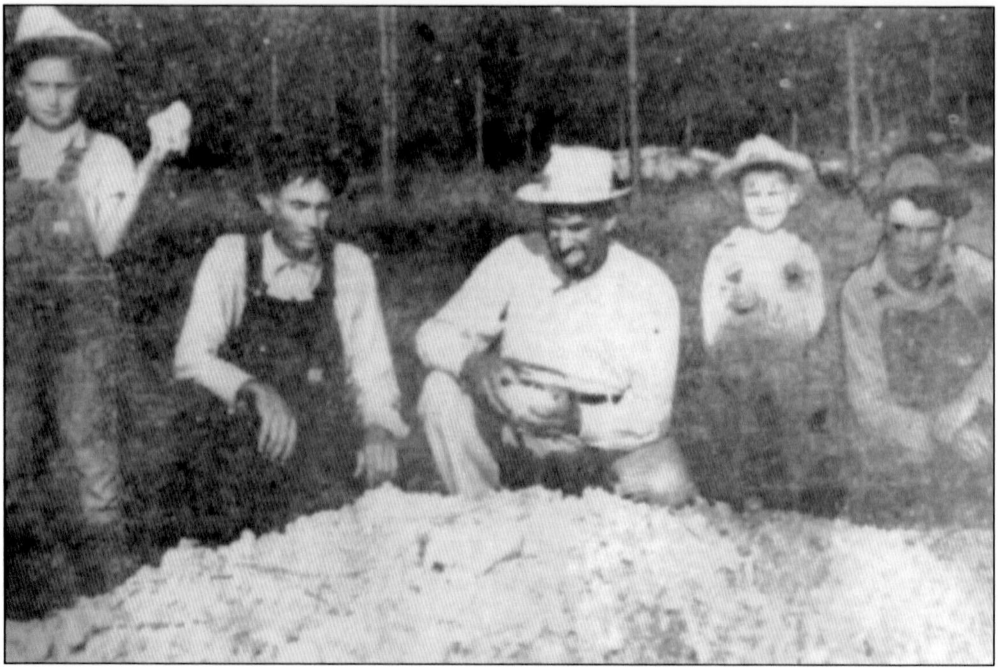

Gold! In 1938, J. Alver Spivey and his neighbor Lucien Wynn discovered gold in the rocks along the creek separating their lands, which were located near Minter. The men and their neighbors mined the rocks containing the gold. The mine never yielded a significant amount of gold and was abandoned.

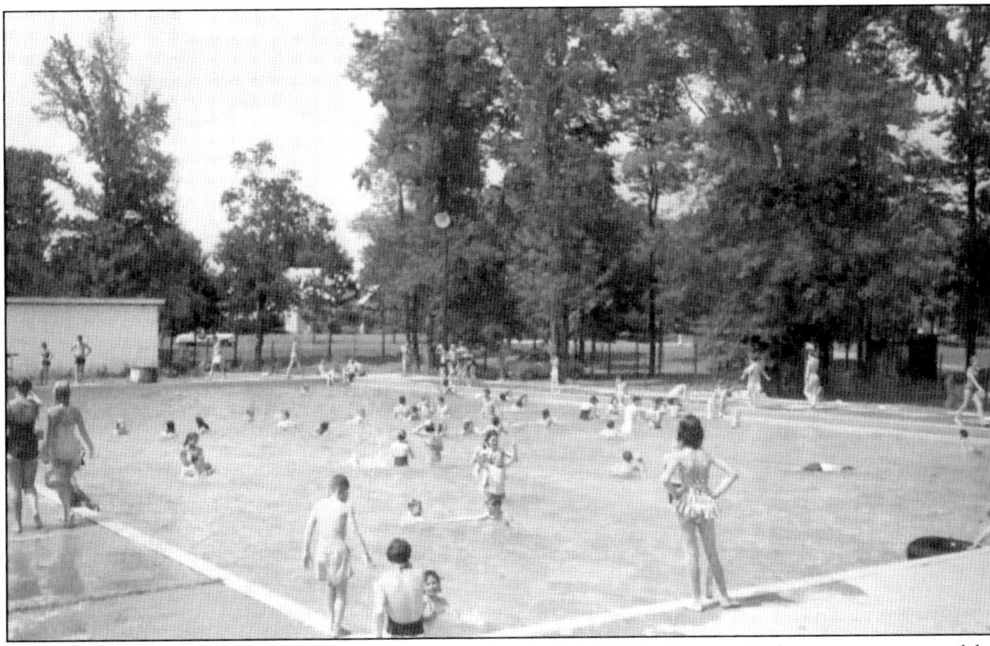

STUBBS PARK POOL. This 1960s photograph shows the swimming pool that was sponsored by the Jaycees. It was built in the 1950s but was later filled in and a tennis court built on top.

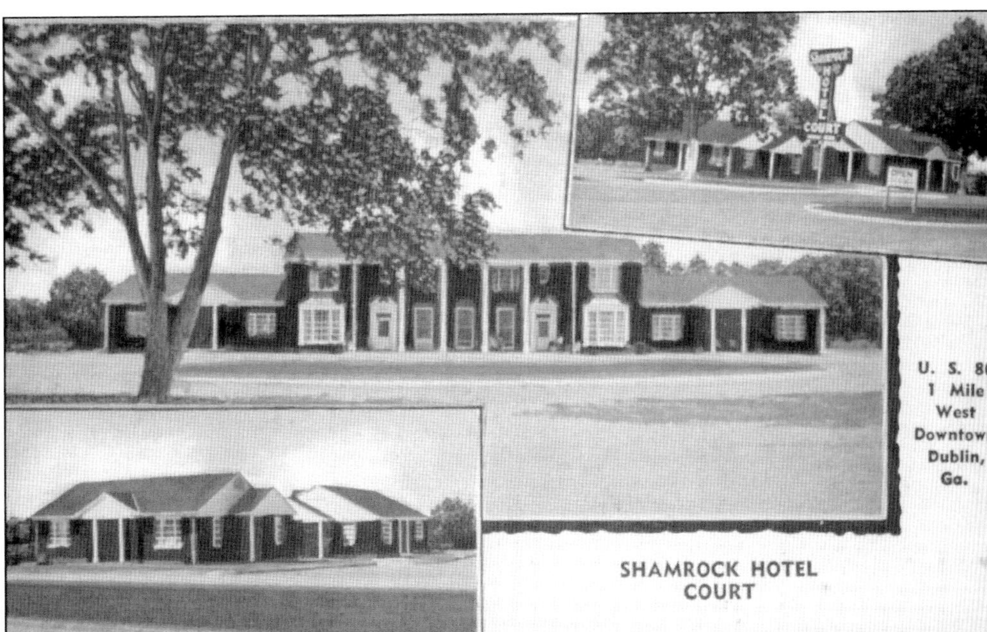

SHAMROCK HOTEL COURT. This attractive motor hotel court was built in the middle of the 20th century primarily to accommodate guests who were visiting friends and family members in the Veterans Hospital across the street. The buildings are now the home of Curry Realtors/Insurors.

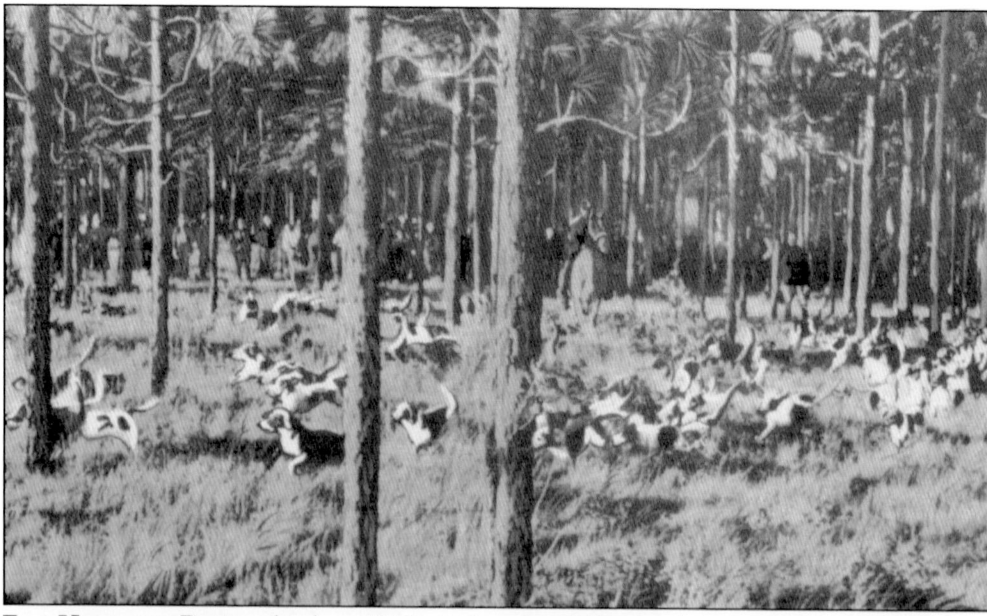

FOX HUNTING. During the late 1930s and early 1940s, fox hunting was a popular sport in Laurens County. Fox hunters from all over Georgia converged on Dublin for their annual hunts.

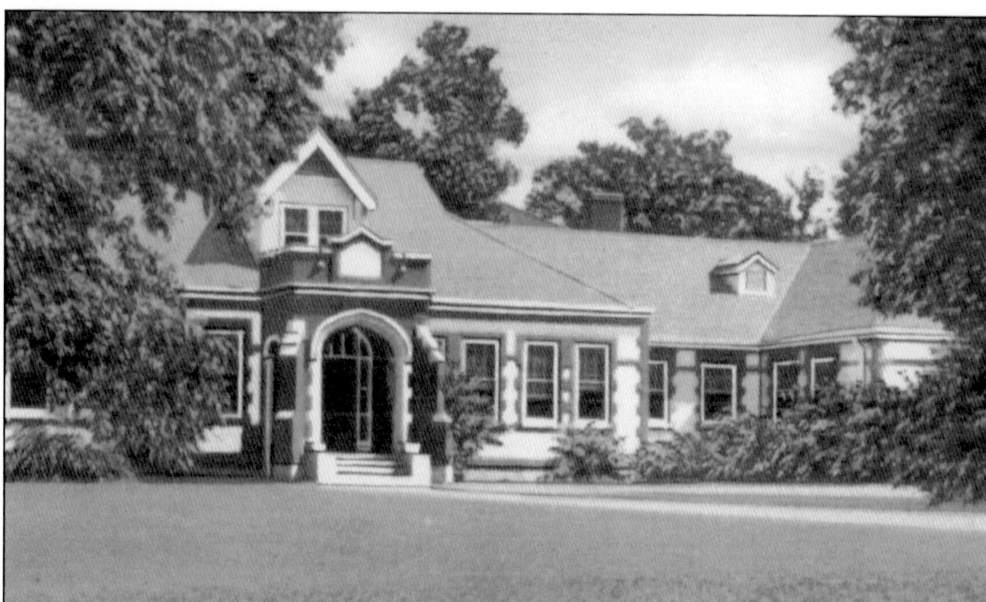

CLAXTON SANITARIUM. Dr. E.B. Claxton established Laurens County's first large hospital in the mid-1930s on Bellevue Avenue. It was used for 40 years but is no longer in operation.

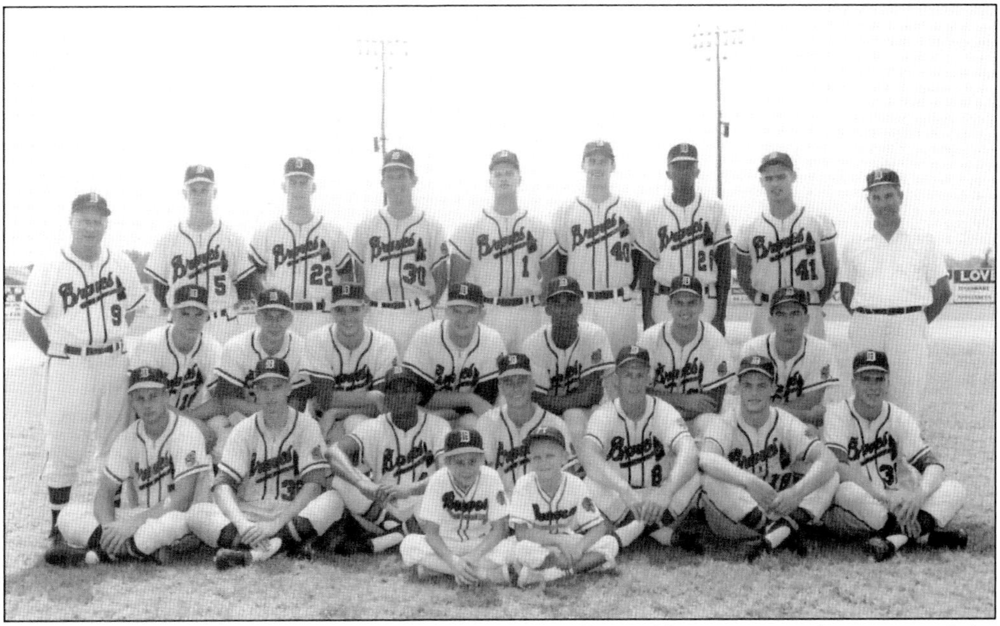

THE DUBLIN BRAVES. This 1962 photograph shows the Dublin Braves, a farm team of the Milwaukee Braves in the Georgia-Florida League. Standing on the left is manager Bill Steinecke, who formerly played in the major leagues. Kneeling on the second row, third from the right, is Bill Robinson, who played for the World Champion Pittsburgh Pirates in 1979 and was an ESPN sportscaster.

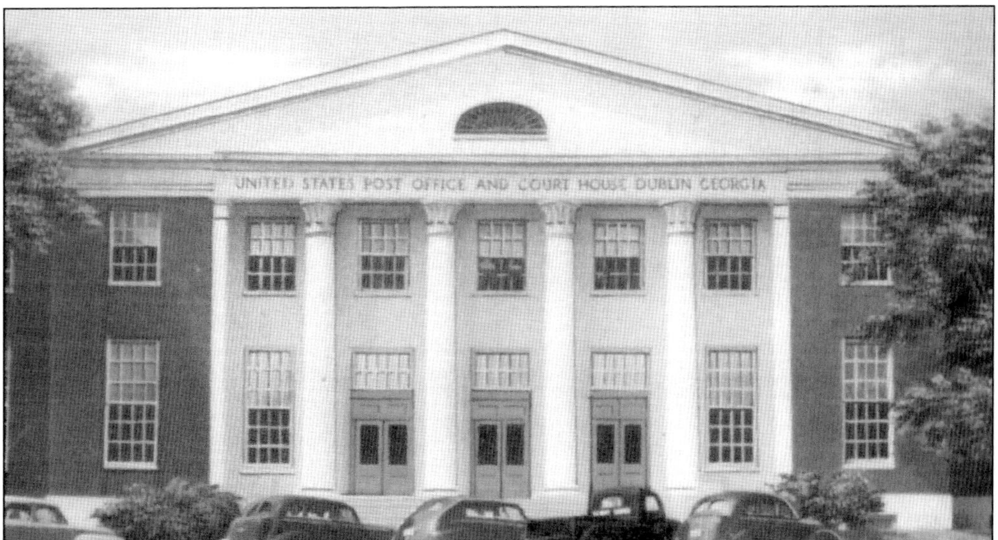

THE FEDERAL BUILDING. This magnificent structure was completed in 1936 to accommodate the post office and federal offices. The building was completed through the efforts of Congressmen W.W. Larsen and Carl Vinson. It was named the J. Roy Rowland Federal Courthouse in honor of the Dublin physician who served six terms in the U.S. Congress.

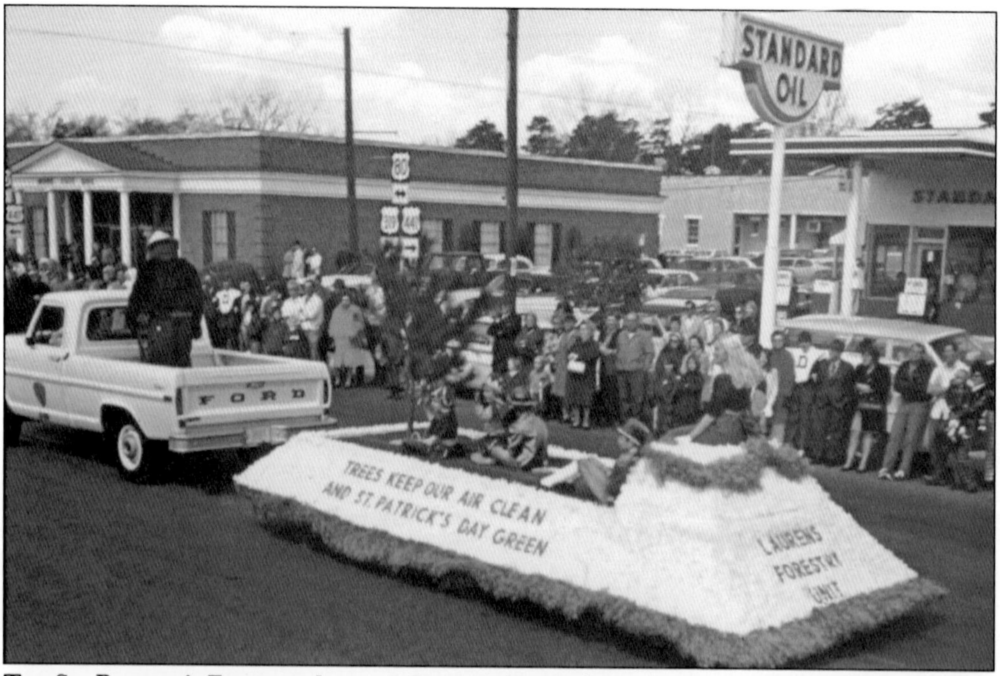

The St. Patrick's Festival. Laurens County's largest festival and the world's longest-running festival celebrating Irish heritage is the St. Patrick's Festival, which is held every March and attracts thousands of visitors and participants.

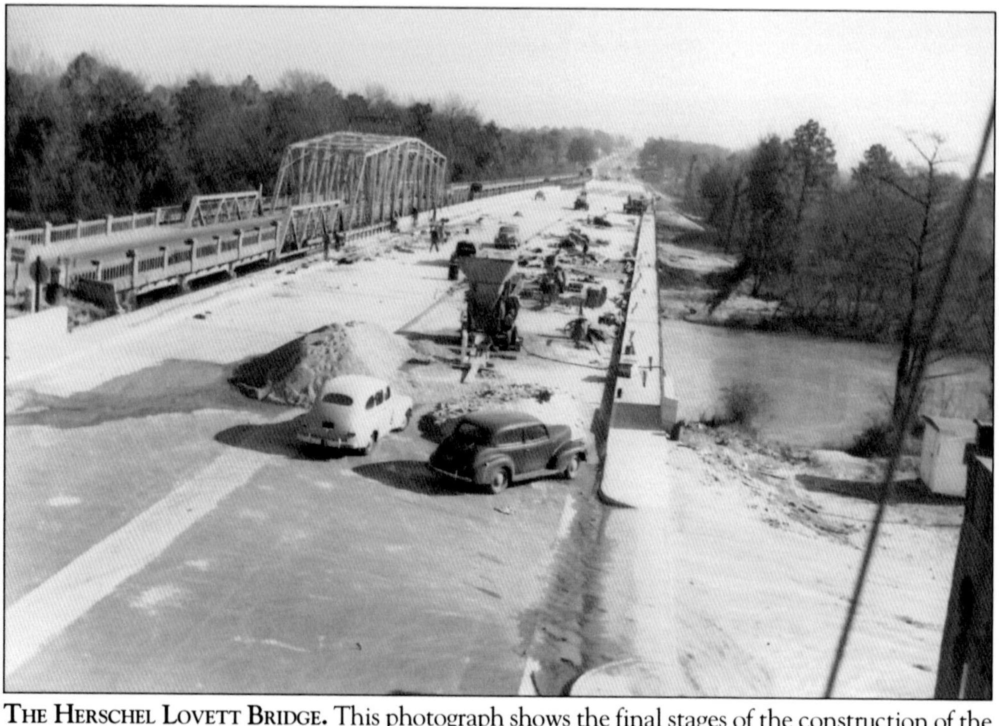
The Herschel Lovett Bridge. This photograph shows the final stages of the construction of the Herschel Lovett Bridge, spanning the Oconee River between Dublin and East Dublin. The bridge was completed in 1952 and was named in honor of a Dublin businessman and politician.

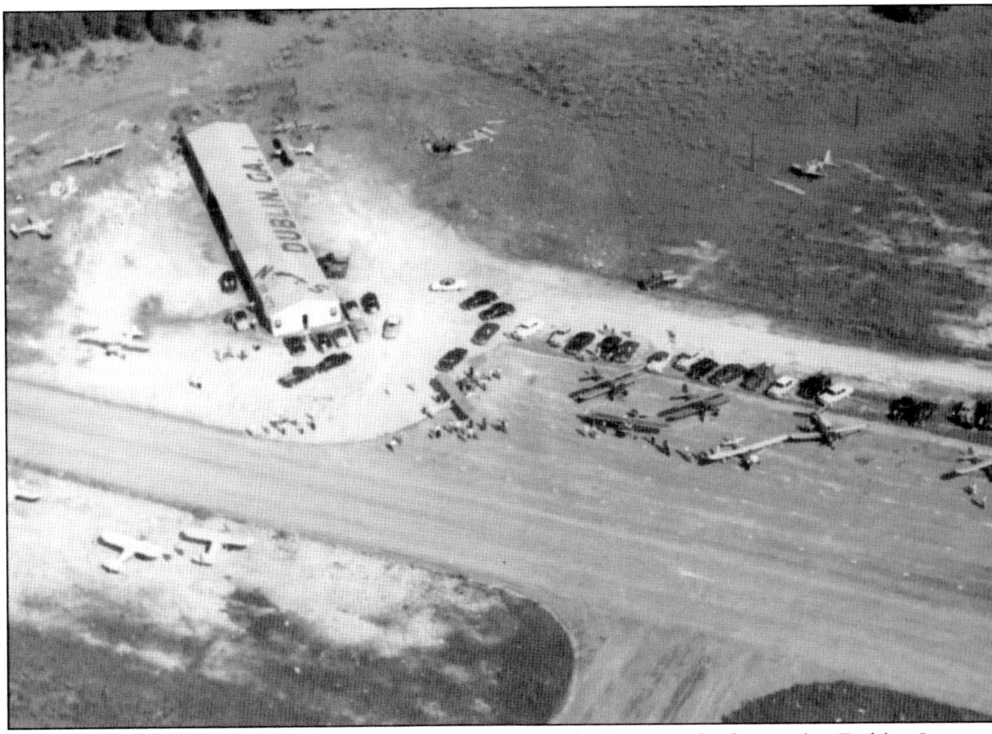

The Dublin-Laurens County Airport. This aerial photograph shows the Dublin-Laurens County Airport in the early 1950s. The airport was constructed in 1943 to accommodate flights of patients in the U.S. Naval Hospital. Through the efforts of concerned citizens, the airport has become one of the best in the state of Georgia.

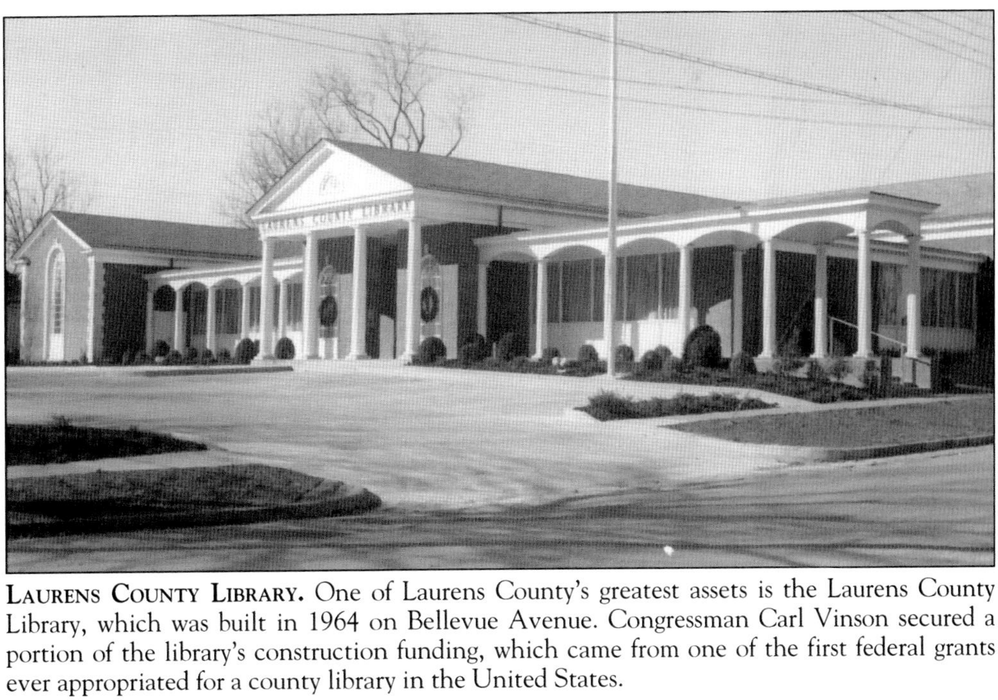

Laurens County Library. One of Laurens County's greatest assets is the Laurens County Library, which was built in 1964 on Bellevue Avenue. Congressman Carl Vinson secured a portion of the library's construction funding, which came from one of the first federal grants ever appropriated for a county library in the United States.

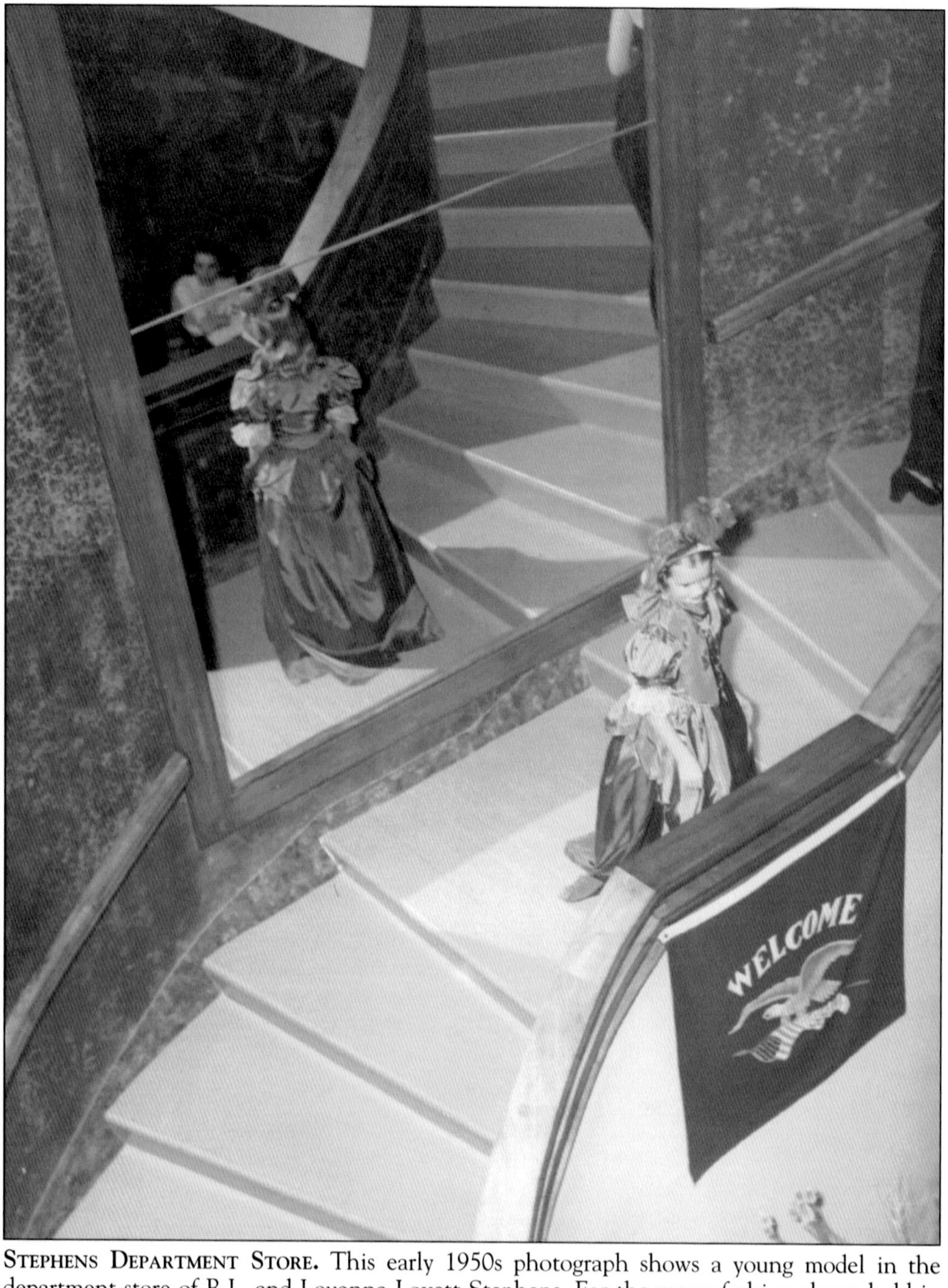

Stephens Department Store. This early 1950s photograph shows a young model in the department store of R.L. and Louanna Lovett Stephens. For the many fashion shows held in the store, Mrs. Stephens designed the staircase so that both sides of a dress could be seen by customers at the same time. The store was one of the most elegant stores in Dublin.

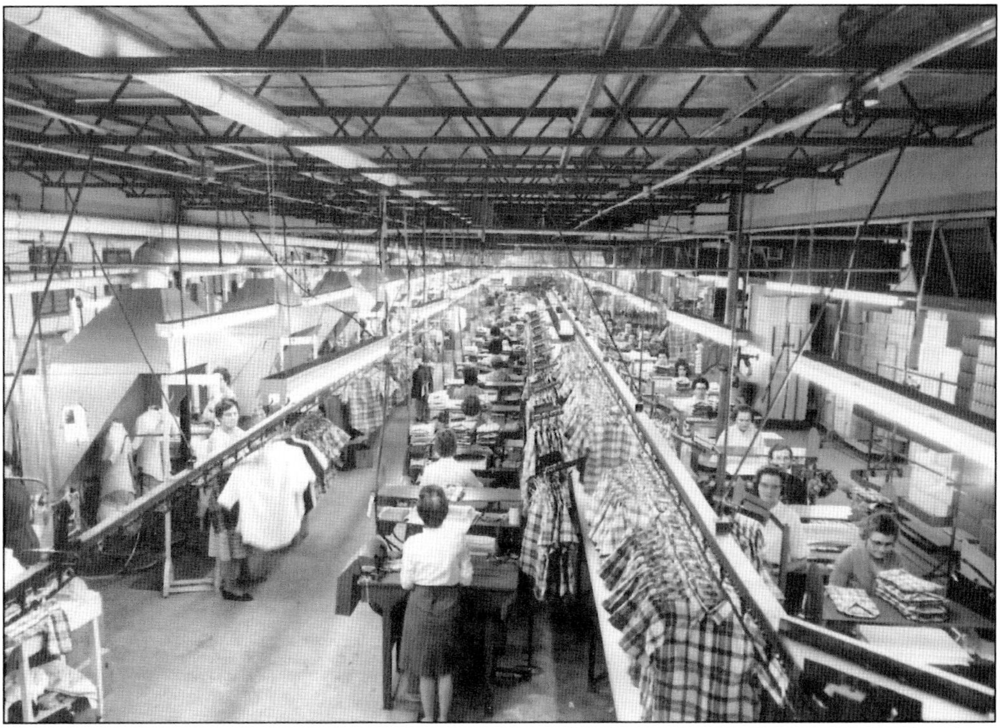

DUBLIN GARMENT COMPANY. This 1960s photograph shows the production line of Dublin Garment Company, which later became Oxford Manufacturing Company. Known as "The Shirt Factory," the building housed an operation that provided many jobs for the citizens of Laurens County for several decades.

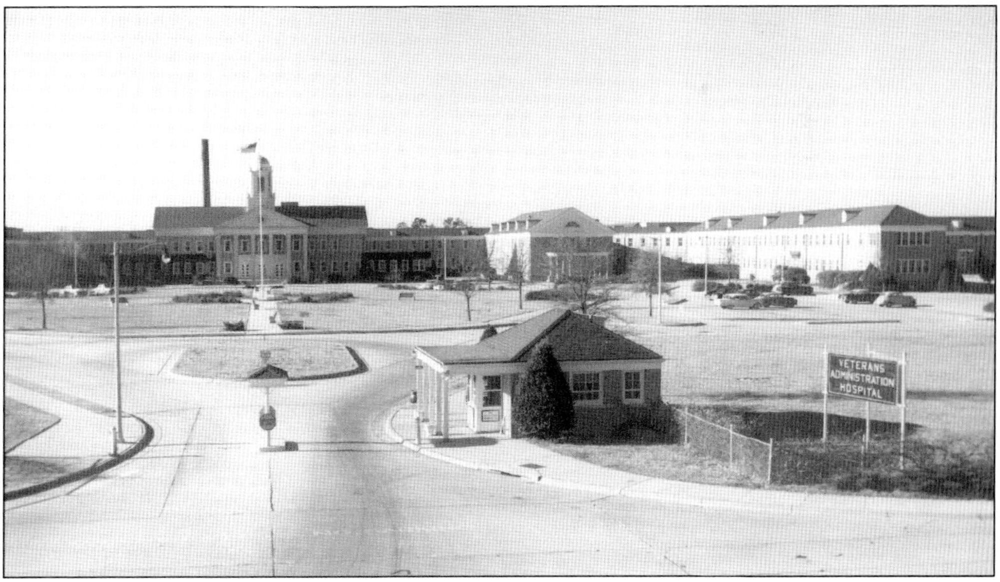

THE VETERANS ADMINISTRATION HOSPITAL. The Veterans Administration took over the U.S. Naval Hospital in 1948. Guards were once posted at the entrance to the hospital in the guard house in the center of the photograph. During Christmas time the grounds were decorated by a multitude of Christmas lights and decorations.

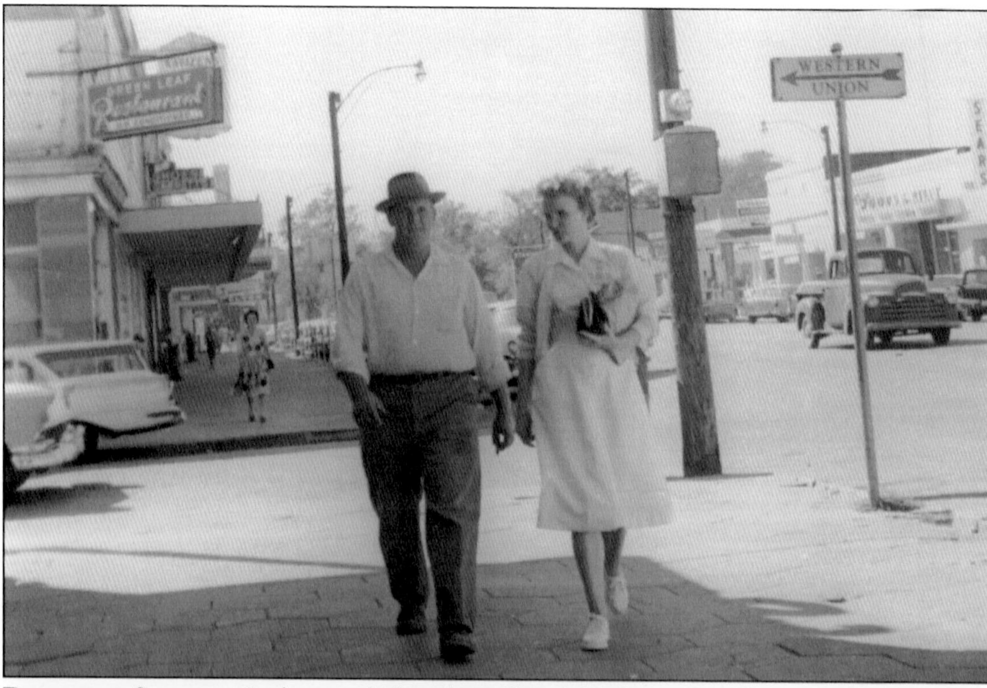

DOWNTOWN SHOPPERS. In the years before the mall and the shopping centers, Laurens Countians converged by the thousands in Dublin every Saturday. Shown in this *c.* 1960 photograph are Wallace and Celestine Dean walking in front of Oatts Drug Store.

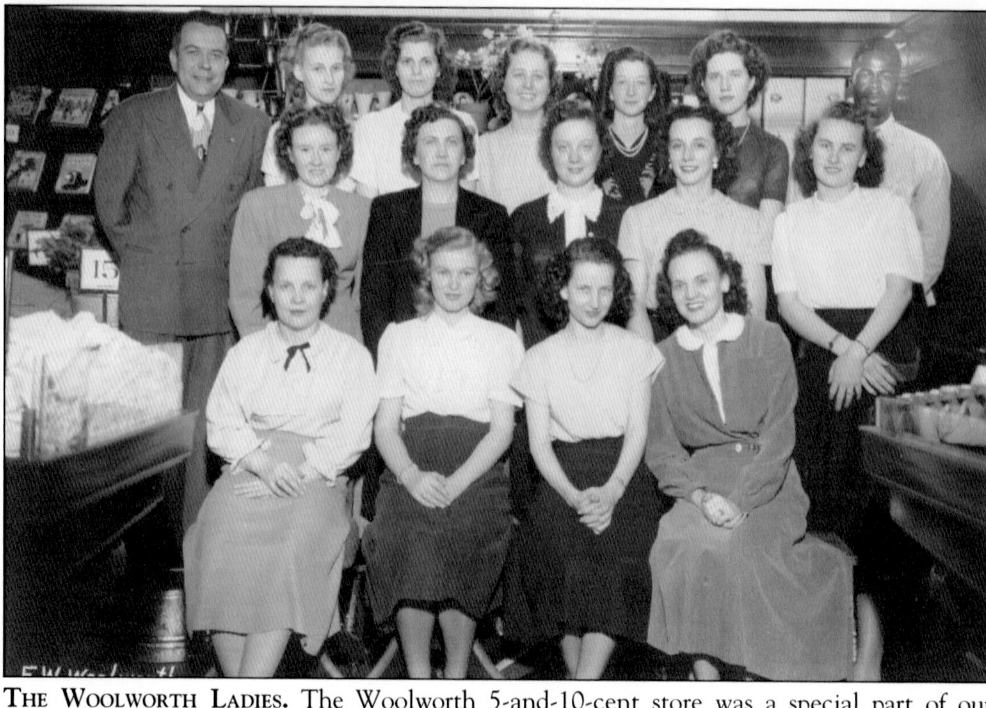

THE WOOLWORTH LADIES. The Woolworth 5-and-10-cent store was a special part of our community. To any kid it was a magical place. This 1949 photograph shows the friendly employees of the Woolworth Store on Jackson Street in Dublin.

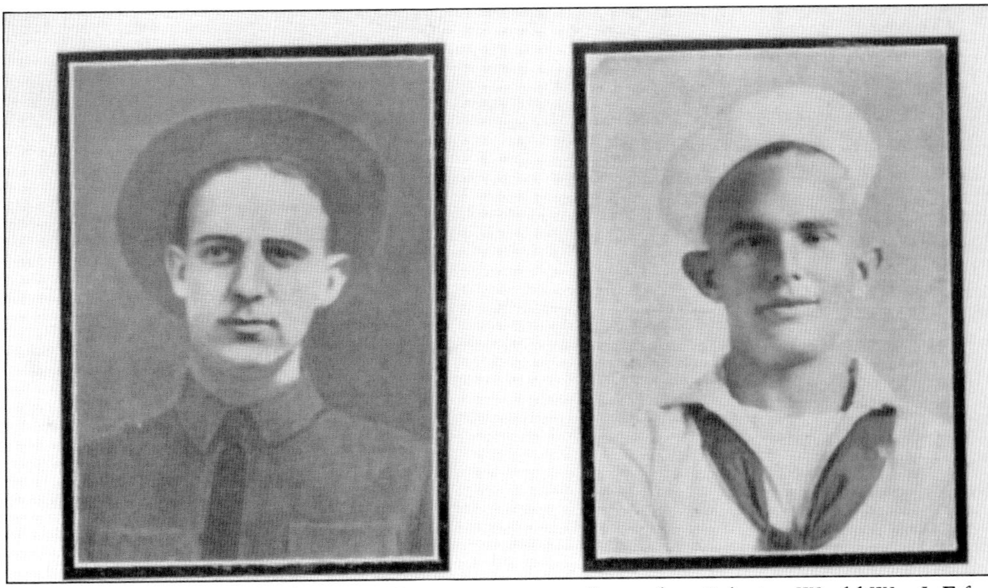

Over There. Thousands of Laurens County men went "over there" during World War I. Fifty-one men never returned. Shown in the photograph on the left is James Mason, the first Laurens County man to give his life for his country. Shown on the right is seaman Robbie New, who died of disease, which killed more Laurens Countians than did battlefield wounds.

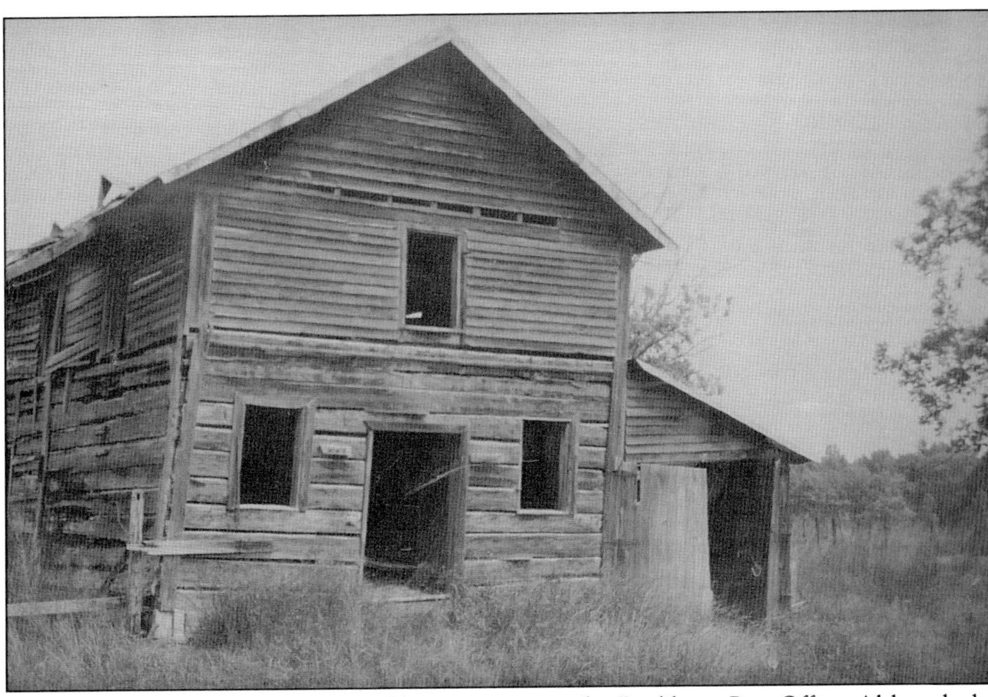

Buckhorn Post Office. This barn-like structure was the Buckhorn Post Office. Although the date of the construction of this building is unknown, the post office was in existence from 1879 to 1903. Andrew J. Thompson was the first postmaster. This photograph was taken by Don Johnston just prior to the razing of the building.

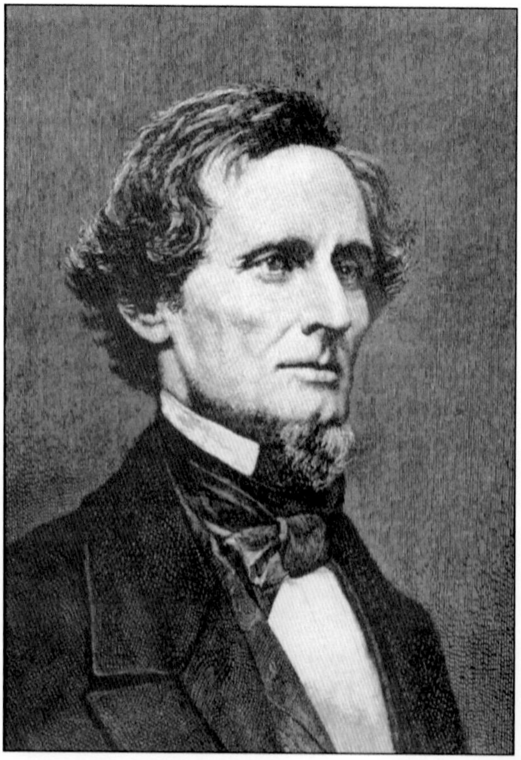

Jefferson Davis. On May 7, 1865, Confederate president Jefferson Davis passed through Dublin during his attempted escape from Federal cavalry. Three days later, Davis was captured in Irwinville, Georgia. Had the Union army arrived in Dublin a day earlier, Davis would have been captured in Laurens County.

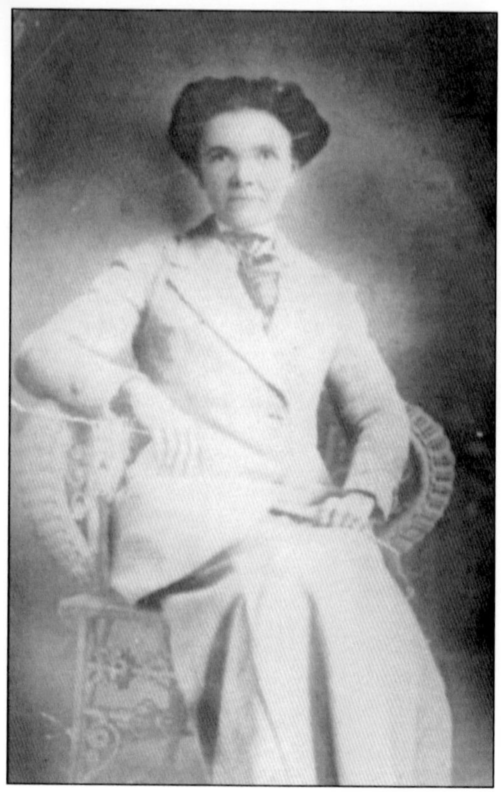

Rebecca Lowery Cadwell Burch. Mrs. Burch founded the town of Cadwell on the new line of the Dublin and Southwestern Railroad. She originally chose the name of Burch for the new town, but the name had already been used by another Georgia town. She chose Cadwell in memory of Matthew Cadwell, her first husband who was killed by lightning while riding his horse, who was buried beside him.

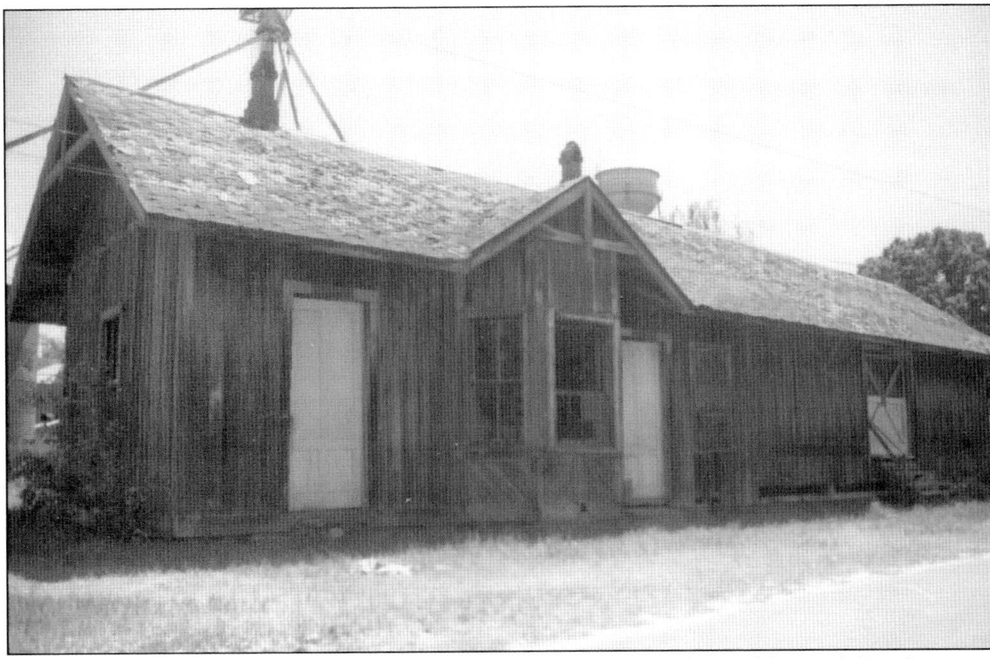

The Cadwell Depot. This photograph shows the depot of the Dublin and Southwestern Railroad just before it was torn down around 1990. The building is a reminder of our need to preserve the important pieces of our history before they are gone.

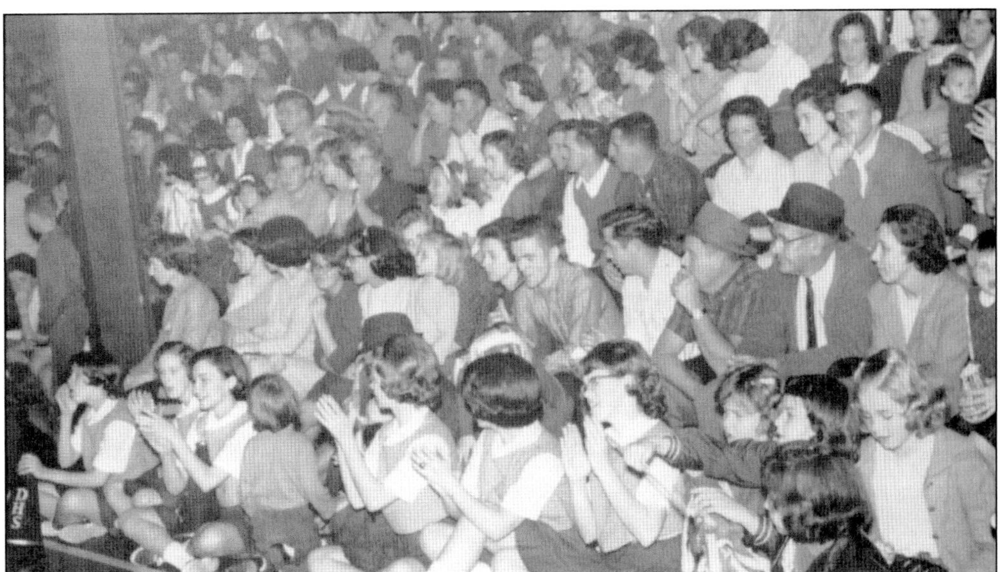

Basketball Fans. For three nights a week from November to March, Laurens Countians filled small county gyms to watch the local schools play basketball. This 1960s photograph shows Dudley Cardinal fans cheering their team to victory.

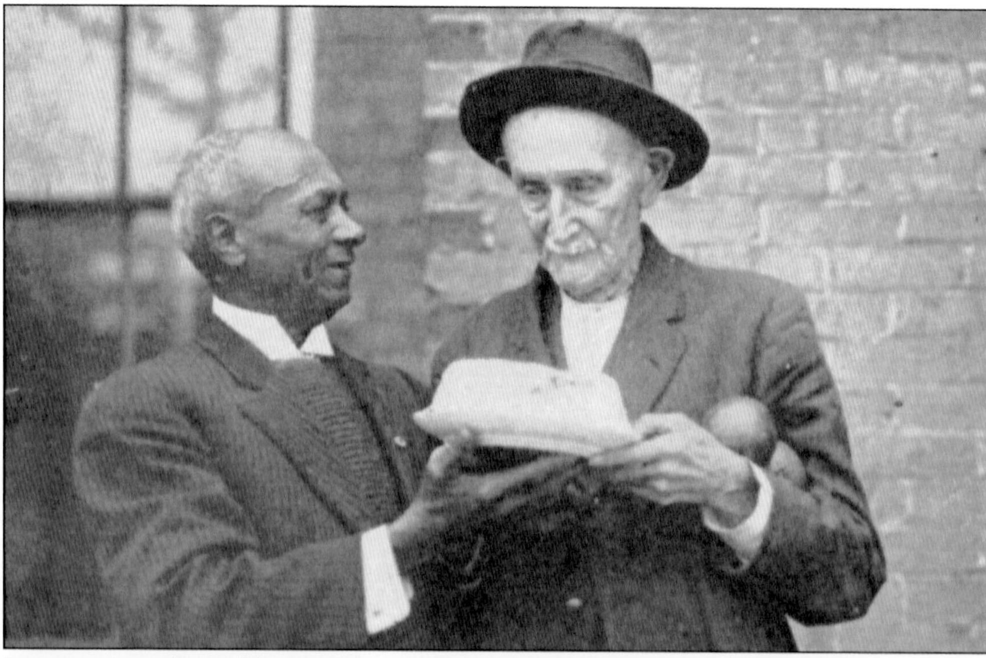

Friends of the Past. Shown in this c. 1920 photograph is "Ten Cent" Bill Yopp and Thomas M. Yopp. Bill was born a slave and was owned by Thomas. The two were childhood friends, fought in the Civil War together, and remained friends for over 70 years. Bill Yopp was a drummer of the 14th Georgia Infantry and is the only African-American Confederate soldier to lie in the National Cemetery in Marietta, Georgia.

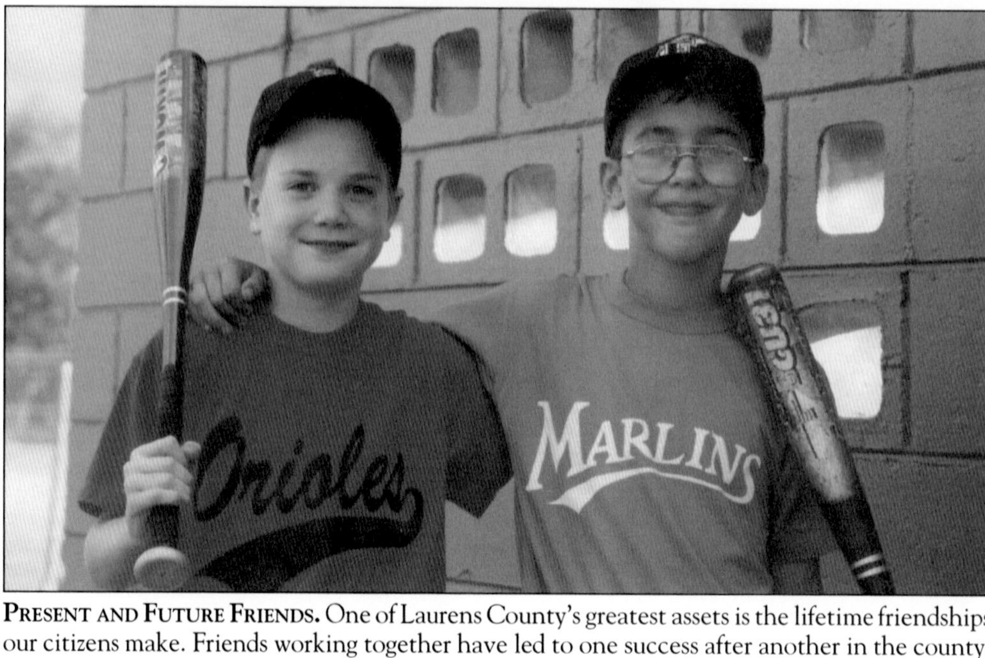

Present and Future Friends. One of Laurens County's greatest assets is the lifetime friendships our citizens make. Friends working together have led to one success after another in the county. In this photograph, Matt Greer (left) and Scotty Thompson (right), best friends and former teammates, prepare to pitch against each other for the first time. This picture from our present reminds us that our most important history is yet to come.